Murder at Montpelier

MURDER AT MONTPELIER

Igbo Africans in Virginia

Douglas B. Chambers

UNIVERSITY PRESS OF MISSISSIPPI   JACKSON

www.upress.state.ms.us

The University Press of Mississippi is a member of the Association of American University Presses.

Maps courtesy of Beth Chambers

Print-on-Demand Edition

Library of Congress Cataloging-in-Publication Data

Chambers, Douglas B.

Murder at Montpelier : Igbo Africans in Virginia / Douglas B. Chambers.

 p. cm.

Includes bibliographical references and index.

ISBN 1-57806-706-5 (cloth : alk. paper)

1. Slaves—Virginia—Orange County—Social conditions—18th century. 2. Igbo (African people)—Cultural assimilation—Virginia—Orange County—History—18th century. 3. Plantation life—Virginia—Orange County—History—18th century. 4. Culture conflict—Virginia—History—18th century. 5. Virginia—Race relations. 6. Montpelier (Va. : Dwelling)—History. 7. Madison, Ambrose, ca. 1696–1732—Death and burial. 8. Murder—Virginia—Orange County—History—18th century. 9. Madison, James, 1751–1836—Family. 10. Orange County (Va.)—Biography. I. Title.

F232.O6C457   2005

975.5′372′08625—dc22   2004015605

British Library Cataloging-in-Publication Data available

Ife Na-azo Na-egbu,
Ife na-egbu Egbu na-dzo Azo

"What saves also kills,
and what kills also saves"

—Igbo Proverb

CONTENTS

ACKNOWLEDGMENTS

Having long ago spent nearly two years living on Montpelier (1986–87), through the courtesy of the National Trust for Historic Preservation at Montpelier, which I gratefully acknowledge, and mostly before the property opened to the public, I was able to gather a range of research materials, part of which formed the core of my master's thesis (University of Virginia, 1991). At that time, however, I found there was very little that I could say about slavery and the Madison-owned enslaved people, though I had "discovered" the murder of Ambrose Madison, as well as the likely African connections of some of the slaves at Montpelier. Research for my dissertation (University of Virginia, 1996), took me in a radically different direction of studies, focusing on probable African-Virginia historical connections in the context of the Atlantic world, and enabled me to center the historical reality of Igbo influences in the formation of early Afro-Virginian slave culture and society. Returning now to the story surrounding Ambrose's tragedy in 1732 in its larger context and to the story of the Madison slaves' community in the century following the charter generation is, as always, the result largely of the work and inspiration of others and perhaps of once again attempting to plow these old fields crosswise.

Some of the research for this project benefited from the support, directly or indirectly, of several organizations and institutions, for which I am grateful. These include the Raven Society at the University of Virginia, the Society of the Cincinnati in Virginia, the National Trust for Historic Preservation, the Virginia Foundation for the Humanities and Public Policy, the International Center for Jefferson Studies of the Thomas Jefferson Foundation, and the Smithsonian Institution. Lastly, the staff of the Special Collections Department, Alderman Library, University of Virginia and of several courthouses across the Commonwealth were always most helpful. Special thanks are due to a number of people, including George Smith; Professors D. Alan Williams, J. C. A. Stagg, William Abbott, Charles and Nancy Perdue, Theresa Singleton, and the late Armstead Robinson; the Hon. Helen Marie Taylor, Pattie Cook, Adam Gaiser, Richie Grinspun, Mel and Dee Cherno; Bronwen Souders, Cinder Stanton, Lorena Walsh, Gwendolyn Midlo Hall, Jerome S. Handler, and of course Joseph C. Miller; Lic. Ernesto Valdés Janet, his family and Proyecto Orúnmila; the people of Accompong Town, Jamaica, and the late Professor Douglas Hall; Shelia Smith and colleagues in the history department, at the University of Southern Mississippi; the two reviewers for the University Press of Mississippi; and as always, Mr. and Mrs. William Greenlee, to whom this book is dedicated.

PART ONE

Igbo Africans

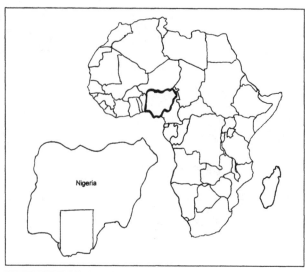

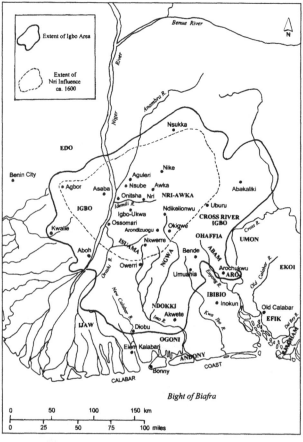

Map 1.   Eboan Africa ca. 1700

CHAPTER ONE

Atlantic Africans and
the Charter Event of Montpelier

Historians always write within the constraints of partial knowledge. For those of us who work in the field of subaltern groups such as African Americans, and especially in the era of the slave trade, the challenges are compounded by the relative lack of documentary sources. As one researcher who studies the relatively well documented slave community of Thomas Jefferson's Monticello remarked, a particularly frustrating aspect of trying to recapture the lives of enslaved people in the Chesapeake is the fact that we may know something as quotidian as their shoe sizes but little else about the slaves as individuals. Slaves whose lives intersected with those of their master or of other white people who put their observations to paper (and which survived) are the people about whom the most is known. But these slaves—often house rather than field workers—were a distinct minority. And yet they have been perceived by many scholars as those whose personal styles of life most closely approximated that of whites. African-born slaves have remained the most invisible of all, even in the era when they were numerous.

In other parts of the African diaspora, especially the Caribbean and Brazil and including Louisiana before about 1820, African-born slaves are more visible in the historical record. For reasons that are not at all clear, masters and other whites in these broad areas paid more attention to their African slaves than was the case in general in North America. These whites noticed and recorded the specific ethnicities of their enslaved Africans. Researchers are (re)discovering many documentary sources that speak to the ethnicity of Africans in the diaspora. These include notarial and ecclesiastical records and runaway slave advertisements as well as some court and penal documents. In general, however, such records do not seem abundant for the Chesapeake. No doubt in part this is because the transatlantic slave trade to Virginia, which always dominated the Chesapeake region, ended in 1775, and the abolition apparently was effectively enforced.

By the time that many descendants of colonial Virginia's "first families" were donating family records in large numbers to organized historical societies and the state library (basically in the generation after the Civil War), commercial and business records predominated, and family reputations were jealously guarded. Furthermore, the court records from the original Black Belt of Virginia (those counties straddling the fall lines of the upper York and James Rivers), were largely burned or otherwise lost during the Civil War. Furthermore, courthouses in general preserved records to the extent that they spoke to principal legal issues, mostly involving land tenure and inheritance and chancery suits and taxation, as well as the abstracts of colonial court decisions. Given the apparent purblindness of the colonial white elite to the Africans among their slaves, the basic public documents in the Chesapeake are often silent on the ethnicities of Africans among the enslaved people. Though there are plenty of lists of slaves, especially those included in inventories of estates of deceased masters in the Chesapeake region, only rarely are the Africans among them specifically noted. And yet, unless they all died shortly after landing or were so quickly subsumed by their Creole children and grandchildren as to rapidly disappear from the social landscape, historically they were there.

As well, the key decades of the second and third quarters of the eighteenth century, when the slave trade to Virginia was at its peak, were the "frontier" years for many of the counties whose records have survived. The extant records of suits and legal cases, criminal as well as civil, often are noted in only the most cursory way. Though these sources are excellent for basic demographic and economic data or for questions requiring aggregate numerical information—in short, for quantitative material—they fall far short of the level of description that could be considered comprehensive for qualitative material. Rarely will any available material reach the level of absolute certitude; rather, we deal within the demands of plausibility, of credibility, of necessarily partial knowledge enhanced and filled in by our understanding of the larger historical context(s).

And so it is with the question of the death of Ambrose Madison in 1732, which I argue was the charter event of Montpelier. Only two very terse sources comprise the whole documentary record for his apparent murder at Montpelier, and both are buried in the official documents of a county other than the one in which the estate is now situated. One is the abstract of the Oyer and Terminer trial of three slaves accused of "feloniously Conspiring the Death of Ambrose Madison."[1] The other is a short note that reports the cost for trying the "three Negroes for Suspition of Poysoning Ambroes Madison."[2] And that is it.

The mystery of Madison's death, for which three slaves were blamed and for which one paid with his life, is compounded by the silence of all of the many secondary sources on the history of the Madison family. Not one of President James Madison's numerous biographers, the many scholars of the period, or even the exceptionally careful local researchers has pursued the question of the plausibility of the African slaves purposefully killing the future president's paternal grandfather. The accusation of poisoning of course did not mean that his death actually came from poison, especially in the eighteenth century, when "poison" could have been a catchall explanation for any unexpected (or drawn-out) death. But given the larger context of central Virginia at this time, it is entirely plausible that the largely African (and therefore likely Igbo or "Eboe") slaves would resort to this means of murdering their master. Even if the slaves did not in fact use poison to dispatch Ambrose Madison, we can never know this. At the same time, of course, it is impossible to prove that the slaves murdered him or that they indeed used poison to kill him. If absolute certitude is required (as boring or perhaps comforting as that may be, depending on the perspective), all that can be said is that Madison died unexpectedly after languishing for some time in the summer of 1732 on the land of what later became known as Montpelier; that his family or others believed strongly enough that there was a conspiracy among at least some of his slaves to kill him to force a formal trial along those lines; that the three accused slaves included one man who was not owned by Madison and that one of the other two was a young woman; that all three slaves pleaded not guilty but were found guilty; and that rather curiously, only the outsider was executed. Rather than casting doubt on (or obversely, simply trying to prove) whether the slaves actually murdered their master, I think a more interesting question is what this event meant in the *longue durée*. How might it follow the logic of the larger historical context of that place and time, broadly considered? How might this event be a window into the world of the central Piedmont in the second quarter of the eighteenth century? What might it suggest about the development of Afro-Virginia slave society and culture when the transatlantic slave trade to the colony was at its peak?

Therefore, I begin with the plausible assumption that the slaves purposefully killed Madison and that they used (or at least were commonly believed to have used) poison to do him in. In the long run, however, it really does not matter. Why? Because the common perception evidently was that they had in fact murdered him and that they did so by poisoning him. The story here is not about how three slaves impulsively bludgeoned a master to death in a moment of anger, for example, or about an accidental killing. Rather, the story is of an apparent conspiracy among several slaves who likely shared (at least in general) a common ancestral African set of traditions, commonly applied in the Creole setting in which they found themselves, albeit with tragic consequences. They responded to whatever crisis precipitated the extreme act of murdering their master, just six months after he and his family had moved permanently to the central Virginia farmstead that the slaves had spent some years developing, by using a necessarily secret technology ("poison") that harked back to their shared African origins.

Understood in terms of these broader contexts, this is primarily the story of a local murder in central Virginia in the second quarter of the eighteenth century. A young white planter had launched his adult life through the patronage of his father-in-law and had, through the partnership of his brother-in-law, moved his family to a new plantation on the western reaches of colonial settlement in the 1720s and 1730s. Within six months of joining the nascent settlement that his new African slaves had seated, he was killed in a conspiracy involving at least two of his slaves.

There is a good chance that the majority of the African slaves at the new plantation, as well as the majority of the enslaved people in the surrounding district, were from the Bight of Biafra in West Africa. As such, the patterns of the transatlantic slave trade suggest that there was every likelihood the more immediate origins of these "Calabar" slaves were in the densely populated Igbo (Ibo) hinterland, especially within the old cultural frontiers of the ancient Nri (Enri) civilization of north-central Igboland.

Some time in the summer of 1732, probably in July, three slaves apparently conspired to poison Ambrose Madison (ca. 1696–1732) in what was then western Spotsylvania County in the newly settled backcountry of the central Piedmont, a rolling and fertile region ranging along the tributaries of Virginia's York (and upper Rappahannock)

Rivers. Of the three, one man, Pompey, belonged to a neighboring planter, while the other two, a man named Turk and a young woman named Dido, were the property of Madison. On July 31, their master made out his last will and testament, though he apparently languished for another three weeks before dying on August 24. Within a week, the county's fellow elite planters (who made up the county court) had secured a *dedimus potestatum,* or writ of authority, from the colony's lieutenant governor in Williamsburg to conduct a formal (if summary) trial of the accused slaves.[3]

The shock of the murder must have reverberated through the white and black communities of the region and perhaps of the colony, as it is the first known case of the killing of a master by slaves in Virginia. Furthermore, the means used to murder Madison would have been especially troubling. The intimacy of enslaved people's contact with their masters, for whom slaves cooked and washed in the house as well as toiled in the fields, made the threat of poison terrifying. If Madison was indeed poisoned, then this case also represents the first known conviction of slaves for the use of poison against their master in Virginia.[4] It would not, however, be the last.

On September 6, seven justices of the county's Commission of the Peace, including the powerful Henry Willis, Robert Spotswood, and Robert Slaughter, gathered to hear the evidence and render a judgment in the trial of Pompey, Turk, and Dido. The slaves were led to the bar, and all pleaded not guilty. After deliberating, the court found all three guilty. The justices apparently decided that Pompey, a slave of Joseph Hawkins, was the principal conspirator.[5] Either he supplied the poison or was the prime mover in Madison's murder, as the justices sentenced him to death by hanging. Turk and Dido, however, must have described some kind of extenuating circumstances or simply convinced the court that they were less directly involved, as the justices decided that the two slaves were "Concerned in the said ffelony, but not in Such a Decree as to be punished by Death." Instead, they were ordered to be whipped with twenty-nine lashes "on their bare backs at the Common Whiping post, and there-after to be discharged." The justices further directed the sheriff, Ambrose's brother-in-law, Thomas Chew (d. 1782), to then "Convey the said Turk & Dido to their said Mistris" (Ambrose Madison's widow).[6]

It is impossible to ascertain Turk's and Dido's motivations for helping Pompey kill Madison. The degree to which the other slaves at Mt. Pleasant, as the plantation was called at the time, joined or acquiesced with or protected the conspirators (or, conversely, exposed them) after the fact is also unknowable. Yet two of Madison's slaves clearly were not afraid to conspire to rid the group of its master in 1732. Killing a white man, of course, was practically a suicidal act. The surprising aspect of the trial was that Turk and Dido each got away with only a whipping. Turk eventually may have been sold, as his name disappears from the set of names used by Madison-owned slaves. But the name Dido was reused by later slaves, appearing in lists in 1766–74, 1782–86, and 1787. And in the white family, Ambrose remained a staple among male Madison descendants well into the nineteenth century.[7] It is likely, therefore, that the central message of the murder (about the limits of the master's power and of the slaves' resistance to it) echoed for a long time among the descendants of both free and slave at Montpelier.

That Turk and Dido, who clearly were involved in the murder of their master, received relatively light sentences or that Ambrose Madison's planter peers perceived some exculpatory evidence in the account of the conspiracy is itself remarkable. For example, planter justices in this same district a few years later, now organized as the new county of Orange, reacted with extreme measures to two simi-lar cases. One, in 1737, involved the murder of a master by an adult slave named Peter, who was not only condemned to death but also subsequently had his head cut off and displayed on a pole at the courthouse building "to deter others from doing the Like." And in January 1746, also in Orange County, the court convicted a female slave named Eve who had attempted to kill her master, Peter Mountague, the previous August by putting the poison in his milk, with Mountague suffering severe illness through the end of December. Though Mountague recovered and lived at least until 1771, Eve was convicted of poisoning him and sentenced not merely to death but to be "Drawn upon a Hurdle to the Place of Execution and to be Burnt" alive, a punishment carried out later in January.[8] One can only imagine what reception awaited Turk and Dido back at the Madison home plantation, but at their trial at least they had convinced the white men whose held sway over the slaves that they should be relatively forgiven.

As the original settlers of that land and perhaps also as collective witnesses to the playing out of the conspiracy against their master, this generation of slaves was a "charter generation." It very likely comprised a core of African adults who had been purchased within a decade before the event as well as several Creole adolescents or young adults and their first-generation Creole children. In 1733, this group of twenty-nine slaves formed part of a larger neighborhood community whose connections stretched across the bounds of particular plantations and slaveholdings. The historical geography of the settlement of the York River watershed and of the transatlantic slave trade to this area that enabled the expansion of settlement into the central Piedmont suggests that the great majority of Africans were from one region of the continent, the "Calabar" coast of the Bight of Biafra. They were transported from the coastal slave trade towns, which were entrepôts for the densely populated Igbo hinterland of present-day eastern Nigeria.[9]

There also clearly were Africans of other ethnicities in this region, including in what became Orange County. For example, there was a runaway named Angola Tom was captured in the county in 1744.[10] However, in general it would appear that Igbo predominated.

The wave of imported Africans in the first half of the eighteenth century to Virginia, dominated as it was by Igbo but with a probable

Central African admixture and the presence of Akan and Mande/ FulBe in small numbers, shaped the contours both of slavery and of the historical development of slave community culture there. Even though Africans of other ethnic backgrounds were in the colony and would continue to arrive in some numbers in the 1760s and early 1770s, the historical world the creolizing slaves created in Virginia seems to have developed largely from a diasporic Igbo base. By drawing on their ancestral material, social, ideological, and other resources to adapt to slavery and make sense of their new lives, communities of Igboized Creole slaves created a distinctive culture informed by "Eboe" or Igboesque principles and paraphernalia.

The internal world of the slaves in the eighteenth century, however, was multiethnic. Just as whites in Anglo-Virginia differentiated among French Huguenots, Palatine Germans, Scots, and Irish, so did ethnic Africans confront differences in Afro-Virginia. The peoples of other African ethnic backgrounds, and not just Central African and Akan and Mande but also Malagasy (Madagascars) and perhaps even an occasional Yoruba,[11] were in colonial Virginia. There were also a few American Indian peoples, including the community of Sapony at Alexander Spotswood's Germanna in the 1720s, Mattaponi and Pamunkey peoples along those rivers, and other individuals scattered among plantation slaves.[12] Personal names testify to identity, including putative community of origin, and even though the evidence is scanty, some afriphonetic names reveal African ethnic backgrounds in particular times and places, especially in the counties of what was becoming Virginia's eighteenth-century Black Belt.[13]

In the region that probably absorbed the bulk of slaves imported during the peak decades of the slave trade (ca. 1710 to the mid-1750s)—Caroline, Essex, King and Queen, King William, New Kent, Henrico, Hanover, Charles City, and Prince George Counties— most courthouse records were destroyed in the Civil War, as were many planters' personal records. These were the core counties of the emerging Black Belt, with the outer ring comprising the adjacent Piedmont counties of (in the mid-1750s) Spotsylvania, Orange, Goochland, Louisa, Albemarle, Cumberland, and Amelia. These secondary destinations were heavily represented by slaves sent in the 1720s–50s. In the latter 1760s, planters imported proportionately more Central Africans (Western Bantu) and some Mande (sent by London- and Liverpool-financed ships) and probably more Akan or Akan-influenced slaves by way of the West Indies (the roughly 4,500 brought to Virginia by American ships, usually in very small shipments). This pattern could account for the local visibility of Congo/Angola names and Akan day names in the colony in the eighteenth century. However, since the flow of people (black especially but white as well) in the years between about 1755 and the 1780s was from the Tidewater to the Piedmont, internal migration would have added to the Igboized-Creole influence. Many of the Tidewater Creoles would have been the children of Igbo brought to the Chesapeake in the 1710s and 1720s. They were brought into areas with a known Igbo presence, such as the central Piedmont, though they would have encountered other Africans, especially Central Africans.

There also is evidence of a relatively early Akan presence. For example, in the years when London merchants financed shipments of some 6,000 slaves to Virginia (1698–1709), the English visitor Hans Sloane acquired (ca. 1700) in the colony an apparently Asante-style drum made of American cedar.[14] Also, in 1710, a recently imported boy named Quamino, whose name evokes the precolonial Akan day name for "male born on Saturday," was taken by his master to the Essex County court to have his age adjudged.[15] Other Akan day names appear in county records at the end of the slave trade era in the 1760s and 1770s, including Quasheba (Cumberland 1773) and another Quamino (Orange 1771).[16]

The concentration of Liverpool merchants in the lower Rappahannock River area and their sources in Senegambia are reflected in the presence of slaves with Islamized names in that part of Virginia. These presumably were Mande and/or FulBe and include names such as Kilbree, Rauhana, Hassah, and perhaps Kadar in Essex County (1717–23), and Fulah, Potah, and Packah in Caroline County (1752), as well as by known Muslim slaves such as Job ben Solomon and Yarrow Mamout in the 1730s Chesapeake.[17]

Some Central African personal names of slaves, like the two children named Congo (Amelia 1768, Cumberland 1773) and Angolo (Spotsylvania 1734) and Gola (Amelia 1763), are evident in courthouse age adjudgment records. These probably also included the common male slave name Mingo (and less common "Catholic" names like Emanuel and Maria). From the 1730s, when Central Africans were taken in greater numbers to Virginia, we begin to see references to places such as Angola Creek. The first such toponym was mentioned in Goochland in 1733 and was retained in eighteenth-century Cumberland County (which Fry and Jefferson included in their 1755 map of Virginia). Another example of the Central African presence lies in the Angola quarter, or farm, that Thomas Jefferson acquired from his father-in-law's estate in 1774 and possibly in such vernacular practices as "bottle-trees."[18]

The long-term cultural influences of those peoples, however, all pale in comparison to that of Igboized Creoles in colonial and early national Afro-Virginia. The Igbo presence in eighteenth-century Virginia was pervasive, especially in the interior Tidewater and Piedmont counties on the upper reaches of the James, York, and Rappahannock Rivers.

By using "poison," the enslaved Africans of Ambrose Madison (and many of his contemporaries) responded not as "Atlantic Creoles" but as "Atlantic Africans" to whatever particular crisis or confrontation caused them to resort to the extreme act of killing their master.[19] Poison, arson, and running away were generic "weapons of the weak," and particularly effective ones for enslaved people resisting their oppression in a kind of asymmetric opposition to the hegemonic power of the masters expressed both individually as owners and collectively as the state itself. But the use of poison especially evokes a different matrix of meaning rooted in African conceptions of efficacy. There are strong associations between poisoning and "conjuring" in eighteenth and early-nineteenth-century Virginia, as indeed there was between poisoning and obeah in the Anglophone Caribbean, in particular Barbados and Jamaica.[20] Both regions received disproportionate numbers of Africans from Calabar; indeed, in the Caribbean, the term *obeah* itself evokes the precolonial north-central Igbo word for "doctoring" (*ôbia*), which combined herbalist knowledge with spiritual/supernatural power and sorcery to resolve problems and punish enemies. Igbo were thought to specialize in such powers and practices.[21] Therefore, it would seem productive to investigate local events such as Ambrose Madison's 1732 murder, which occurred during the height of the slave trade to Virginia in general and of the importation of Calabars in the York River watershed in particular, as a "charter event," precisely in terms of an Atlantic perspective. The slaves who conspired to poison Madison did so not as "Atlantic Creoles" but as Atlantic Africans.

An Atlantic perspective alters our historical view of these worlds in novel ways, both for this particular event and of the general social-historical context of its times. To tell this story, I explore a series of connected transformations that date to the same proximate period, the second quarter of the eighteenth century.

In effect, better-connected Virginia planters financed their expansion into newly claimed lands above the fall lines of the rivers by establishing new commercial links with British merchants in Bristol. At roughly the same time, Bristol merchants were consolidating their move into the transatlantic slave trade. They "bought into" this dangerous but tragically profitable overseas trade by concentrating their resources on the coast of Calabar in the Bight of Biafra. This new reach by Bristol traders, at first financed to a large degree by Virginia planters, had a cascading effect on the peoples and polities along the Calabar coast as well as in the hinterland. The peoples within the ancient and pacifistic Nri civilization, which may in fact date to the tenth century C.E.,[22] clearly came under great stress and experienced a marked rise in social violence. A new people or menacing "trade diaspora" emerged from the east, the Áro, who came to dominate the internal phase of slaving for the transatlantic trade throughout Igboland, with tragic consequences for many and surprising opportunities for some.

By beginning with the history of the African region from which it is likely that most of the slaves in central Piedmont Virginia originated, it is possible to approach the story of this murder from an Africanist perspective. Though the event at the heart of this story happened in Virginia, some measurable proportion of the slaves within the extended community around Montpelier had been enslaved within the past decade. The Madison slaves were surrounded by a set of interconnected slave Quarters that represented a world in large part unto itself. To understand the historical significance of the slaves' conspiracy against their master, the emerging culture of these enslaved people, at least in collective terms, must be outlined. Even with the catastrophic changes that enslavement, transportation, and resettlement would have wrought—the consequences of people being torn from their roots and thrown down half a world away—I assume that the enslaved survivors drew on ancestral cultural resources to make sense of their new lives. As such, they were Atlantic Africans rather than somehow cosmopolitan Atlantic Creoles.

Though displaced into the diaspora, enslaved Africans throughout the Atlantic relied on ancestral cultures to make sense of their new lives. These practical and esoteric knowledges remained meaningful in succeeding generations. In times of crisis people reacted in essentially conservative ways, at least culturally. Unlike Ira Berlin's conception, in which displaced Africans expected to experiment with new cultural behaviors and/or learned early and often how to behave like the whites to negotiate a newly racialized world, I see instead people who responded to events and situations as Atlantic Africans. The process of creolization was a long one, and it took several generations. The idea of Atlantic Creoles makes sense for the middle decades of the seventeenth century, when Virginia was a society with slaves and black people were few and far between. But the real charter generation arrived with the flood of Africans in the early eighteenth century, when the transatlantic trade transformed the Chesapeake into a slave society. Igbo dominated this generation and to a large degree laid the foundations for Afro-Virginia culture and society.[23]

Historical creolization in Virginia was a group phenomenon. In the 1970s, Sidney W. Mintz and Richard Price imagined how isolated individuals had responded in largely ad hoc ways to totally unfamiliar situations, sharing little but their slavery with other culturally isolated individuals. We now must imagine how groups of Africans like those living in the set of interlinked communities around Montpelier, for example, drew on ancestral ethnic-cultural resources to adapt to slavery. Since not all people of Atlantic African ethnic backgrounds were equally represented in such creolizing slave communities, we can focus on the roles and resources of those groups most heavily represented in various times and places to explain historically the creolization of distinctive regional slave subcultures.

In this regard, the Chesapeake presents a conundrum. On the one hand, African slaves in Virginia apparently did not utilize recognizably ethnic public institutions (or at least those recognizable by modern historians, generally with at most a passing knowledge of African history), particularly to resist slavery.[24] On the other hand, the enslaved people did not initially create a collective identity as a "new people" out of some internal frontier experience. In other words, Afro-Virginians never became a neoteric or cenogenic society (that is, new without roots) like the Seminole Maroons in Florida, the Garífuna in Central America, the Saramaka in Suriname, or others.[25] Yet there was just too much of what Sterling Stuckey called "Africanity" in the lives of Afro-Virginian slaves to see them as simply the "assimilateds."[26]

Therefore, it is useful to distinguish among primary, secondary, and tertiary creolization in Virginia. During the Atlantic crossing and initial resettlement, enslaved people would have learned that they were Eboe, for example, probably for the first time, as was the case among Sigismund W. Koelle's informants in nineteenth-century Sierra Leone.

The succeeding generation in Virginia, however, seemed to choose or perhaps appropriate "Guinea" to describe where they had come from and either gave or accepted that appellation to denote places in the colony, especially in the Piedmont. For example there were various "Guinea Creeks" in Goochland and Cumberland Counties. This name also was used for some of the Quarters on which the slaves lived. For example, there was the Guinea of John Wayles's slaves in the early 1770s, where Sally Hemings was born, and other places such as the Guinea (now called Guinea Station) in Caroline County. Before long "Guinea" was used to mark many other things with African origins that the slaves commonly used. These ranged from a particular variety of chickens (Guinea keet) to Indian corn (Guinea-wheate) to eggplant (Guinea squash).[27] Other slaves incorporated Guinea as part of their given names, including two Guineys (a man and a girl) in Caroline County (1744, 1752) or the Guinea Will at Jefferson's Poplar Forest in 1774.[28]

By the late eighteenth and early nineteenth centuries, in a third stage of creolization, one sees another shift in the use of *African*. When the few black Christians (led by free blacks) started their own churches, they often put the term *African* in the name, as was the case in Williamsburg in 1791 and Petersburg in 1797. And of course, when Equiano published his life story, he chose to call himself "the African."[29] The use of *African* in the title of the First

African Baptist Church in Richmond (1845) is one of the last examples of Afro-Virginians asserting affective ties with "Guinea" by historical metaphor, as the term then was in the process of being replaced by *Colored*, which would remain the main choice for institutional and collective nomenclature for more than a century.

The process of historical creolization in eighteenth-century Virginia, therefore, did not mean a one-to-one transfer of Igbo culture, which was impossible anyway, but did effectively mean the Igboization of slave community and culture. Although we can see certain Igboisms in Afro-Virginian slave life, Igboesque creolisms were more prevalent as Africans drew on ancestral physical, material, social, and ideological resources to adapt to slavery in the Chesapeake.

In the end, this book is really a set of stories about belonging and social memory. It is also about the limits of power and of resistance within the violent world of chattel slavery. Furthermore, it is an exercise in demonstrating the new uses that the remarkable outpouring of research on early African American and African diaspora history is producing. For the first time, it is possible to follow groups of enslaved peoples out of Africa as well as to work backward from particular points within the diaspora with new levels of assurance concerning the likely provenances of captive slaves and to do so across time and space. As a discipline, African diaspora studies is now on the verge of attempting event-level analysis.[30]

From the slaves' perspective in this story, the key institution, if you will, of their common ancestral tradition was the system of Igbo "doctoring" (*ôbea*) and of "sacred science" men (*díbia*), who specialized in poison as well as the divining/healing arts. Enslaved Africans could never simply re-create their lost worlds wherever they found themselves. But they did create a number of African-derived common traditions from their loosely shared ancestral ones wherever they wound up in sufficient numbers to do so. Given that the slaves in this story apparently poisoned their master and that poisoning was associated with the African-derived religion of the slaves in the pre-Christian period and indeed may be seen as an expression of that religion's core ideology, it is useful to begin with the beginning. This beginning is in the Igbo hinterland of the Calabar coast.

But also we must understand that this murder was a charter event of a particular place and time. It was a founding event in what became a large plantation slave community that eventually developed deep roots in the area. There are strong indications that the enslaved people continued to remember how the Africans killed the first master Madison at Montpelier, no doubt in revenge. And this social memory, this story, was likely carried well into the nineteenth century before apparently becoming lost in the twentieth. Given that these events involved the family of a future major figure in the early political history of the United States, as it was the grandfather of the Father of the Constitution who was killed, this larger story is even more compelling. The preservation of the Montpelier estate, now open to the public under the able administration of the National Trust for Historic Preservation, presents unusual opportunities to explore the consequences of the world(s) that produced this murder.

An African-oriented understanding of the murder of Ambrose Madison, in the historical moment when Igbo slaves likely predominated in central Virginia, requires a sense of the several layers of history and social memory that "Eboe" slaves would have brought with them into the diaspora. In short, to see these slaves as Atlantic Africans—that is, as enslaved people displaced from one part of Africa (Igboland) who wound up in one part of the Atlantic world (Virginia), a subdiaspora of a subdiaspora—we need to have some specific sense of the world from which they were torn. In the end, the use of poison connects these two imaginary cartographies; thus, the significance of poison concludes part 1 of the story.

Part 2 shifts to Virginia, using the numbers and patterns of the slave trade to suggest the great likelihood that many of the Africans taken to the central Piedmont came from the Bight of Biafra and therefore were largely Igbo. Furthermore, the generation of Madison-owned slaves living at the time of their master's murder were themselves a charter generation. They were succeeded by a creolizing generation that also reached far beyond the bounds of this one plantation to create a larger community. The third generation, which was probably the first truly Creole (locally born) one, may well have kept the story of Montpelier's charter event alive, at least well into the nineteenth century. The final chapter suggests that such a generalized long memory and the significance of Africans in general and of Igbo in particular can present new ways to conceive of the historical development of early Afro-Virginia society and culture. As a kind of historical bas-relief, we may begin to see figures who stand out, if only a little, from the general African background of slaves in Virginia.

For the more general reader, some of the apparatus required to tell this story may be annoying. As one of the few comprehensive records surviving for historians, plantation and mercantile and number-driven public documents figure prominently in the telling of this story. And as the point is to use this murder to peer into the larger world of which it was a part, a whole cast of characters necessarily walk in and out of these pages. That many of the whites happened to have been some of the most prominent men of their times and of prerevolutionary Virginia in general both eases and complicates the telling of this story.

For professional colleagues and other students of those times, the account of Madison's murder in its fullest context serves as a challenge to pursue further Africanist interpretations within American history. When considering archaic African American cultural history, especially in the era of primary creolization, the emphasis on the African side must indeed be commensurate. In thinking of people, places and things as *lieux de mémoire* (sites of memory), particularly for largely nonliterate peoples, and in understanding that slave communities tended to extend across social and physical landscapes rather than to be restricted to particular plantations, one may imagine new vistas populated with Africans as well as Creoles. I have included the various data in the appendixes to encourage further research into the Madison-owned enslaved people and their community.

To all readers I would note that the orthography I use for Igbo words does not include the complex semantic tones in that language, of which there are four. They are rather loosely evoked by attempting to include the more obvious stresses.[31]

That many of the Africans among the early slave communities in the central Piedmont (and indeed throughout colonial Virginia) were quite likely Igbo now seems without doubt. The central question of course, is what did this mean then, and for them, and what may it mean for new understandings of those lost worlds, and for us? In addition, how did things change in the broad African homeland as the effects of the forced migrations that brought slaves to the Americas in such numbers rippled among those who remained free? And what does the world that produced this murder suggest about our understanding of the historical process through which Africans became African Americans, what I call historical creolization? How may we pick up the challenge offered by W. E. B. Du Bois early in the last century to mend the broken threads of African and American histories, a challenge perhaps unfulfillable in his own time yet approachable in ours? Even though this particular story perforce is atypical, an African lens helps to clarify the picture.

CHAPTER TWO

Out of Calabar: The Igbo Hinterland

T he main African ethnic group, or set of historically related peoples, taken out of Calabar in the transatlantic slave trade were Igbo. The coast of the Igbo hinterland, called "Calabar" by Europeans, stretched over 100 miles from the eastern delta of the Niger River, with its endless mangrove swamps and lagoons, to the broad estuary of the Cross (or Calabar) River.[1] Just inland of the coast itself was a series of towns, including Élem Kalabári (New Calabar), Bonny, and the set of settlements collectively called Old Calabar that served as entrepôts for trade goods and were the main coastal slave trade sites. The coastal kings and other big men, who became powerful and rich by controlling trade with Europeans, also controlled the supply of slaves. By the second quarter of the eighteenth century at the latest, their reach had extended far beyond the local districts to the heavily populated interior of the Igbo heartland, including Nri-Awka and "Ísuàma."[2]

The Igbo peoples, especially those from within the cultural ambit of the ancient Nri civilization, were a distinct ethnohistorical group whose members shared distinctive ancestral traditions and drew on the same or very similar material, social, and ideological resources to adapt to the conditions in which they found themselves as slaves in the diaspora. They were a people that modern scholars have begun to study as a separate "nation" in the African diaspora.

The Igbo diaspora as a whole originated in the Nigerian hinterland of the Calabar coast. This was an immense forced migration, amounting to about 1.3 million of the 1.7 million people exported from the Bight of Biafra during the era of the Atlantic slave trade. During the eighteenth century, as the flow of enslaved Igbo turned into a tidal wave, the American market shifted rather dramatically from the Chesapeake region to the West Indies, especially Jamaica. But in the first half of the eighteenth century, between a quarter and a third (29 percent) of the estimated 93,000 Biafran Africans sent into the diaspora wound up in Virginia. The apparent Biafra-Virginia nexus was even more concentrated in the quarter century after 1716, when more than 55 percent of shipments sent from Calabar with a known destination went to Virginia.[3] Between 1716 and 1740, Virginia was the major market (destination) for Biafran Africans. Slaves taken from this region were at least six times more likely to wind up in Virginia than in the next two major markets for these Africans, Jamaica and South Carolina.[4]

From the perspective of Virginia, the Bight of Biafra was the most important source of slaves for planters in the colony. Of the roughly 83,500 Africans taken to Virginia in the century after 1676, about 37,000 came from the Calabar coast, and of these, perhaps 30,000 were Igbo. Most Biafran Africans (and Igbo) were taken in the first half of the eighteenth century, when the transatlantic slave trade to Virginia was at its height. Even though the Virginia market generally was a minor one in the Anglophone Americas, the flow of slaves from the Bight of Biafra during these decades was a demonstrable wave of Africans to the colony, and the Virginia market was significant for the initial expansion of the slave trade along the Calabar coast. In the forty years after 1716, 57 percent of Africans sent to Virginia originated in the Bight of Biafra and thus came "out of Calabar." This wave of Biafran Africans and thus of Igbo resulted in 30,000

Calabars (of whom a likely 25,000 were Igbo) landing in Virginia in one long generation. This Biafra-Virginia connection was especially concentrated in 1716–30 and 1741–50, when Biafrans constituted 62 percent and 75 percent of imports to the colony, respectively, or about two-thirds of the slaves in those cohorts combined. The forced migration of largely Igbo peoples in one wave had important conse-quences for the historical development of Creole Afro-Virginia slave culture and society, especially in the district around Montpelier. The timing of this wave also had significant consequences for people throughout Igboland, especially in the central and northern regions.

Although fiercely localistic in their home areas, Igbo-speaking (and presumably -acting) peoples, once thrown into the diaspora, embraced a collective identity derived from being a member of "my own nation," as Igbo-born former slave Òlaúdah Équiáno put it. As the early English explorer W. B. Baikie explained in the 1850s, "In I'gbo each person hails . . . from the particular district where he was born, but when away from home all are I'gbos."[5]

Koelle, a German missionary, solicited information about the same time from Igbo speakers who had been "recaptured" and sent by the British to Sierra Leone in the 1820s and 1830s. They told him that "certain natives who have come from the Bight [of Biafra] are called 'Ibos.' " Koelle noted, however, that in "speaking to some of them respecting this name, I learned that they never had heard it till they came to Sierra Leone." Before being drawn into the slave trade such people knew "only the names of their respective districts or countries."[6]

The structure of the export trade in slaves from Calabar, in which Igboized coastal big men brokered exchanges between newly arrived European captains and their agents (supercargoes) and a series of Igbo-speaking headmen in the interior villages or slaving specialists such as the Aro, combined with particular social and political changes in the broad region to make Igbo peoples the Calabar coast's principal source population of slaves. By the 1710s or 1720s at the latest, local slavers' reach extended relatively far inland. Their alliances with intermediaries, especially the fearsome itinerant Aro traders and their allies, who were protected in their travels by the divine sanction of the supreme deity (Chukwu) and hence called themselves Ùmuchúkwu (children of God), enabled the slavers to conduct captives along formal paths and roads to the heads of the creeks and lagoons flowing to the coastal towns. Hailing from the oracle of Arochukwu (Ibíniukpábi), the Aro and their dependents relied on the muscle of their armed porters (and their relations) as much as on their reputation for retribution. The Aro established a series of settlements throughout the Igbo heartland in the middle decades of the century and ran major and minor fairs (regional markets) at larger villages all across Igboland in the eighteenth and nineteenth centuries.[7]

The slave trade out of Calabar reached further inland over the centuries. In the sixteenth century, individual Kalabari and associated coastal villages apparently had raided each other for slaves. One village, perhaps apocryphal, called Agbániye Ejíka (Fishing Village) or Bi'le was remembered as the most disruptive and warlike in this initial phase of violent accumulation. One anthropologist has written that in this early period, "Bile got its slaves by sacking neighbouring Delta villages, rather than by trade with the hinterland."[8] Oral traditions mark the disruptions of this predatory period and contrast with the later expansion of New Calabar under the new dynasty founded by King Amákìri I. Whereas the early Bi'le attacks had scattered villages, perhaps creating refugee settlements at the heads of the coastal creeks, in the seventeenth century coastal New Calabar colonized other village groups and offered protection from the ravages of slave raiding in return for acknowledgment of Elem Kalabari's suzerainty. This small shift in regional power is remembered in a twentieth-century song: "Agbaniye Ejika Ama Fama Te—Amachree Ama Paka Mam" (Fishing Village Destroyed Towns—Amakiri Founded Towns).[9]

Precolonial Igboland had two major overlapping trade systems, each of which linked people in the densely populated central plateaus with sources of outside goods that were controlled by various other peoples on the peripheries of the region. In the Niger River system of cowrie-based canoe trading, the minimonarchies of Aboh, Asaba, and Ossomari rose out of trading villages on the Niger and incorporated cultural influences of various organized polities, including Bénin to the west and the ancient Nri civilization to the east.[10] By the late seventeenth century in central and northern Igboland, African brokers (increasingly Aro) demanded payment in a distinctive assortment of trade goods based on *manillas* (iron and/or copper ingots shaped like anchors), iron bars, and guns as well as cowries.[11] The early leading market towns in north-central Igboland included Àzumíni, Ùzuakóli, and Ohúhu, all on the middle or upper reaches of the Imo River and its tributaries in the Igbo heartland, whence merchants conducted slaves to rulers and other brokers at Kalabari, Bonny, and by the 1820s, the new coastal kingdom of Opobo. By the early eighteenth century, the Aro were funneling increasing numbers of people from their trade "colonies" along roads to major market towns like Béndè and from there to the set of settlements in the Cross River estuary known collectively as Old Calabar. In ensuing decades, the final destination was largely Bonny.

The largest interior market towns, which also served as collection points for coffles of slaves destined for the coast, such as Bende (Mbénté-Úga),[12] lasted four days every twenty-fourth day—that is, one *izu* (customary Igbo four-day week) every three *izu ùkwu* (big eight-day weeks). In general, markets were scheduled so that itinerant traders making rounds could attend several of them in succession. Bende, already well established by the 1670s, was said to be "two to four days" journey north of Bonny. In the mid–nineteenth century, Bende was still "a grand depot for slaves, as well as for palm-oil and provisions, and supplies with the former New Kalabar, Bonny, and Andony, as well as other neighbouring countries." The same observer also noted that when the "foreign slave trade was being actively carried on, [Bende] was in the zenith of its wealth and importance, and even since had declined but little, as it still remains the centre of the home slave mart for the coast, and the south of I'gbo."[13] Located halfway between the Imo and Cross Rivers and the hub of an immense regional trade, Bende was under the firm control of the Aro, perhaps from its founding.[14]

The Aro can be described as a "state" or a "trade diaspora," though one important scholar argues that they were "more economic imperialists than colonizers."[15] As a people they were of a mixed background. In fact, they were sui generis, having forged themselves out of several unrelated lineages, some of them Igbo and others from the lower Cross River, including Ibibio. The central village, AroChukwu, was founded around the 1620s and served as a metropolis for a culture that emphasized its connection with the pan-Igbo supreme deity (Chukwu) through their proprietary oracle, Ibiniukpabi. With their fealty to the Aro emblem of authority, to the council of lineage heads and the kings who presided over it, and to extended lineages within the whole, the men were imbued with the cultural imperative of the Aro—that is, the cultural concept of *mmúba* (expansion, proliferation).[16] To be "Aro" was to participate in a collective identity; they were highly assimilative and emphasized trade and merchant activities as a means of self-aggrandizement.

Founded in the early seventeenth century, AroChukwu was located in the far southeastern corner of Igboland, closer to coastal Old Calabar than to far Nri (Àgúkwu) in the Igbo heartland. The Aro first established daughter settlements throughout the east, before turning toward the west later in the century. By the 1720s, Aro had initiated expansion into central Igboland, and in the 1730s–50s several powerful and enterprising "merchant warlords,"[17] or agents, established important settlements in the upper Imo area on the outskirts of the Nri-Awka region. Two of these men, Mazi Ìzuógu (ca. 1710–80), and Íchiè Íkèliónwu (fl. ca. 1750), founded two of the largest settlements, NdeIzuogu and NdeIkelionwu, respectively.[18] The success of Ikelionwu in subordinating existing villages to his control at Omógho and in slave trading, spurred the rapid settlement of at least a half dozen more Aro settlements in his vicinity, about twenty miles southeast of Awka, and all became known as Aro Ndéni (NdeEni).[19] Although by the nineteenth century, some 150 Aro settlements were distributed throughout what is now eastern Nigeria, the ones in central Igboland were "unusually large."[20]

It is clear that the initial expansion of the Aro in the latter seventeenth century came, in part, from gaining control (or perhaps establishing) the regional market town of Bende and from the subsequent supply of slaves to the emerging entrepôt of Old Calabar. The massive expansion of Aro settlements in the eighteenth century and their concentration in the central highlands to the west of their core was even more closely tied to the supply of slaves for the coast, especially Bonny. The establishment of NdeIzuogu and NdeIkelionwu in the second quarter of the eighteenth century, followed soon by the other villages of NdeEni, both caused and reflected the rapid rise in the export of slaves, particularly at the newly prominent port of Bonny. Aro adopted the Èfìk/Ibíbio secret *èkpè* masqueing society, which enforced decisions of the elders, among other responsibilities, and adapted it to slaving. The Aro employed a general strategy of demanding annual tributes in slaves from villages that accepted subordination in return for protection from the ravages of slave raiding. Consequently, these Aro settlements flourished. But they often did so by creating or at least by directly manipulating the conditions of social violence and discord and displacement that attracted refugees and other desperate peoples to Aro protection. The violence that undergirded Aro expansion reflected the close historical connection of this regional shift in power "with the expansion of the Atlantic trade."[21] It is also of central significance that the mid–eighteenth century era of dramatic Aro penetration occurred mainly into the areas under Nri cultural influence and in a time of

extended drought and famine. These changes correlate rather dramatically with both the rise of Bonny and the massive expansion of
slave exports from the second quarter of the century.

On the Calabar coast, the main slave trade site in the eighteenth
century was the town of Bonny. It was strategically situated on an
island at a central point on the coast. The rise of Bonny in the late
seventeenth and early eighteenth centuries was based on creating ties
with interior Igbo peoples, including Aro merchant warlords, and by
cornering the market on trade with the Europeans. Ìbáni principal
men, who headed their own "canoe houses" under the paramountcy
of one (or often two) local kings, apparently first built their trade on
connections with southern Igbo, in particular the Ndóki and Ngwá
communities east of the middle Imo River, initially for yams, later for
slaves, and eventually for palm oil. Members of the main masqueing
men's society in this area, called *okónko* or *ekpe Aro,* referred to each
other as "friends of the Aro."[22] The early role of these southern Igbo
as intermediaries is marked by oral histories that emphasize that the
immediate descendants of the founding king of Bonny, Asimini, were
Ngwa Igbo and that they gained office by persuading Europeans to
trade at the town. Asimini is said to have given his daughter in
marriage to one "Opoli of Azuogu in the Ndoki country," and she
returned to rule Bonny as Queen Kambása. Her son, Kumálu, whose
name later became common among children in Ngwa-Igboland, succeeded her as king. The name Kumalo suggests a ruthless, even evil
ruler who strikes like lightning, and it seems to evoke the violence
inherent in slaving. It is also a typically Aro name and may signify the
signal importance of creating connections with the Aro through the
Ndoki.[23] All of this must have taken place in the seventeenth century,
as these changes predated the Pepple (or Perekule) dynasties of the
precolonial era. As late as the mid–nineteenth century, the Ibani still
referred to the Ndoki as *Amina mina* (brothers).[24]

Before benefiting from the ties with Ngwa-Igboland, however,
Bonny and its allies had to fight a series of wars to defeat the

neighboring Kalabari, Okríka, Ogóni, and Andony peoples (and perhaps others), who occupied land between the sea and Isuama. These conflicts are remembered in Bonny oral histories, which explain the rise of the littoral village group in mythic terms. To "widen the river" at Bonny Point, the founding king Asimini was forced to offer a daughter in sacrifice, thus starting a new tradition of offering a virgin every seven years to propitiate the gods of the sea. A new war cult, established to honor the war god *Ikúba*, whose totem was the monitor lizard or iguana (as well as the house of skulls that so fascinated later European visitors), was also a function of Bonny's new reach into the interior.[25]

Elem Kalabari's traditions assert that Bonny stole the European trade from them. They describe the conflict in terms of a struggle in spiritland between the tutelary gods of each group—that is, Ikuba of Bonny and Òwoàmekáso of New Calabar: "After *Oruyingi* [Mother of the gods] had given birth to all the gods of the *ibe* [named peoples] in the delta, she asked them to make requests for the benefit of their people. Owoamekaso asked for a book that would attract European ships to Elem Kalabari. After they left the presence of Oruyingi, Ikuba became jealous and tried to seize the book. In the ensuing struggle, Ikuba was able to make off with the larger fragment of the book, and so got the bigger ships calling at the port of Bonny, only smaller ships being able to go upstream to Elem Kalabari."[26]

The region that likely was most severely affected by slaving throughout the hinterland was central and northern Igboland—in particular, communities within the cultural ambit of the ancient Nri civilization. Centered at the village known in the colonial era as Agukwu (Great Lion), the Nri civilization may date as far back as the ninth-tenth centuries. Several archaeological sites excavated in the early 1960s revealed large caches of intricately decorated pottery, ivory tusks, forged metal objects, bead ornaments, and other regalia and burial practices that strikingly resemble royal Nri material culture.[27] The one human face object from Igbo-Ukwu, of bronze, shows facial scarification that mirrors the distinctive hachure of Nri men.[28]

Nri was both a place and a culture. As a place it was a union of several villages located between two small lakes in the Anambra River Valley. As a culture it was centered on a priest-king who claimed a special relationship with the deified Earth Force (*Áni*, var. *Álè*). Therefore, he was associated with the founding or introduction of crops and with practices that defined institutional culture, such as yams and title societies (with their ennobling facial scarification), and the system of "abominations" (or taboos, *nsò*) as well as with the cult of achievement (*ìkénga*) and, most importantly, a pacifist ideology that abhorred the shedding of human blood. Nri were in effect the first Igbo, seen in central and northern Igboland as the eldest brother, the most senior community that controlled the most ancient *ófo* (staff of ancestral authority). The priest-king (*Ézè Nrì*) delegated to his representatives, often the most accomplished local men who had achieved high status in a complicated titled society, the *ozo* society, the power to render judgments in disputes, remove the ritual pollution that breaking taboos wrought, set the agricultural calendar, and regulate markets and control the elements, all to keep the peace and assure prosperity.[29]

The representatives of the *Eze Nri* received a special and distinctive facial scarification called *ichi*. The *mgbùríchi* (mbreechi), those marked with the ennobling hachure, were singled out as men who were full citizens; above all, the hachure denoted (spiritual) royalty and qualified one to be a representative of the priest-king and eligible to receive the spiritual inspiration to become king. As the eighteenth-century Igbo-born Olaudah Equiano recalled, the "elders or chiefs" in his home district were "styled Embrenché; a term, as I remember, importing the highest distinction, and signifying in our language a mark of grandeur. . . . Those Embrenché, or chief men, decided disputes and punished crimes; for which purpose they always assembled together."[30] To be within the Nri cultural ambit meant to ascribe to the *nso* ideology, and its institutional apparatus: the *Eze Nri*, the yam spirit (*ífèjíóku*, var. *njókku*), the *ozo* title society, the *ikenga* cult, and the *Àgbála* oracle of the blacksmiths at Awka, among other beliefs and practices.[31] As one customary praise song performed during the multiday scarring ritual suggests, *ichi* marks were closely associated with royal status: "*Nwaichi nyem ma aguu agbunem/ Ichi Eze, ichi Nwadiokpala*" (Ichi child give me food so I will not starve/Facial scar for kings, facial scar for first sons).[32]

Pioneering Nigerian ethnoanthropologist M. Angulu Onwuejeogwu neatly summarized the core religiopolitical concepts of the Nri civilization:

> The concept of peace, harmony and truth was ritually symbolized and enacted in the ceremonies of the *ozo*-titled men, who were also the political elite. Nri men who had taken the *Ichi* title always carried in their hands the spear of peace called *otonsi*. With the spear of peace in their hands and the *ichi* marks on their faces, they were identified as the "sons" of Eze Nri, *Nwa nri*, who controlled the mystical force. They travelled generally unmolested from one Igbo settlement to another as agents of Eze Nri to perform political and ritual functions associated with the removing of abomination, the dissolving of the codes of abomination and the enacting of new codes, the ordaining of ritual and political officials, the crowning of chiefs, the making of peace and the creating of markets and shrines. In the performance of these activities Nri people spread into different parts of Igbo land and Eze Nri held some degree of control over the external and internal politics of the older Igbo settlements.[33]

In short, these settlements saw themselves as under the spiritual protection of the *Eze Nri*. And the prestige and power of the *Nwà Nri* came from their ability to ensure peace and prosperity and to safeguard the people from the misfortunes that plague human existence.

At its height, Nri influence extended across the densely populated region generally in a great arc from beyond the Niger in the west to Nsukka in the north, Bende in the east, and Owerri in the south. By the twentieth century, however, the area where Nri lineages were still found had contracted to the plateau region at the headwaters of the Imo River and west of the great escarpment that divides northern Igboland longitudinally from Nsukka through Enugu and Awgu and above a line roughly westward through Okigwe, Orlu, and Oguta and across the Niger north of Aboh.

The history of the Nri civilization can be divided into four periods.[34] The first is the formative period, comprising the reigns of the first three *Eze Nri* (Ìfikuánim, Nàmóke, Buífè), or roughly 1225–1425.[35] This was the initial period of primary migration and of the introduction and institutionalization of divinely inspired priest-kingship in the original or core settlements. This period was marked by the articulation of many of the institutions of Nri social and political culture.

The second, or classical era, roughly 1425–1700, began with the distinguished reign of Jìmófo I, a great leader who spread Nri influence throughout northern Igboland and established the *ikenga* cult of achievement. This era included a period of severe drought (ca. 1500–1530), which was followed by the magical reign of Fenenu (ca. 1530–1630),[36] who acquired many wives as well as the ability to fly and lived so long that it is said he "refused to die." But he was arrogant and eventually was cursed by the Council of Advisers (the *Nzèmábuo*), which led to his death. During Fenenu's reign, the Nri first came into contact with the Delta Igbo and other coastal peoples.[37] He was succeeded by Agu (r. ca. 1630). Even though his ascension marked the apogee of the Nri civilization, "when Nri was real Nri" (*oge Nri bu Nri*), Eze Agu was the first to abdicate his title because he refused the rigors of the office.[38] The classical era closed with another innovation, the dual kingship of Àlíke and Àpia (ca. 1635–1710).[39] They are remembered for living a very long time and for profoundly valuing human life, banning the ancient practice of abandoning "deformed" babies and the ritual sacrifice of slaves because they defined all people as human with the universal right to life. During their reign, and likely toward the latter part, slavery and slave trading became an issue, and they defined the status of a slave for the first time. They formally declared that such a person was "an unfortunate human being held in captivity" and therefore that it was an abomination to kill or bleed a slave. Alike and Apia also authorized the selling of slaves. By doing so, the kings acknowledged for the first time that the organized slave trade had reached the UmuNri.[40] The formal recognition of slavery and slave trading marked the end of the classical era of Nri.

The third period was an era of crisis from the early eighteenth through the early twentieth centuries. It was marked by ritual anomalies and was inaugurated by the supreme abomination of the murder of a sitting *Eze Nri*, Èzimílo (r. ca. 1710–25).[41] He had ascended to the title as the dark clouds of social violence and slave trading were gathering across central Igboland. His murder brought a severe drought and famine throughout the land, understood as collective punishments, which continued through the reign of his successor, Èwenétem (r. ca. 1725–75).[42] At the close of the eighteenth century, an even more serious abomination occurred. The newly installed *Eze Nri* Ènweleána (r. ca. 1790–1889), who had forcibly deposed his successor, Nwánkpo,[43] formally authorized the use of force. He created an anti-Aro [anti-NdeIkelionwu] military alliance (the *Amakom*) and then launched a war against the Aro. Hence, a very long interregnum occurred after his death.[44]

But the sense of things falling apart continued into the modern era. Shortly after the coronation in 1889 of Obalike, the British arrived in a series of punishing military expeditions, and in 1911 British forces disgraced the Eze Obalike in the supreme crisis of the Nri civilization. The British forced him to leave his shrine residence (the first *Eze Nri* ever to go outside the palace during his tenure) and travel to Awka. There, the British demanded at gunpoint that he formally renounce the powers of the *Nwa nri*, which he did.[45] His death in 1926 marked the advent of the modern era and triggered a further crisis of succession with a contested coronation and the secret installation of a second *Eze Nri* (1935–36). Thus, an unreconciled divided kingship existed between about 1935 and 1947.[46] The succession crisis has continued, though a new *Eze Nri*, Enwelani II, was officially coronated in 1988. The current crisis pits the people of the two oldest villages of Nri (Diodo and Akámpìsi), who still contest the coronation of Enwelani II, against the leaders of the other villages and lineages, the *Ádama*, and secular political authorities.[47] In the 1980s and 1990s, Chief Ònwanétilòra Anágo Okóye (1912–2002), who was initiated into the *ozo* council in 1944 and eventually gained the title of *ísìnze* (the most senior *ozo* in Nri), served as chief-priest until his death. Though there was a time of relative stability in the late colonial and independence decades (1947–70s), the modern period has been characterized by deepening crises, especially over succession. This trend has been exacerbated by the general secularization of Igbo (and Nri) society, the accommodation with Christianity, and the intervention of secular political machinations.[48]

The long period when "Nri was real Nri," or roughly the fifteenth through seventeenth centuries, occurred before the advent of slaving for the transatlantic slave trade and by the Aro in central Igboland. The emergence of slaving and the need to clarify slave status, probably in the latter seventeenth century and certainly by 1700, quickly gave way to one deepening crisis after another, beginning in earnest in the second quarter of the eighteenth century. This was also the period of extended drought, sustained Aro expansion into the Igbo heartland, the rise of Bonny on the coast, and the momentary importance of the Biafran slave trade to Virginia.

The further expansion of Aro merchant warlord settlements beginning in the mid–eighteenth century was reflected in the growing power of their client village groups in the Nri area. This shift resulted in the massive increase in the exportation of slaves from the coast of Calabar that continued through the rest of the century. By the 1790s, slaving was so destructive that even the Nri had to resort to violence to defend themselves. The added exigencies of sustained drought and even famine through at least the first half of the eighteenth century also probably helped pave the way for Aro influence. The consequent slave raiding and trading and the general increase in social violence directly undermined the core cultural premises of the Nri civilization, with tragic consequences even for those who escaped enslavement. By the twentieth century, perhaps only half of the area that had once been part of this civilization still maintained its ancestral connections with the "first Igbo."

In the eighteenth and nineteenth centuries, the rise of a new meritocratic elite in the heavily populated interior regions of Nri-Awka and Isuama (north-central Igboland), whose wealth was fueled by the importation of commodity currencies such as iron bars and copper rods, brought by new traders such as the Aro, encouraged the export of people as slaves. The community culture of Eboan African society, with its volatile mix of gerontocracy and meritocracy, of fatalism and localism, of *ôbia* (doctoring) and *aja* (sacrifice) and respect for *ikenga* (cult of achievement), lent ideological support to a growing system of exchange that increasingly transferred large numbers of people as slaves to the coast. As elsewhere, slavers in Igboland manipulated the political fragmentation of the region and benefited from the legality of enslaving one's enemies as well as of groups defined as Others. The destructive reach of the transatlantic slave trade extended deep into the Biafran hinterland and ravaged communities as far as 150 miles from the coast. Again, the key turning point was the first half of the eighteenth century, the same time that transatlantic shipments from Calabar were flooding far-off Virginia with Igbo slaves, many of whom would have been enslaved from communities within the ambit of the Nri civilization.

The transformations that were ultimately both cause and effect of the growing transatlantic slave trade "out of Calabar," including the rise of Bonny in the central littoral, the ascendance of Aro throughout the Igbo hinterland, and the slow collapse of the ancient Nri civilization, all crystallized in the first half of the eighteenth century. This was precisely the period when slave exports from the Bight of Biafra were sent disproportionately to the Chesapeake region of North America and to Virginia in particular. Not only were the great majority of these enslaved people likely Igbo, but they came from villages and village groups in the central and northern regions, and many of these people shared historical and cultural experiences rooted in the way of life of the "first Igbo."

CHAPTER THREE

Village-Level Society in "Eboan Africa"

The Nri were the "first Igbo" for a number of reasons. They were said to be the descendants of the oldest ancestors (the *ṅdi íchiẻ*), or the elder brothers of Igbo, whose sacred king, the *Eze Nri,* owned the original ancestral staff of authority (*ofo*). They were connected directly with the introduction of such essentially "Eboan" things as *nso* and the ideology of abominations; yam cultivation and *ṅjókku;* the *ofo;* the multitiered *ozo* titles system, with its *ichi* marks and other insignia of exalted rank; and the drum and perhaps human sacrifice. The Nri, in short, were the arbiters of Igbo custom (*òmenáni*), or what the ancestors said was done.[1]

Igbo people recognized that *omenani* was a function of local arrangements. As one proverb states, "The bush fowl of a village cries in the dialect of the village." Or put another way, "The hawk of Ezálo catches a fowl of Ezalo and goes to the cotton tree of Ezalo." Each village or village group might do things in its own fashion, produce its own footprints, which made local custom seem ever new. Often, however, the appearance of particularism merely colored a more fundamental unity of form and function. As another proverb collected early in the twentieth century put it, "I am a drum; if there is no wedge, the drum has no head."[2]

Eboan Africans, as Equiano termed the people of village-level Igboland, relied to a great extent on yam agriculture. Although Igboland was just one part of the larger yam belt of West Africa, the cultivation of *Dioscorea* was of particular import for the Igbo, for whom it indeed was "the king of crops."[3] Yams were central to the social conception of being Igbo and signified the deepest sense of Igboness. For example, traditionally, whenever an Igbo man's life was in peril outside of his local community, he could shout for "Igbo who eat [domesticated] yams" (*Igbo néri jí*) and expect immediate assistance.[4] In the early twentieth century, many Igbo still made eating yams a key to understanding shared ethnicity.[5]

Yam agriculture was time-consuming and required constant attention. The work included making clearings by burning the surrounding bush, making the mounds in which the seed yams were planted, tying up the runners with stakes, weeding, and harvesting and storage. A series of other crops, including cocoyams (but no cassava until the twentieth century), guinea corn, plantains, black-eyed peas, watermelons, various fruits, and the oil palm tree and cotton, were intermixed with yams. By the mid–eighteenth century, Eboan Africans also produced cotton and tobacco. Though Eboan agriculture centered on the production of yams, which all primary and secondary sources emphasize was characteristic or essential to Igboland, regional agriculture was actually a mixed-farming system with a continuous round of work. In fact, yam agriculture was largely inseparable from oil palm cultivation. This is one reason why constant human habitation of a particular area resulted in the reduction of the tropical rainforest to what became known as oil palm bush. Oil palms provided kernels and oil of course, but also the basic beverage of Igboland, palm wine (*mímbo*).[6]

Foodways were an important way of defining *omenani*. Igbo did not eat just anything, and what was edible was often a consequence of what the ancestors said was edible. The proverb "If vultures were edible birds, our forebears would have eaten them all up" captures this perfectly. Another common proverb closely identified folkways with foodways: "The type of firewood that is native to a village is the one that cooks the food of the people who live there." In fact, the relationship between the common garden crop okra (from the Igbo word *òkrò*), the pods of which were used to thicken soups and which Igbo thought had aphrodisiac properties, and the wisdom of the ancestors as distilled in proverbs was itself proverbial.[7] An early colonial anthropologist recorded this somewhat enigmatic proverb in 1911: "Those who cook okro soup have done, there remains those who only beat the (empty) plate." He explained that this meant that those who knew proverbs are dead; the living know few proverbs, which were "the oil for eating speech."[8]

The food staple throughout Igboland was *fufu*, boiled and pounded yam. Variously described as yams "boiled & then beaten into a consistence like dough" or "pounded until they become like a stiff dough," *fufu* in Igboland was invariably made of yams, not cassava.[9] Heavily peppered soups served in calabash bowls, greens "of the Calilue kind," and stews rounded out the Eboan diet.

The built world in Igboland—houses, juju structures, and living compounds—also reflected a local logic based on a rectangular model. There were no round structures or round buildings, as were preferred to the east and north. Captain Hugh Crow, who traded extensively at Bonny in the 1790s and 1800s, described the houses there as being "six or seven feet high," which means they must have been between about twelve and thirteen feet wide (using standard assumptions about vernacular architecture), or twelve feet on a side. Present-day "traditional" Igbo houses tend to be square, and if historical Igbo built on a twelve-foot-square model, such an Igbo protoform was nearly half again as large as the supposed "West and Central African norm" of ten feet square for building units in the diaspora.[10] All available evidence suggests that Igbo built on the template of rectangles, with compounds coming to resemble minivillages behind fences or walls that enclosed house yards. Most daily living took place in such yards, as people tended to live out-of-doors, and there women planted their garden plots of kitchen crops, including *okro*.

For most people in historical Igboland, the world was circumscribed by the limits of family compounds. As Equiano remembered, they typically were "a large square piece of ground, surrounded by a moat or fence, or enclosed with a wall made of red earth tempered." Neighborhoods or villages were composed of adjoining compounds together with the outlying fields, which often were "some hours walk from our dwellings." Adjacent villages, or the village group, comprised "one little state or district."[11]

The extreme localism of most Igbo meant that personal loyalties rarely extended further than one's village or group of adjoining villages. This discouraged large-scale state formation but encouraged a culture of honor and the investment of political power in the village-level patrilineage. As Igbo in Owerri say, there was "a king in every lineage" (*Eze no na nchi*).[12] In fact, every village had its leader (*eze*) or set of leaders (the holders of the Nri-based *ozo* title, of which the *eze* title was the highest), which Europeans later saw as so many little kings and chiefs, just as every compound had its headman and every lineage its *òkpára*. As Samuel A. Crowther noted, "A king is acknowledged in every district of the Ibo country," and there also was a "superior class of men, who have paid enormous sums to obtain this rank." He also observed that "every headman appears to be master in his own quarters."[13]

Furthermore, these leaders expected and exacted respect from their lesser fellows, often in the form of special greetings and acts of obeisance. In 1831, the Obi of Aboh, on the Niger River, had detained the Lander brothers as valuable contraband. When more whites showed up the following year, he felt constrained to ask R. A. K. Oldfield, one of the white leaders who kept pestering the Obi for some canoe men, "what he was to call me." As William Allen noted, everywhere in the Niger Igbo area, the people were "punctilious in salutations and greetings." "It is a great insult," wrote Crowther, "to salute these gentlemen with the common salutation, except by the title they bear." Achieving the *ozo* title enabled the holder to receive an ennobling facial scarification, the *ichi,* which William B. Baikie wrote, "entitles the possessors to respect."[14] Such respect or esteem extended to the entire class of titled men, to their children, and to the secret societies that the men constituted, such as the various masquerades and *okonko* or *conko* (clubs).[15]

The material world in Igboland was marked by the use of iron (blacksmiths were powerful people) for basic tools such as hoes, machetes, and diggers (plows were not known). Village specialists also crafted distinctive low-fired earthenware ceramics and carved calabashes as vessels and carved wooden items. Igbo wood carvers were known for their intricately designed wood panels and doors and for ceremonial stools and *ikenga* figures. People generally slept on mats or on raised platforms or benches. Musical instruments ranged from locally made brass bells and gongs to short four-holed flutes, distinctive xylophones, and finger pianos as well as stringed banjolike instruments and various kinds of drums (often of the hollowed-wood rather than membrane type).[16]

Strongly patriarchal gender roles were clearly marked and defined in these Eboan societies. As one proverb states, "Do this do that does not allow a woman to grow a beard."[17] Women potted, grew "edoes" (cocoyams) and all the kitchen crops and tended the other crops, and did the cooking as well as the market work. Men planted and harvested yam crops and controlled the oil palm and its products. Men also did carving and smelting crafts and much of the public palaver and juju work, including sacrifice. Both sexes were circumcised, sometimes in infancy and in other places at puberty or before marriage, and clitoridectomy apparently was universal. Obesity was considered a mark of beauty, especially female beauty, and the institution of seclusion in a "fattening house" as preparation for marriage seems to have been universal. Marriage itself was a process, with no single distinct ceremony but rather a series of rites that connected one kindred to another for the purpose of creating children, reincarnating the *úmunnè* (patrilineage), and providing for future *ndi ichie.*

One of the oldest known proverbs collected in Igboland, in the 1850s, was about how people should respond to new situations. Drawing on the imagery of the *okóko* (guinea fowl), of the house yards so common throughout Igboland, and of the group of fellow *okoko* who surely would be there, the proverb said, "A new fowl when brought into the yard, walks gently and looks steadily on the old ones, to see what they do." Such beings, of course, would learn to crow in the language of that village. This imagery of learned performance, of useful things passed down by the group yet in their performance perhaps (as Equiano thought) "ever new," undergirds another saying, that dates to the early years of the twentieth century: "The song I sing, the chorus is not difficult to sing."[18]

Historical village-level society—that is, the artifacts, learned behavior, institutions, and beliefs of the people in the Igbo hinterland— had an essential character. Its performance also derived from (and expressed) a dynamic logic of its own. Based as it was on ritual (the acting out of certain universal and generally held beliefs) and on custom (the definition and enforcement of particular ways of doing things), this community culture defined what it meant to be an Eboan African. As the enslaved Igbo Equiano remembered, this definition was both universalistic (centered on general forms of public performance) and particularistic (ever new). Its performance was a function of internal Igbo dynamics and was the consequence of a historical logic largely unaffected by European cultural influences.

Equiano believed that dance, music, and poetry (proverbs) defined Igbo-speaking people as Eboan. These performances also took for granted the existence of a historical public, of a group of people culturally conversant with one another and bounded by time and space who would understand the performance. As an Igbo proverb states, "A new man does not sing" (*Onye ofo edekwe*).[19] In other words, Eboan community culture was something that existed in its performance, that was historically real, and that people recognized as guiding their behavior in concrete ways. As Equiano understood, in historical Igboland every person by definition belonged to a group, and every group had its rituals, customs, beliefs, and ways of life—in short, its community culture.

The lack of direct contact with Europeans in the Igbo heartland was mirrored in the lack of a specific Igbo word denoting "white man" or "European." Whereas Efik and Ibibio peoples had combined two indigenous words, *kara* (encircle, rule, abuse, master) and *mb* (plural) to form *mbákara* (white man, European), Niger Igbo peoples eventually appropriated the surname of the mid–nineteenth century English explorer W. B. Baikie (*béke*) to denote all Europeans. Various other terms used by Igbo in the nineteenth and twentieth centuries to gloss "whites" or "Europeans" included *óyibo* (stranger) and *ónye-òcha* (white-color person).[20] As late as 1911, however, Igbo in the Isuama heartland still called all whites *nwàmbé-ke* (children of *beke*) and often used *beke* to mark new things that Europeans had introduced to Igboland.

In the early and mid-nineteenth century, the relative lack of European material culture in the Igbo interior also clearly was remarkable. Even after nearly 150 years of extensive slaving and trading with intermediary groups such as the Aro and Ńkwerre and on the Niger River with canoe merchants direct from Nembe, Bonny, and New Calabar, many (perhaps most) Igbo people used locally made cloth and other products made by local craftspersons and acquired in nearby village markets rather than from headmen on whom they theoretically may have relied to redistribute imported European goods.

The Lander brothers wrote in 1831 that unlike people in contemporary Yorubaland and Hausaland, for example, the "Eboe people have a savage appearance."[21] Igbo men and women tended to wear white or blue lengths of locally made cloth (either cotton or the fiber of a forest plant called *úfa*) and loincloths. Igbo women looked especially exotic to early Europeans, with elaborate coiffures and heavy ivory or brass anklets. In 1841, Allen noted "the Ibu fashion among the women of wearing enormous anklets." In the 1850s, Baikie wrote that "one custom peculiar to this district [riverine Igboland] is, that all women who can afford it, wear ponderous ivory anklets, made from the thickest parts of large tusks. These are so very weighty as to give a strange character to the gait, and a peculiar dragging motion to the leg." In walking several miles inland from Onitsha to another village in the mid-1850s, Rev. John C. Taylor was struck by the unusual local cloth and clothing styles of the people. He described one woman as wearing "a sort of country cloth deeply dyed [reddish-brown] with camwood, two broad plates made of brass, as leg-rings, and her hands strung with ivory as white as snow." When Taylor arrived at the village, the local headman wore no hat or trousers (or, presumably, shoes) but had one major piece of European wear, "a soldier's red coat of an English regiment." The rest of that leader's ceremonial dress was a long cotton sheet (*tobe*) "studded with feathers, and a little cloth around his waist."[22]

Cotton textiles of many various kinds had been a staple commodity currency in the coastal trade for slaves for more than a century, yet locally made cloths seem to have predominated among the general populace throughout historical Igboland. Equiano wrote that in the 1750s women in his region wove locally grown cotton into coarse ("calico") and fine ("muslin") cloths. Such cloths, he noted, were "usually dyed blue, which is our favourite colour."[23] Around 1800 at New Calabar and Bonny, Crow noted that the "clothing of the lower orders [of Igbo who came there] is made of a kind of thread, manufactured from grass." In 1841, most of the people (Omun/Ekoi) along the east bank of the Cross River across from the "Eboe Country" did not wear "clothes of European or cotton manufacture, their covering being of their own grass-cloths." Moreover, the

European cloths that Captain Becroft and J. B. King did see in Omun were, in their opinion, "in an inferior style, as silks and the finer qualities of cotton cloths are excluded by the traders of Old Calabar from this market." In the same year, while going up the Niger, Captain William Allen observed that beyond the delta, in Igboland, "the people are better clothed in the native costume; European articles of dress being rare." As late as the 1850s, people in the Onitsha area made their own cloth, the best of which was "nearly all white: no dye is used to checquer and stripe them as in the upper parts of the river."[24] Many, perhaps most, Igbo people therefore seemed to wear locally made coarse cotton (*ákwa*) or cottonlike (*ufa*) cloths, which generally were produced by women. Some of these textiles were dyed a deep indigo blue, but much of what people wore in Igboland was undyed white.

In the Nsukka region of northern Igboland, oral traditions recorded in the 1970s credited the Aro with bringing the first woven cotton cloths (*ékwa-éru* [*akwa-aro*]) to the region. These new cottons supposedly supplanted the older cloths made of a local fiber called *áji*, which a modern local village historian in the region defined as "a fibrous material used by the ancients to cover themselves of their nakedness." Yet those same traditions assert that Nsukka (and by implication, Nri-Awka) people acquired their cotton-weaving technology (especially distinctive vertical looms) from their northern Igala neighbors.[25] An Igbo weaver born in 1909 explained that in "pre-colonial days we made use of cloth which was made locally. This was hand-woven. The weavers made cloth from the cotton plant *mkpúlu olúlu* which we planted in our farms." An Igbo man born in the 1880s described the antiquity and ubiquity of locally handmade cloths in historical Igboland:

Even before the arrival of the white men we wove our own cloth. . . . Our weavers made cloth from the cotton plant, which looked similar to the white man's cotton. We grew this plant in our farms and when they were harvested they were spun into threads and later woven into cloth. . . . There was also the *ufa* plant. The bark of this plant contained fabric-like materials out of which cloth could be woven. This plant was very abundant in the forest. All we did was to get to the forest and collect them in bundles. When we returned we had them split, soaked, boiled and the rough portions removed. . . . A weaver peeled off a piece which she made into long threads. These threads were arranged in bundles and with a needle were woven into cloth. *Ufa* cloth used to be very white though some people dyed it. The *ufa* plant is no longer in the forest since the arrival of a certain type of plant that has now almost exterminated all other plants.[26]

The limited importation of some woven cotton textiles by Aro and Nkwerre traders in the era of the slave trade may even have spurred the development of this "traditional" cotton-weaving craft throughout the interior of Igboland. If cotton cloths imported initially by the Aro and their agents in fact supplanted the previous cloths made of local natural fibers, such imports also seemed to spur the production of locally made cotton textiles. Perhaps as early as the mid–eighteenth century and certainly by the early nineteenth century, Igbo peoples in the areas most closely connected with long-distance trade to the coast relied largely on local textile crafters (usually women) to supply common cottons. The fact that women also were the major petty traders throughout Igboland and ran the ubiquitous local markets would have encouraged the availability of such coarse cottons for everyday use rather than cloth carried by traders from the coast.[27]

Markets throughout the interior followed a historical Eboan logic. As one modern historian put it, "the kind of trade which had been basic in 1500 was still basic in 1850."[28] Most markets were held once every fourth day, with larger intergroup markets and regional fairs alternating in a continuous cycle based on the ancient four-day Igbo week.[29] These local village markets formed a hierarchical market ring where women went to trade basic foodstuffs and local manufactures in a regular sequence on *Èkè* day, which was the customary rest day. On the Niger in the 1840s, for example, every village had "a market, generally once in four days; but the principal feature is in the large fairs held at different points on the river, about once a fortnight for what may be called their foreign trade, or intercourse with neighbouring nations."[30]

Higher-level or "senior" markets attracted longer-distance trade and a greater diversity of goods, but those were still mostly concerned with general provisions. Equiano accompanied his mother on her market rounds and remembered that "the principal articles of [trade], as I have observed, are provisions."[31] Even the largest fairs, such as those at Bende and Uburu, lasted for four days every twenty-fourth day—for one *izu* every three *izu ukwu*.[32] Each village "owned" its market, which was under the protection of that village's tutelary deity, who punished those who violated local rules or refused to honor the locally accepted currency. The largest markets were owned by the most powerful village groups, with the Aro owning the biggest of the regional fairs.[33]

Unlike at Bonny, moreover, where coastal traders shifted their activities around 1800 to a seven-day week, people at Old Calabar maintained a four-day pattern.[34] One uncomprehending visitor at Old Calabar in the 1820s recounted that there were "two grand festivals here, which take place every eighth day in succession. . . . The succession of these festivals is curious enough; that which takes place on Thursday in this week, will be on Friday in the next week; and the one on Friday this week, will be on Saturday in the following week, and so on."[35] In the 1850s, as many as two thousand people attended the "great market-day" at Onitsha. As one astute observer wrote about a relatively poor village in central Igboland in the 1930s, the "seething crowd of an Ibo market with its chattering and its gossip—and its transaction of business withal—epitomises much of Ibo life."[36]

This pattern of local markets held every fourth or eighth day dated at least to the seventeenth century. James Barbot, writing of the Calabar coast in the 1690s, noted that in the Igbo interior, "there are two market-days every week, for slaves and provisions." The local historian of Onitsha, S. I. Bosah, believed that Onitsha's market, also held every fourth day, was founded in the seventeenth century. The basic pattern of local markets run by women every four days stayed the same in the nineteenth century and by the early twentieth century had become something that people fought to keep. In the 1920s, one colonial officer related that the "Eke day" was seen as a customary right that local Igbo asserted was nonnegotiable even in the new circumstances of what they had come to call "Government time."[37]

The goods sold at most of these markets also reflected an Eboan African logic. Village markets were vents for surplus as well as a collective means for redistributing subsistence goods. Women exchanged foodstuffs, including yams and other vegetables as well as palm oil, fowls, and goats, to buy something else. They also traded local crafts such as cloths, woven mats, baskets, and earthenware pots. This "usual miscellany of African productions, with the same noisy and eager system of barter," characterized village markets throughout the region up to the 1850s. As Equiano remembered of his childhood a hundred years earlier, "we have few manufactures," he wrote, "for the most part . . . calicoes, earthen ware, ornaments, and instruments of war and husbandry." On the Niger River in the 1840s, "earthenware jars, calabashes, cotton cloths, and grass mats of native manufacture, were the principal things brought to the markets."[38]

In the 1850s in central Igboland, goods of European manufacture were still rare and valuable enough to provoke violent takings by the hosts of the most powerful markets. Even though theft was one of the most serious crimes in the region, supposedly seen as a prime abomination by the deities and punishable by excruciating

death or sale into slavery, in 1858 women from Onitsha who had
carried European goods to the Nkwerre market were plundered by
their hosts.[39]

The Onitsha market women had gone to Nkwerre, at least twenty
miles away, with another troop of women from nearby Ńsúbè.
At the time, Onitsha was a much less powerful village group, with a
smaller market and nothing like the connections to iron smelting,
itinerant blacksmithing, and the *úmuchúkwu* (Aro "god men") that
people had at Nkwerre. When the Onitsha women showed up with
a large cache of European manufactures as well as the usual "good
native articles" to sell, the locals "envied them, and determined
to plunder their goods." Apparently, each Nkwerre woman at the
market "contrived to get something; and the poor [Onitsha] women
were obliged to take to their heels, and escape for their lives." The
Ńsúbè women, however, were not routed from the market. The
men of Onitsha threatened to go to war over this affront to their
women's honor but then quickly allowed the "people of Nkwerre"
publicly to apologize and to pay "ample compensation" to restore
the peace.[40] The Nkwerre presumably plundered the foreign goods
either because they could not afford to buy them or because they
could not afford to let Onitsha women become suppliers of such
goods to their market.[41] It may also be that women who marketed
European-made goods were seen as usurping a male trading prerog-
ative and thus violated a *nso* (taboo) of Nkwerre.

Even in Bonny in the decades of the greatest import of European
manufactures (1790s–1810s), many of the people there lived outside of the bounds of European things. Men and women both wore
a "piece of cloth . . . *in their way,* invariably tied round the waist."
People on the coast generally did not use knives and forks and slept
on mats on the floor, in the same fashion as people on the Niger to
the west. The main market at Bonny (and perhaps at Aboh) was full
of traders, "buying & selling Beads, Cloth, Guns, Knives, Mugs &
other articles of English, French & Spanish manufacture, as well as

provisions, etc." But at the same time, most people owned only "a few calabashes, some earthen culinary utensils of home manufacture, a wooden mortar or two, and a few mats, together with their fetiches, or charms." Bonny's principal traders, it seems, hoarded European manufactures, often storing them in cellars under their houses. At Old Calabar, the most powerful trade king, Duke Ephraim, had "several warehouses full of goods, some of which he has had in store for years, such as wines, spirits, liqueurs, sail-cloth, cordage, manufactured goods, copper rods, iron bars, etc. etc." Some of this cache he distributed on the day of his weekly "festival," but much of it he seemed simply to hold.[42]

In general, then, the lack of European material-cultural influence derived from the lack of personal contact with white people. In the coastal entrepôts, only the principal men dealt in trade with whites, and women continued to run the local markets.[43] Furthermore, not until 1896 did the first white men go into the interior of southern Igboland (through Ngwaland to Bende), and on that expedition they were swamped by local crowds straining to see these exotic creatures. The leader of that expedition, Major Arthur Leonard, later described the Igbo as "a medley of tribes so singularly alike in their sociology, yet differing from each other in language and dialect."[44] In the era of the transatlantic slave trade, and well into the twentieth century, that "sociology" was profoundly rooted in a world largely insulated from direct personal or cultural contact with Europeans.[45]

Throughout Igboland, people attempted to gain mastery of their Eboan African world through the performance of ritual. The people prepared offerings, poured libations, and performed sacrifices to the spirits of their individual and collective ancestors (*ndi ichie*) as well as to "feed" and placate the many forces, gods, and "invisibles" (*ndi muo*) who inhabited the animistic Eboan African world.[46] Equiano wrote, "Those spirits . . . such as our dear friends and relations, they believe always attend them, and guard them from the bad spirits or their foes." For this reason, he said, "they always before eating, as I have observed, put some small portion of the meat, and pour some of the drink, on the ground for them; and they often make oblations of the blood of beasts or fowls at their graves."[47]

The core of historical Igbo ritual performance and thus of Eboan community culture, was sacrifice (*aja*). Throughout Igboland as well as in heavily Igboized Elem Kalabari, Bonny, and Old Calabar, public ritual killings of consecrated victims, occasionally including even humans, was ubiquitous.[48] Personal *aja* included pouring libations, apparently at every meal. Sacrifice was a fundamental religious act. As one modern scholar wrote, sacrifice was "the soul of Ibo cult," "the essence of their worship, and the heart of their religion."[49] Sacrifice was performed most commonly by diviners (*obea* or *dibia*) as part of asking or demanding (*a-juju*) something from the multitude of invisible forces, powers, and spirits (*muo*) who inhabited the Igbo world. More importantly, though less commonly, people engaged specialists from Nri to make sacrifices to cleanse or remove "abominations" that had occurred as a result of breaking taboos. Sacrifice in historical Igboland reaffirmed the ideal existence of the invisibles largely because people thought of *aja* in terms of "feeding" the benevolent spirits (the *muo*) and of placating the bad or evil spirits (the *mó njò*).[50]

Unlike other peoples in West Africa, however, Igbo generally did not eat the physical remains of sacrifices; thus, the religious act of *aja* was not a function of "eating the gods" but rather of petitioning and of "feeding" them.[51] Indeed, sacrifice in Igboland tended to reaffirm the close connections between the gods and the people, between the invisibles and the visibles, rather than expressing the separation of the profane world from that of the sacred. As one recent scholar wrote, in Igboland, "the gods and men live a symbiotic life. . . . Men feed the gods and the gods provide health, fertility of soil and reproduction."[52] As elsewhere, though, sacrifice in Igboland also underscored the connections among the people, who struggled to live in a world inhabited by a host of invisible as well as visible beings. In this Eboan world, nothing happened by chance; therefore, leaving anything to chance was dangerous.[53]

Sacrifice was the principal way that people in Eboan Africa attempted to create order out of the events of their individual and collective lives. Sacrifice, the ritual killing of consecrated victims to feed the spirits, to placate the powerful forces (visible as well as invisible) in Igboland, and to petition for answers, structured much of historical Igbo ritual life. Igbo people understood that they sacrificed living things because the deities demanded it. The more powerful the deity or the more powerful the need for "asking" (*a-juju*), the more valuable must be the sacrificial victim. Conversely, some sacrifices, called *ichu aja* (joyless sacrifice), were of rotten or disfigured or ugly things, such as rotten eggs, sick chickens, abortive lambs, or lizards. These joyless sacrifices were done specifically to distract otherwise malevolent spirits, "much as a dangerous dog is given a bone to keep it busy."[54]

Eboan people sacrificed for any number of reasons. The most specialized sacrifices were to remove the "abomination" of having violated a taboo (*nso*), usually thought of as a transgression against *Ana* (the ground, Earth Deity). These usually required the services of a Nri man because the *ndi Nri* were the only people with the power to remove such pollution. People also sacrificed regularly to the *ndi ichie* and the *ndi muo,* offering not just libations at every meal but also sacrificing at periodic personal and collective rites, when misfortunes struck, and at funerals, festivals, harvests, and other calendrical events. At Bonny in the 1820s, for example, people performed sacrifices "at different periods, which are governed by the Moon." At such times they would "offer up Goats & Fowls as a sacrifice to their departed Progenitors, & the more especially if they had performed any signal achievements." At one large festival at Bonny in 1826, in which the king distributed rum, cloth, beads, and brass manillas to the general population, "Goats, Dogs & Fowls were

sacrificed in immense numbers—long poles on which were suspended dead carcuses of the canine race met the eye at every turn."[55]

Equiano also recounted that sacrifices were common, marking
special events, especially days of thanksgiving. Most sacrifices were
performed by the lineage heads (*okpala*) and other leading men:
"They have many offerings, particularly at full moons; generally two
at harvest before the fruits are taken out of the ground: and when
any young animals are killed, sometimes they offer up part of them
as a sacrifice. These offerings, when made by one of the heads of a
family, serve for the whole. I remember we often had them at my
father's and my uncle's, and their families have been present. Some
of our offerings are eaten with bitter herbs. We had a saying among
us to any one of a cross temper, 'That if they were to be eaten, they
should be eaten with bitter herbs.' "[56] These sacrificial rites often
included other forms of mass or collective performance, especially
dancing and singing. In the 1820s at Bonny, Richard M. Jackson
described at length (and in somewhat dramatic and disparaging
terms) the "high Jujew Festival" held there in mid-February, including what must have been a masquerade (*Mmuo*), perhaps by one of
the secret societies of southern Igboland (such as *okonko*).[57] He was
most impressed with the singing, dancing, and firing of guns that
accompanied the sacrifices at the various shrines or temples in the
town:

> Before the Jujew Houses Women & Children danced to the sound of
> their own voices, & the shrill accompaniments of their native music.
> A few Men at intervals sent forth most discordant bellowings from the
> teeth [tusks] of Elephants, formed into trumpets. The Priests at times
> issued from the sanctuaries where their Heathen rites were perform-
> ing, & ringing small Bells attached to their garments, commanded
> silence; they then addressed a few extemporaneous words to the
> multitude, who when they had concluded, made the "welkin ring"
> with their boisterous acclamations. . . . Before dusk the Town was

completely in confusion; drunkenness had usurped the Throne of Reason, & we retired from this extraordinary scene, amid the firing of Guns, the discharge of Musketry, and the shouts of the Negroes.[58]

On the upper Cross River in the 1840s, people celebrated important events in riotous fashion, with drumming and gun firing, and most likely sacrifices of some kind. One night, perhaps in response to the 1842 arrival of Europeans Becroft and King and their frightful steamship, the locals prevented the whites from sleeping "by the frequent discharge of muskets and continued noise of native drums, which the inhabitants of the town below kept up without intermission until morning."[59] At Onitsha in 1858, people celebrated the success of a man named Oríkabùe, who had just earned a high-status title, by dancing and singing (and presumably by sacrificing as well). Rev. Taylor's description does not mention sacrifices, which may, however, have been performed before he arrived on the scene: "I heard the sounds of drummings, accompanied with wild music. As I approached nearer to our little abode, I saw the people were in high glee, marking their faces with stripes of red ochre or *uri,* and white clay. The deafening sounds of musketry, the playing of swords and spears, the decoration of Orikabue's house with pieces of handkerchiefs, young men and women, old men, women, and children, all vigorously employed in jigging, clapping their hands, and uniting in the boisterous mirth, each in their turn dropping into the circle—all these things were done in honour to Orikabue for his commissional title as *Jasére.*"[60]

The most common reason for sacrificing, however, was to petition the spirits. People sacrificed to ask a particular spirit for something or for an explanation of why something has happened or to find out what the person, a family member, a village, or a village group needed to do to placate that spirit or to ensure the continued goodwill of that deity or of the deities in general. In Eboan Africa, ignorance was anything but bliss, yet knowledge always had its price.

Sacrifice therefore was intimately connected with the concept of *a-juju,* or asking, which is why so much of Igbo magicoreligious practice was called *juju.*[61]

We can distinguish between two domains of Eboan juju. One level was apparently associated largely with male power and public performance—that is, *aja* (sacrifice) in its strict sense. This public cult also had a series of objects and shrines (oracles) that men used to express their authority through their representation of the ancestors as well as other invisible powers. Another level was private sacrifice, including pouring libations, and personal cult, which people expressed by reading omens and signs and wearing charms. This second kind of juju may have been dominated by women.

The term *juju* clearly meant much more than simply "fetish" or "idol." Juju referred to almost anything that had sacred or supernatural power, including the lesser deities, oracles, shrines, and fetish houses (including *mbari*) that dotted the landscape. Objects like the ritual staff of patriarchal authority (*ofo*); wooden figures of the cult of achievement (*ikenga*); clay fertility charms (*ibúdu*); charmed ceramic pots or "god basins" and other amulets; iron; and substances such as poisons (*nsi*), cut hair and clipped nails, and "protective medicines" (*ogwu*) in general, as well as sorcery, fell under the generic description of juju in historical Igboland.

In general, however, *juju* meant spiritual power—more specifically, the power invested in the multitudinous lesser deities as well as in the objects vested with that power (known colloquially as "medicine").[62] Leonard defined such medicine as the "spiritual means for gaining ends that are superhuman—beyond or outside the scope of humanity, in other words." More recently, Francis A. Arinze defined such medicine (specifically *ogwu*) as "useful things charged with powers which man can exploit."[63] For example, the most powerful nineteenth-century oracle, where people went to petition the Supreme Deity (Chi-ukwu) as a last resort, *Ibinokpabi* of Arochukwu, was known as the "Long Juju." This was the case even though the people of Aro called themselves *umu-chukwu* (God's people; lit. "children of God") rather than something like *umu-juju*. Whites and other Europeans, however, commonly were thought of as juju.[64]

The use of the term *juju* to describe "the gods we can see" and "spiritual power" (medicine) can be dated at least to the seventeenth century. At New Calabar in 1699, people surrounded themselves with idols and ritual objects to which they sacrificed and which they called *juju*. Barbot wrote that every house in the settlement "is full of idols, as well as the streets of the town. They call them Jou-Jou, being in the nature of tutelar gods. Many of them are dried heads of beasts, others made by the Blacks of clay and painted, which they worship and make their offerings to." To the east, at Andony (later Opobo), people also called their fetish-houses "Jou Jou," which Barbot's associate Grazilhier in 1699 observed were "full of the skulls of their enemies killed in war, and others of beasts; besides a quantity of human bones and other trash, some of them moulded with clay, and painted as at [New] Calabar."[65]

Among the Kalabari, moreover, the most powerful juju traditionally came from the north. In general, people thought that the further away a "medicine" originated, the greater its power. At New Calabar, one chief confided that Igbo juju was the most effective for witchcraft and that the "most dangerous rites are usually practised by means of medicines bought from Ibo doctors." The ethnographer who recorded the chief's statement also noted that in the early twentieth century at least, Igbo peoples "dread jujus and witchcraft far more than do Kalabari."[66]

Throughout Igboland, as the diversity of concepts and objects subsumed by the term suggests, juju was a panethnic element of Eboan African life. As Crow noted for Bonny, "the natives attach the greatest confidence to their fetiches . . . and touch themselves with them on various parts of the body, for they believe that they see and watch all their actions." He noted that the Igbo at Bonny were especially cognizant of the spiritual power of things. "The Eboes,"

Crow wrote, "when employed at any kind of labour, continually talk to their tools, and that in an earnest manner, as they were addressing a human being. Other inanimate objects they will address in the same manner, even to their canoes and the ground on which they tread."[67] In the Niger River area in the 1840s, every house or compound had one or more carved wooden or painted ceramic "Fetiches, or idols . . . as well as amulets, or charms, suspended from sticks in the quadrangular courts. Many of the idols had pots of water and food placed near them."[68]

Such sculptural jujus were also placed in secluded glens near streams or in elaborately decorated rectangular buildings at the entrances of villages, as were various other objects, including ceramic images, European plates, bottles, manillas, and cowries. Other kinds of jujus or charms, made mostly of skulls and bones and often including chickens "staked to the ground," were placed at crossroads "to ward off an anticipated evil, or to check or break the spell which has produced disease."[69]

In the 1840s, William Allen stumbled across a big ceramic juju, or "large earthen idol, placed in a thicket surrounded by high trees," near the Niger River. His description of this encounter suggests that by the middle decades of the nineteenth century, perhaps reflecting the supremacy of the Aro throughout Igboland, juju was increasingly connected with Chukwu. Allen wrote, "Some persons who were near when we moved towards the direction of this sacred spot, made earnest signs for us not to approach, exclaiming, 'Tshuku-Tshuku,' and just as we had obtained a look of the figure, one of the Ju-ju men, or priests, came up in a menacing manner, and would not allow us to remain, or further to examine the neighbourhood. He appeared to be very much exasperated, and disposed to punish our temerity."[70]

Oath making was another major form of juju. In a society of rules rather than rulers, people made and were proud to keep contracts with each other. In general, people relied on their honor (and the honor of others) to give and to get good conduct, then sealed these contracts with personal and collective oaths.[71] Oath making was a serious act—indeed, a sacred one—because the promise made was backed by divine sanction. Revenge was the proper and expected punishment for breaking an oath, and such revenge was one of the chief functions of the jujus, especially the ancestors. As Leonard noted in 1906, for Igbo people, making an oath was "a matter so sacred that, just as the keeping of it brings its own reward, the breaking of it involves its own punishment."[72] Another ethnographer was struck by the importance of honor (oathing) among Igbo in Owerri, writing of their "tendency to ritualistic, formal behaviour" as evidenced by "their constant resort to a formal oath in one type of relationship after another." In southern Igboland, men would perform oaths of innocence, which they called "drinking juju," by pouring a little gin, declaring that the juju will kill a liar, and then drinking the gin to prove innocence.[73] Such oaths were honorable acts, requiring courage and responsibility, and they linked people both within and between local communities.

Oaths were equally important in the nineteenth century. Crow explained that men at Bonny performed oaths or what he called "swearing the fetish," to bind themselves to a particular obligation (perhaps for purposes of trade). "This is done by the party," wrote Crow, "whose veracity is put to the test, taking his favourite fetiche, and drinking what is termed the oath-draught, which is followed by an imprecation, that the fetiche may kill him, if he do not perform the obligation he has promised." Similar ceremonies, usually involving some kind of imprecation or long preamble followed by a sacrifice, were prerequisites to negotiating the terms of trade between each European ship and the principal men of the area, what was known as "breaking trade."[74]

When Major Leonard in 1896 announced to the coastal treaty chiefs his intention to go to Bende to find out why the Aro had stopped the trade to Bonny and Opobo, the local leaders responded

with "incredulity" and "a storm of excitement and argument" about
how such a journey was too dangerous. The only way that Leonard
could get any of the headmen to agree to go was if the party would
stop and make formal oaths of friendship at each village along the
route. In other words, the coastal chiefs "decided unanimously that
the safest and surest, in fact, the only, way to pass through the country
as far as Bende was to swear Ju Ju in every town." Some of these coastal
leaders, of course, may have had conflicts with leaders of interior villages or village groups. But even if they did so, they realized that, in
the words of Samuel Crowther (writing of Onitsha in the 1850s),
"such quarrels are settled with oaths, which in many instances are as
binding as oaths of enmity." In effect, these chiefs made Leonard
operate within their terms of ritualized honor, and this he did, using
an "oath-draught" of a bottle of "German beer which had been rendered noxious by means of all kinds of vile decoctions."[75]

The ceremonial oath or "imprecation" made by Leonard's inter-
preter Albert Jaja of Opobo to the assembled chiefs and their people at the first town on the journey and their ritualized response
were probably typical. Jaja stood before the whole village population and declared to the leaders, "If you, or any of your people, do
or wish us any harm, our Ju Ju, which in its revenge is terrible and
deadly, will most assuredly kill you all, even down to the first born;
but if you do and wish well to us, may the longest life, combined
with the greatest prosperity and happiness, be yours." The local
chiefs each then tasted a couple of drops of "the liquid nausea."

The chiefs of Into Ozo then brought out their juju, which was a
most sacred ceramic relic but which appeared to Leonard to be
"a meagre piece of a broken pitcher": "This absolutely miserable
object, upon which, however, all the assembled chiefs looked with
awe and veneration, as if within its plastic grasp lay the fate of all
their lives, was carried right round the members of our party by two
chiefs of the town, one of them calling down every available curse
and imprecation if our contact with them proved in any way hurtful

to any of their people. If, on the contrary, however, it turned out to be beneficial, every conceivable blessing was to be showered on us." The ceremony concluded with an exchange of gifts and with the assignment of a couple of villagers as "guides sent in charge of us by the chiefs." Leonard noted that the assignment of such guides was as important as the actual swearing of comity, for "they took upon themselves the responsibility of our welfare and safety, until they in turn had handed us over safely to the next town."[76]

In the interior areas of Igboland, such oaths most commonly were sworn on an *ofo*. This clublike wooden staff, always made from a particular tree (*Detarium senegalense*), symbolized the authority of the ancestors and the collective identity of the patrilineal kindred (*umunne*). Held in trust by the lineage head, usually the oldest living male (the *okpara*), the *ofo* was the main symbol of the central cult of all Igbo, the cult of the ancestors.[77] The *ofo* was also integral to public oath making. Because revenge often was a function of the ancestors (to whom one always had to answer for one's behavior) as well as other juju, swearing on the *ofo* was to call directly on their vigilance. In the 1850s Taylor even defined *ofo* directly in terms of Igbo honor when he described these artifacts as "one of the sacred sticks held by the Ibos, used during the time of making oaths."[78]

Another constituent element of honor, vengeance, was also thought of in terms of the group, especially the other members of one's *umunne*. Across Igboland, the ideal of "a life for a life" operated to enforce group solidarity. The *lex talionis* also reinforced both the culture of honor in general and localism in particular. As Crowther noted, in comparison to the Yoruba and Hausa people, whom he knew well, the concept of *lex talionis* or the "law of *life* for *life* among the Ibos is very strong, and is more to be dreaded than any other." In other words, Igbo had to answer to each other and for each other's behavior.[79]

One of the most important groups, however, especially in terms of defining what it meant to be Igbo in the era of the slave trade, was the *ôbia* or *dibia*.[80] These men (and occasionally women) were the diviners, the doctors, the petitioners who specialized in finding out why things happened in daily life and in determining what needed to be done to placate the gods in a given situation. In short, they were the juju men par excellence.

The *dibia* or *ôbia* was the person, usually a man, who could communicate directly with the spirits. Known across Igboland and the heavily Igboized coastal settlements as powerful and dangerous and thus both feared and respected everywhere, such "doctors" served as the most common link between the visibles and the invisibles. Privy to secret information, purportedly including a separate ritual language, and often idiosyncratic in their lives (and thus thought to be gifted or touched), *dibia* combined their sacred knowledge of the spirit world with a practical pharmacological knowledge (which presumably required them to spend time collecting herbs from the forest) to divine what ailed someone, determine the necessary remedies, and then apply them. Not only were the "Oboe doctors, or Dibbeah" able to "cure diseases by charms," but they could "foretell things to come, and discover secrets" and in general were the "great ally of the people against witchcraft."[81]

Indeed, the various and sundry sacred science or magicoreligious abilities of *ôbia/dibia* changed very little across time and space from the 1750s to 1820s/1850s and into the 1920s. In southern Igboland in the 1920s, an "Ibo chief" told P. A. Talbot that "With our people a native doctor is called Onye Dibia. All know witchcraft, but some are good and only make medicine to help men. Others can make both bad and good medicine and yet others only busy themselves with bad ones. . . . Every Onye Dibia has great power, because everyone fears to offend him on account of his medicines."[82] At Onitsha in the 1850s, the "doctor, or priest, called *Dibia,* is another person of consequence, and is very much feared by the people. He has a great sway over the people, from his pretension to be able to foretell things to come, and discover secrets." At Bonny in the early 1800s, the *dibia* also combined the sacred and the profane and by their powers held "the populace in the most absolute awe and subjection." Crow emphasized the *dibia's* curative medical abilities and wrote that although "they apply certain remedies, chiefly decoctions of herbs and cupping, which they perform with a small calabash, after having made incisions, they depend upon charms, in a great measure, for relief."[83] His vivid description of a *dibia* curing rite shows the role of sacrifice in healing. After killing a male fowl by slitting its throat, the *dibia* "then threw himself into many strange postures, and while muttering some incantations over the sick men, he sprinkled the blood on their heads." Presumably that *dibia* also gave the afflicted persons some physical medicine, as Crow noted that in general *dibia* "make much use of pod pepper, palm oil and various kinds of herbs for the cure of diseases."[84]

Olaudah Equiano, remembering his childhood in the 1750s in northern Igboland, wrote much the same description of *dibia,* although he seemed to also conflate the other major group of ritual specialists, the *mgburichie* (Nri men) and what was called *ífè-ji-njokku* (yam-spirit rites): "Though we had no places of public worship, we had priests and magicians, or wise men. I do not remember whether they had different offices, or whether they were united in the same persons, but they were held in great reverence by the people. They calculated our time, and foretold events. . . . These magicians were also our doctors or physicians. They practised bleeding by cupping, and were very successful in healing wounds and expelling poisons. They had likewise some extraordinary method of discovering jealousy, theft, and poisoning [which] is still used by the negroes in the West Indies."[85]

The institution of the *dibia* was intimately connected with the Igbo concept of the *chi.* This invisible force was a complementary will or sacred double—in short, a unique personal god who was imparted to each living thing by the Supreme Creator, *Chukwu,* and who guided behavior. Notwithstanding all the other juju, in particular the lesser deities and the ancestors, the *chi* had the greatest daily impact on the individual. The *dibia's* great gift was his ability to talk with spirits and to find what they wanted; the *chi* was frequently the first spirit consulted. As a proverb says, "If one agrees to a thing his chi will agree to it too." In the historical Igbo world, nothing happened by chance. Therefore, to find why one chose to do something or why one had experienced a misfortune (or fortune, for that matter), it was necessary to consult a *dibia.* Another proverb stated, "One sees the spirits through the *dibia's* eyes," and what the *dibia* often saw was an invisible demanding to be placated or fed. The *dibia,* therefore, knew what and how much to sacrifice, as another proverb makes clear: "The spirit that eats seven, refuses when he is given eight."[86]

The *dibia's* control over medicine (*ogwu*) and his ability to communicate with the spirits to find out what to "feed" them may have made *dibia* increasingly important in Igbo life as contact with Aro traders increased in intensity in the eighteenth and nineteenth centuries. In fact, *dibia* may have played a major role in the increasing use of oracles and petitions to *Chukwu* and of relations with the Arochukwu and, therefore, in the displacement of the older Nri hegemony with a new one based on petitioning (*a-juju*) and sacrifice (*aja*). This is evident especially in the contrast between the pacifist role of the Nri, one of whose main functions was to remove the abomination caused by the shedding of human blood, and a secondary function of *dibia,* which was to provide the special *ogwu* that facilitated warfare.

Taylor recorded one example of such war medicine when the men of Onitsha prepared for an armed conflict in 1858: "The young and middle-aged men are directed to lance their breasts, hands, and backs, and instil medicine into the wound, which they look upon as an antidote against shots and arrows." In other times and places, including among the Aro and their allies, the *dibia* supplied the taboo-breaking *ogwu* for warfare.[87]

The *dibia* most often were responsible for divining what needed to be sacrificed and usually called for the sacrifice of a fowl. In fact, the fowl "is the classical Ibo sacrificial victim." Guinea fowl were ubiquitous domestic animals, and as a proverb stated, "What a person feeds on, that he gives the spirits."[88] There was a marked symbolic association of fowl and humans, however, as any number of proverbs make clear. Even the way *okoko* and some humans were sacrificed seems quite similar, although human sacrifice was rare and was reserved only for special occasions.[89]

The rise of *dibia* to great power throughout Igboland in the era of the slave trade, however, may have come in part from arrogating the ability to "sacrifice" humans and then having them sent away instead of killed (and thus avoiding the required intervention by a Nri man). A successful sacrifice to the spirits was signaled by the appearance of vultures, who carried the sacrifice to the *muo* world; the appearance of Aro and other interior traders demanding to be pleased and placated with people might have seemed like the vultures sent by the spirits for a sacrifice.[90]

Moreover, *dibia* and juju were closely connected with the secret societies and masquerades, whose members generally were the most powerful in the village and village group. The only other figure that would have had the kind of authority to send people away or to instigate seizures would have been each compound's headman (*okpara*) or the *ndi Nri*. However, the secret societies and *Mmuo* (masquerades) likely were instrumental in such seizing. Not only could the powerful local men act with impunity and anonymity in *Mmuo* and with the sanction of the local *dibia*, but they had the personal connections with outside long-distance traders directly connected with the slave trade to the coast.

In the many little worlds of Eboan village-level society, grounded as they were in localism, a generalized ethic of honor (and its obverse, vengeance), and the ubiquity of the invisible but living spirits, where nothing happened by chance alone, the real or imagined threat of "poison" was a constant fact of life. Even today, when nearly all Igbo are modern Christians, there are practicing *dibia*, especially in the countryside, and it is not uncommon to hear an unusual or unexpected or accidental death explained as the consequence of poisoning. Even Equiano explicitly remembered the method for determining who had caused the death of someone—that is, for discovering whether a death had resulted from poisoning. And he noted that the general method used in his village in Igboland, which he thought might "serve as a kind of specimen of the rest," was, apparently from his own experience (or perhaps from hearsay), "still used by the negroes in the West Indies."[91] When Equiano published his memoirs in 1789, he included his Igbo name in the manuscript's title and referred to himself as "the African." And when he summarized the first chapter of his life story as "some account of the manners and customs of my country," Equiano specifically wanted his audience to know that these customs "had been implanted in me with great care, and made an impression on my mind, which time could not erase, and which all the adversity of fortune I have since experienced served to rivet and record. . . . I still look back with pleasure on the first scenes of my life, though that pleasure has been for the most part mingled with sorrow."[92]

CHAPTER FOUR

The Significance of Poison

Throughout the Black Atlantic, the use of poison was strongly associated with African religiomagical or sacred science practices in a Creole setting. As one historian of slave crimes in colonial and early national Virginia has written, "Newly imported Africans often brought with them strongly developed conceptions of crime, justice, and judicial institutions"; furthermore, "slaves who used poison adapted a West African practice to the circumstances of Virginia's racial slavery."[1] The use of poison in the Chesapeake region was also closely associated with "conjure," the African-derived system of healing and sorcery. The significance of poison is that it points to the hidden historical reality of the non-Christian religious system of the vast majority of slaves. It also suggests the continuing cultural dominance of Africans in the creolizing population during the era of the transatlantic slave trade (and beyond), in their own way.

The Virginia House of Burgesses acted formally in 1748 to outlaw any administering of medicines by slaves, because "many negroes, under pretence of practising physic, have prepared and exhibited poisonous medicines, by which many persons have been murdered, and others have languished under long and tedious indispositions." The prohibition brought increased prosecution; indeed, the vast majority of slave trials for poisoning occurred after 1750. But an analysis of 179 such trials before 1784 shows that they were concentrated in the Piedmont and South Side regions, which after mid-century had the largest proportions of Africans in the slave population.[2] For example, between 1732 and 1766 in the contiguous Piedmont region comprising Caroline, Spotsylvania, and Orange Counties, when African adults and their Creole children were knitting together a distinctive Afro-Virginian society in their collective confrontation with chattel slavery, a trial for poisoning occurred on average every three years.[3]

In general, slaves in Virginia had access to a number of poisonous substances, including wild pulses like raw pokeweed and Jamestown (jimson) weed as well as manufactured simples such as arsenic, mercury, and lye.[4] These substances apparently rarely killed outright but rather caused victims to languish for extended periods. A description from the 1780s in South Carolina is strikingly apropos for central Virginia half a century earlier: "The Negroes have various poisons of which they make an abominable use, often destroying one another, and sometimes avenging themselves for cruel treatment of their masters. These poisons, which act little by little upon the internal organs, produce a kind of degeneration that ends with death."[5]

In an example from Monticello in the 1790s, Jefferson's secretary and plantation superintendent, Thomas Mann Randolph, wrote that such poisonings "were numerous in this part of the Country within my knowledge" and associated these acts with local conjure men. When Jefferson's head driver, George, and his wife, Ursula, were poisoned, Randolph wrote, "The poisons of the Buckingham Negro conjuror appear to have a power of unstringing the whole system beyond recovery in a short time; of destroying the elasticity or rather the Vital Virtue of muscular fibre & nervous thread in a few weeks or days as completely in a healthy African slave as the abuse of natural gratifications for years in the luxurious rich, or

quantities of Ardent Spirits in those who are just above labor. . . .
The poisons of the Conjurer have the most astonishing effect in
producing melancholy & despair—perhaps greately operative in
the catastrophe."[6]

In the eighteenth-century world of the slaves (and indeed of
most whites), such "medicines" also required a spiritual or supernatural component to work effectively. Not every slave was knowledge-
able about administering medicine or poison in particular: specialists
were known generically as "doctors" and colloquially as "conjure men"
and healed as well as killed. A nineteenth-century source defined
conjure as "to use arts to engage the aid of supernatural agents," and
it seems clear that poisoning was, as Randolph recognized, one of
the conjure man's chief arts.[7]

Conjure in the Chesapeake region, with its essential element of
poisoning, may well be seen as a creolized variation of ancestral religiomagical practices, adapted by Atlantic Africans to the realities of
slavery in Virginia. This conjure appears to be a living variant, along
with Anglophone Caribbean obeah, of ancestral Igbo *ôbia* as prac-
ticed by *dibia*.[8] Usually glossed as "doctor" or "doctor-diviner" and
perhaps in the modern idiom best understood as "sacred science
men," these "touched" adepts combined a wide range of functions
from divining to healing to sorcery by communicating with the spirits and communing with supernatural forces (as discussed in more
detail in chapter 3). The *dibia* also applied a profound knowledge of
plant medicines (including poisons) to resolve conflicts, heal the
sick, placate the spirits, and punish the wicked. Igbo *ôbia*, like North
American conjure and Caribbean obeah, was normally a beneficial
institution.[9] It was largely understood as doctoring through the use
of sacred medicine (Igbo *ógwu*), though the supernatural force or
forces on which it drew were essentially morally neutral.[10]

However, poisons (animal, plant, and probably supernatural) were
one of the key components of this secret knowledge/wisdom/power.
Ideally, Igbo *dibia* were protected from any ill effects of malevolent

"doctoring" (and the use of poisonous *ogwu*), as presumably were conjurers and obeah men, because they acted only when invited and worked within the practical maxim that "what kills also saves." As two central Igbo *dibia* proverbs state, *ekuleku aha-egbu dibia* (acting on invitation does not kill or hurt or harm the *Dibia*), and *Ife Na-azo Na-egbu, Ife na-egbu Egbu na-dzo Azo* (What saves also kills and what kills also saves). A third Igbo *dibia* precept, *I jikoo ogwu awale, ulu isaa o bulu nsi* (If you combine seven different good luck charms, the outcome will be poison"), neatly juxtaposes the two sides of the same coin that was Igbo *ôbia*, as well as its two Atlantic African derivations, conjure and obeah.[11]

The significance of poison as an adjunct of conjure (or obeah) also lay in the fact that in the eighteenth century—and, indeed, well into the nineteenth century—the great majority of slaves lived within a sacred cosmos that was only barely, if at all, informed by Christianity. Even historians of early African American Christianity recognize that until about 1800 (or even into the antebellum era), very few slaves in North America were Christian.[12] Assuming that these non-Christian Africans and their descendants were not simply nihilists, the combination of conjuration and the other elements of folk supernatural understandings, including the importance of signs and omens, of charms and other truck, indeed constituted a religion qua religion (and not simply superstition, epiphenomenal root-doctoring). These beliefs and practices—what we may term this orthopraxis—persisted into the twentieth century.[13] Its historical existence suggests that the core ethos of historical (or archaic) African American culture derived as much from particular African ideological resources as from the general slave experience itself. This African-inspired sacred reality would have been especially immanent in such places as Mt. Pleasant in the 1720s and 1730s, when enslaved people lived largely apart from whites and, partly out of necessity, in a world mostly of their own making. At Montpelier, the recovery of a blue glass bead, a pierced Spanish coin, and a terra-cotta (or perhaps colonoware) tobacco pipe, all from slave-associated sites at the original Mt. Pleasant homesite, point to a slave community still heavily influenced by African conceptions of knowing, even among the house slaves.[14] As one general (though condescending) description of the world of field slaves in Virginia in the third quarter of the eighteenth century put it, "The field slaves are badly fed, clothed and lodged. They live in small huts on the plantations where they labour, remote from the society and example of their superiors. Living by themselves, they retain many of the customs and manners of their African ancestors."[15]

In 1732, Ambrose Madison's slaves, Turk and Dido, chose to conspire and to use poison to murder their old master rather than simply to use a knife or an axe handle, for example. The killing was not a momentary crime of passion. In reaching outside the immediate community for conspirators in the poisoning, perhaps because Pompey was a conjure man or was in some way closely connected with Turk and Dido and was simply willing to die to help them, the slaves at Mt. Pleasant demonstrated a kind of malice aforethought and an intention to murder their master, no doubt in revenge. They also reveal themselves as Atlantic Africans in colonial Virginia.

PART TWO

In Virginia

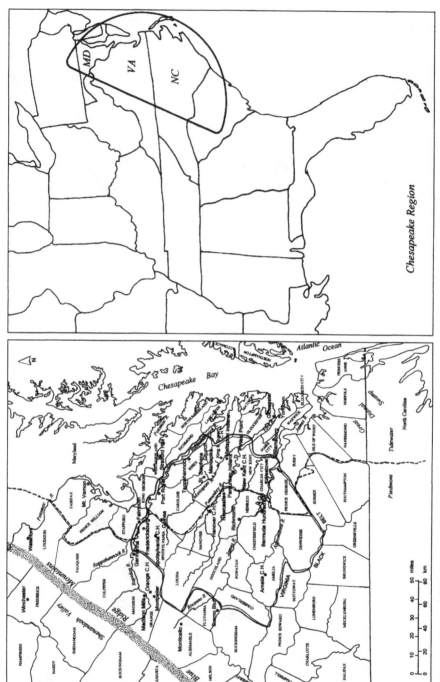

Map 2.   Eastern Virginia ca. 1750–1820

CHAPTER FIVE

The Seating of Mt. Pleasant and the
Development of a Regional Community

In 1719, the slave ship *Anna & Sarah,* owned by the prominent Bristol merchant Abraham Hooke, arrived in the York River with 159 slaves, most of them probably Igbo, from Calabar.[1] The next year, or possibly in 1721, Ambrose Madison (who also lived in the Mantapike neighborhood of King and Queen County) bought two adult women from this shipment from his neighbor, planter-merchant John Baylor, paying fifty pounds for the pair of African slaves, who were most likely "Eboe."[2] When they first landed, these two women, whose names are forever lost, probably were even more unhealthy than the average slave on the *Anna & Sarah,* since they were not sold immediately but rather were retained by Baylor. As a powerful regional consignment agent, Baylor had the personal resources to stockpile and resell African slaves. He specialized in Africans from Calabar and even financed his own ships to West Africa.

During the time they waited at Baylor's for someone to purchase them, not knowing what their futures held, these two women must have become like sisters. They had shared the shocks of enslavement and the terrors of transportation to the coast and even more so in the stinking holds of the same slave ship across the Atlantic.

Together they had faced separation from their shipmates and the further physical and psychological realities of the "seasoning time" of saltwater slaves in Virginia. Eventually they were sold to the same master, no doubt destined for a distant Piedmont quarter.

The settlement of the York River watershed, including the Mattaponi and Pamunkey Rivers and the Rapidan to the Rappahannock, was effected largely by upper Tidewater planters, who took advantage of their social and political connections to claim large tracts of newly surveyed land above the fall lines in the 1720s. Over the next two decades, these planters put their new lands into tobacco production with newly imported Africans.[3] The period from the 1710s through the 1740s or early 1750s also was the height of the transatlantic slave trade to Virginia, when shipments from Calabar, financed by Bristol merchants, dominated imports of enslaved Africans, particularly to the York River.[4] About half of the approximately 84,000 Africans landed in Virginia were taken from the Bight of Biafra between 1716 and 1745; two-thirds arrived from there between 1716 and 1755 (see tables 5.1–5.3). In these years, Africans from Calabar constituted a clear majority of imported shipments of slaves.

This dual shift of the expansion of colonial settlement from the upper Tidewater to the central Piedmont and to the reliance on Africans from Calabar, especially among Bristol shipments and in the York River watershed, derived from the increasing dependence on Bristol merchants in the second quarter of the eighteenth century. The shared political, economic, and social connections among the planter elite, several of whom also were the largest slave trade agents, enabled these men to engross the largest land patents and then to send cohorts of newly imported Africans to those newly claimed lands. The planters often followed several years later to take control of their fortunes, and together they constituted a kind of loose "chain migration."

During the key generation (1710s–40s) when masters sent groups of newly acquired slaves to clear the new farms and then later joined

TABLE 5.1

Number of African Slaves Imported to Virginia, by Quinquennia,
1646–1775

Years	Number of Ships	Number Disembarked
1646–50	1	137
1661–65	1	81
1671–75	3	562
1676–80	8	1,518
1681–85	1	110
1686–90	9	1,351
1691–95	2	623
1696–1700	4	1,190
1701–5	26	4,352
1706–10	26	5,380
1711–15	3	591
1716–20	43	6,126
1721–25	27	4,902
1726–30	43	8,316
1731–35	39	8,069
1736–40	45	8,919
1741–45	23	5,037
1746–50	18	4,677
1751–55	35	7,520
1756–60	19	4,162
1761–65	39	9,179
1766–70	11	1,937
1771–75	9	2,649
1646–1775	**435**	**84,247**

Source: Eltis et al., *Transatlantic Slave Trade;* Query, "5-year period, Where
slaves disembarked = Virginia."

TABLE 5.2

Africans Imported to Virginia 1646–1775, by Period

Year	Number of Years	Number of Ships	Number Disembarked	Percentage	Average/ Year
1646–1700	55	29	5,251	6.2	95
1701–15	15	55	10,323	12.3	688
1716–45	30	220	41,369	49.1	1,379
1746–75	30	131	27,304	32.4	910
1716–55	40	273	53,566	63.6	1,339
1756–75	20	78	15,107	17.9	755

Source: Eltis et al., *Transatlantic Slave Trade.*

TABLE 5.3

Transatlantic Slave Trade to Virginia, 1716–1755, by Quinquennia

	Number of Ships	Virginia		No. Embarkation Known	Biafra Percentage
		Embarked	Disembarked		
1716–20	43	7,444	6,126	5,533	62.8
1721–25	27	5,909	4,902	4,766	51.7
1726–30	43	10,104	8,316	4,552	71.1
1731–35	39	9,634	8,069	5,464	48.2
1736–40	45	10,726	8,919	3,935	34.6
1741–45	23	6,165	5,037	1,696	82.8
1746–50	18	5,638	4,677	4,236	70.5
1751–55	35	9,322	7,520	7,314	51.1
Total	**273**	**64,942**	**53,566**	**37,496**	**56.7**

Source: Eltis et al., *Transatlantic Slave Trade.*

these already existing communities, including the plantation that came to be known as Montpelier, Bristol merchants dominated the Virginia slave trade. Though the history of slave trade merchants and the colonial "colonels" who were their primary consignment agents has yet to be written, on the upper York and Rappahannock Rivers, prominent men such as John Baylor (1650–1720), Augustine Moore (1685–1743), and George Braxton (ca. 1680–1761) on the York, and John Tayloe (1687–1747) and Robert "King" Carter (1663–1732) on the Rappahannock generally earned commissions of 8 percent on the sale of shipments sent to them.[5] Many of these colonial agents (including Baylor and Carter) apparently took their commissions in imported slaves, enabling the agents to quickly build up sizable slaveholdings. They then sent these newly imported Africans to various upland quarters.[6]

As the British economic historian Walter Minchinton stated long ago, by the early 1720s, "Bristol dominated the trade in slaves to Virginia," and this would remain the case through the early 1750s.[7] Between 1716 and 1755, Bristol ships represented 60 percent of the slavers coming to Virginia and brought two-thirds of the 53,500 Africans landed in the colony (see table 5.4).[8] But the Bristol slave trade was always more important to Virginia than the Virginia market was to Bristol merchants. In the 1710s, merchants in the outport of Bristol were investing an estimated £50,000 sterling per year in slaving voyages in general and by the 1730s were investing some £150,000 annually in the African trade.[9] However, their trade in slaves to Virginia between 1716 and 1740 represented a relatively stable annual investment of some £14,000 sterling, declining to an estimated £10,500 between 1741 and 1755).[10] Of about 1,200 shipments financed by Bristol merchants between 1701 and 1750, only 156 (or 13 percent) were sent to Virginia. Through the principal era of the Virginia slave trade (1701–75), only 10 percent of the annual capital invested in slaving voyages by Bristol merchants was used for shipments intended for the colony; Bristol's principal markets were Jamaica and St. Kitts.[11]

TABLE 5.4

Bristol Dominance of the Virginia Slave Trade, 1716–1755

	Virginia		Bristol		
	Number of Ships	Number Landed	Number of Ships	Number Landed	Percentage
1716–20	43	6,126	28	4,308	70.3
1721–25	27	4,902	16	2,867	58.5
1726–30	43	8,316	30	6,172	74.2
1731–35	39	8,069	24	5,891	73.0
1736–40	45	8,919	20	4,877	54.7
1741–45	23	5,037	17	3,725	74.0
1746–50	18	4,677	12	3,276	70.1
1751–55	35	7,520	16	4,133	55.0
Total	**273**	**53,566**	**163**	**35,249**	**65.8**

Source: Eltis et al., *Transatlantic Slave Trade.*

It seems clear that Bristol merchants entered the slave trade to Virginia by supplying less-regarded Calabar Africans, whom Virginians were willing to buy (having little choice, given the relative marginality of the Chesapeake in the eighteenth-century British Atlantic world). It is also clear that in the thirty years after 1716, Bristol merchants concentrated their trade on the York River (see table 5.5), though they also sent some shipments to their agents on the upper James and Rappahannock Rivers. In short, Bristol merchants tended to provide the enslaved Africans who increasingly were put to work producing the relatively more valuable "sweet-scented" tobacco in the interior Tidewater and central Piedmont, which brought higher prices in the London (and later Glasgow) markets.[12]

TABLE 5.5

Bristol Slave Trade to York River Region, 1716–1745

	Total		To York River		
	Number of Ships	*Number Landed*	*Number of Ships*	*Number Landed*	*% Landed*
1716–20	28	4,308	22	3,422	79.4
1721–25	16	2,867	11	1,734	60.5
1726–30	30	6,172	18	3,662	59.3
1731–35	24	5,891	13	3,372	57.2
1736–40	20	4,877	15	3,895	79.9
1741–45	17	3,725	12	2,565	68.9
Total	**135**	**27,840**	**91**	**18,650**	**67.0**

Source: Eltis et al., *Transatlantic Slave Trade.*

If the proportion of Bristol-financed shipments to Virginia and to the York River watershed, both representing about two-thirds of the known sample, establishes that Bristol merchants "dominated the trade in slaves to Virginia," then the proportion of Africans from the Bight of Biafra (Calabar) establishes a similar dominance among the shipments. As table 5.6 shows, a sample of 37,500 Africans landed in the colony between 1716 and 1755 (at the height of the import trade) shows that Biafran Africans dominated. Nearly 57 percent of Africans with a known coastal provenance were brought from Calabar, with a massive concentration in Bristol shipments (approaching 80 percent) and a correlation with shipments to the York River region. This double domination, of Bristol voyages and shipments of Biafran Africans, continued for forty years and fueled the settlement of the fertile central Piedmont.

TABLE 5.6

Calabar Dominance in the Virginia Slave Trade, 1716–1755

	Virginia Embarked (Known)		Bristol Percentage Biafran	York River Percentage Biafran	Bristol–York River Percentage Biafran
	Number Biafran	Percentage			
1716–20	5,533	62.8	80.0	76.9	84.7
1721–25	4,766	51.7	92.0	55.8	91.1
1726–30	4,552	71.1	94.3	75.4	100.0
1731–35	5,464	48.2	62.4	46.4	58.1
1736–40	3,935	41.1	75.3	47.1	72.2
1741–45	1,696	82.8	100.0	100.0	100.0
1746–50	4,236	70.5	78.5	65.9	100.0
1751–55	7,314	51.1	73.7	46.1	50.6
Total	**37,496**	**56.7**	**78.9**	**61.6**	**79.5**

Source: Eltis et al., *Transatlantic Slave Trade.*
Note: All percentages are of Africans embarked whose coastal provenance is known.

Between 1718 and August 1720, one important colonial slave trade agent, Colonel John Baylor, had a hand in selling nearly 1,500 Africans imported on nine ships, of which eight were financed by Bristol merchants and seven were from the Calabar coast.[13] From his plantation and tobacco warehouse on the Mattaponi River, in the Mantapike neighborhood of King and Queen County, Baylor had gotten himself deep in debt. Although in 1718 he was (along with his occasional business partner, Colonel George Braxton) the biggest tobacco broker on the Mattaponi and was described in 1720 by King Carter as the "great negro seller, and in all respects the greatest merchant we had among us," the market value of the 1,470 Africans on the nine shipments was more than five times Baylor's total worth.[14] In fact, just two shipments sent by William Challoner in 1719 and 1720 (both from Calabar), with a total of 225 slaves, would have been about equal to the value of Baylor's whole estate.[15]

The structure of the slave trade to Virginia tended to concentrate Africans in relatively bounded regions in the colony. The Bristol–Calabar–York River nexus in the era of primary westward settlement meant that a large proportion of Africans in the central Piedmont, including the area around Montpelier in what would become Orange County, were likely to be from Igbo and cognate communities. Though thrown into trying circumstances in a new and unfamiliar land and confronted by the tyranny of their masters, some large proportion of "saltwater" slaves would not have been cultural strangers. Indeed, the chances of drawing strength from shared numbers increased even as the numbers of Africans imported grew in the generation after 1720.

In 1721, Ambrose Madison married Frances Taylor (1700–1761), the youngest daughter of Colonel James Taylor (1674–1729). During the same year, Thomas Chew married another of Taylor's daughters, Martha (b. 1702). A year earlier, Thomas Chew's father, the locally prominent planter Larkin Chew (1676–1729), had purchased four slaves (two men and two women) just landed from Calabar, very likely with the intention of giving them to his son when he reached his legal maturity.[16]

By marrying the two Taylor sisters, Madison and Chew acquired a powerful benefactor in Colonel Taylor. He was a local power who in 1714 had secured the prize office of surveyor for both King William and King and Queen Counties (the upper York River backcountry) under the patronage of Henry "Harry" Beverley (d. 1730) of Newlands, Spotsylvania County. He was the brother of Robert Beverley (d. 1722) the historian of Beverley Park in King and Queen County and one of Governor Alexander Spotswood's closest associates. In 1716 Robert Beverley and Taylor accompanied the governor on the famed "Golden Horseshoe" trek to the Blue Ridge Mountains.[17]

Upon their return, Taylor set about surveying the lands they had traversed. In 1723 he turned in a massive survey of more than 142,000 acres to the newly formed Spotsylvania County court. The largest single patent was for 24,000 acres, known as the Octonia Grant, for a company of speculators led by Harry Beverley. Between 1721 and 1726, eight grandees of King and Queen County (Alexander Spotswood, Harry Beverley, John Baylor, Gawin Corbin, Augustine Moore, William Todd, and James Taylor) individually patented 115,000 acres south of the Rapidan River in the newly formed Spotsylvania County, with Taylor as the principal surveyor.[18]

In this "great survey," Taylor had reserved a one quarter parcel of Todd's 20,000 acres, adjoining Baylor's patent of 6,500 acres to the east and the Octonia Grant to the north, and about three miles from Taylor's 8,500 acres to the northeast.[19] In 1723 Taylor gave the (officially) 4,675 acres to his sons-in-law, Ambrose Madison and Thomas Chew, who jointly patented it as such,[20] though later it was found that Taylor had added a further 2,000 acres without Todd's permission. Although Todd discovered the surveying discrepancy, which effectively transferred the extra 2,000 acres to Madison and Chew, in 1726, Taylor stalled until the case was finally heard before the Governor's Council in Williamsburg in 1728.

The councilors were sympathetic to Todd's complaint that Taylor had committed fraud. Todd testified that for two years he had complained to Taylor to "do him right," but Taylor had refused to do anything, claiming that his sons-in-law owned the property in question, and they repeatedly refused to let Todd resurvey it. The stall tactics gave Madison and Chew time enough to clear and record their title (using the old metes and bounds), which they did in 1727.[21] The council then ordered that Robert Brooke, surveyor for Essex and Caroline Counties, go over the old survey lines. If he found that Taylor was at fault, then Brooke was to resurvey "all the other lands which the said Taylor did survey at the same time with the entry aforesaid" (the entire "great survey"), which clearly would have upset the whole land market in the Rapidan River watershed.[22]

The acting governor and president of the Council in 1726–27 was none other than King Carter. He had secured patents for some 40,000 acres in Spotsylvania and no doubt would have been sympathetic to Taylor. When the case was heard on 11 December 1728, the governor and president of the council was William Gooch, who had arrived in the colony just over a year earlier, and Carter was not present. In the final disposition of Todd's petition in 1729, however, when the council specifically upheld Taylor's original survey lines, thus securing the additional 2,000 acres for Madison and Chew, Carter was in attendance. In his will, Ambrose bequeathed 1,000 acres to each of his two daughters, Frances and Elizabeth, and in 1737 Thomas Chew deeded 2,850 acres from the original patent to the widowed Frances Madison and her son, James, (about 500 acres more than half of the land). Thus, Ambrose Madison apparently received the extra 2,000 acres from Taylor's fraudulent survey. It is not for nothing that one historian has called this generation of colonial "land hunters" (including the surveyors and indeed some of the councilors) "some of the canniest land speculators in all the province."[23]

Patentees were required to "improve" their new lands within a certain period to receive full title. Within three years, prospective owners had to meet one of the following conditions: (1) clear and tend 3 acres for every 50 patented; (2) keep three cattle or six sheep for every 50 acres until meeting the first condition; (3) build a dwelling house measuring twenty by sixteen feet if the land was not cultivable; (4) fence 3 acres of pastures for every 50 acres; or (5) spend £10 current money (or about £7.50 sterling) per every 50 acres to improve the land. Therefore, to gain title to their "4,675" acres, by 15 November 1726 Madison and Chew had to clear and tend 280 acres; keep 280 cattle or 560 sheep; build the dwelling and declare that their land had "no part fit for present cultivation" (a highly dubious assertion); fence in 280 acres for pasturage; or spend £935 current money (about £700 sterling) to bring the land into cultivation.[24]

In 1725, Madison tallied up the debts owed to him, which totaled £614.15 current money (ca. £460 sterling). Later that year, with the deadline for seating the western patent starting to loom, he bought another eight newly imported Africans, probably at West Point, where the Mattaponi and Pamunkey Rivers converge to form the York.[25] Madison presumably sent these new slaves to the western quarter, as he continued living in King and Queen or perhaps in what is now Caroline County. Chew remained on family lands in St. George's Parish (present-day Spotsylvania County).[26]

Clearing new land for cultivation was arduous work, and given that these western quarters were absentee owned, it is likely that the slaves relied as much on their own knowledge and skills as on the directions of their overseers. One visitor in Virginia in 1724 described the process: "When a tract of land is seated, they clear it by felling the trees about a yard from the ground, lest they should shoot again. What wood they have occasion for they carry off, and burn the rest, or let it lie and rot upon the ground. . . . The land between the logs and stumps they how [hoe] up, planting tobacco there in the spring, inclosing it with a slight fence of cleft rails. This will last for tobacco some years, if the land be good. . . . Tobacco and Indian corn are planted in hills as hops and secured by worm fences, which are made of rails supporting one another very firmly in a particular manner."[27]

The slaves at Mt. Pleasant (and the adjoining Chew quarter) also built a relatively permanent house for the overseer, their own cabins, and other structures such as barns and sheds. These were likely to be of "earthfast" or post-in-the-ground construction, a style that also was used in precolonial Igboland. According to one description from late-seventeenth-century Tidewater Virginia, "Whatever their rank, & I know not why, [planters] build only two rooms with some closets on the ground floor, & two rooms in the attic above; but they build several like this, according to their means. They build also a separate kitchen, a separate house for the Christian slaves [indentured servants], [and] one for the negro slaves."[28] The slaves also would have contributed to the building of a gristmill on the Chew half of the patent and to the building of at least one road that could accommodate carts.

In 1726, Madison and Chew petitioned the Spotsylvania Court to evaluate their improvements, filing for adjudgment just two weeks before their legal deadline. The commissioners tersely described four Quarters, two established by each patentee. Chew's were on the southern side of the mountain ridge that divided their lands and included the gristmill, and together his improvements were valued at £245. Madison's two quarters were on the northern side of the mountain. One was a minimal settlement valued at only £40, perhaps only a slave cabin or two and some newly cleared field. The other Quarter, called Mt. Pleasant, was the main settlement. It was apparently well organized and extensive, as the commissioners stated that the improvements there were worth the relatively large sum of £340. Because both Madison and Chew had also spent £200 each in direct expenses, presumably for recently imported African slaves, the total valuation of £1,025 exceeded their required costs, and they cleared their title to the patent lands.[29]

Between 1728 and 1730, Madison and Chew negotiated their way through Todd's suit while employing overseers to run their western quarters. Colonel Taylor died in early 1729, and three years later, apparently in March or April 1732, both Chew and Madison moved to their lands at the "little mountains." Madison made the Mt. Pleasant settlement his seat, likely moving into the existing overseer's house, and this became his home plantation.[30] Ambrose Madison was in his mid-thirties; his wife, Frances, was thirty-two; and they had three young children: James, age six; Elizabeth, age four; and

Frances, age three. Though Madison's new plantation was on the Rapidan, it is clear that his principal commercial interests remained tied to the York River, as a London merchant addressed him in 1731 as "Mr. Ambrose Madison, Merchant, York River."[31]

In making the move to Mt. Pleasant in 1732, Madison and his family and their "home" slaves would have joined the already existing community of perhaps ten to fifteen slaves, plus an overseer. The Madisons apparently settled into a house that had been built around 1726. It was located on a low ridge about one-third of a mile southwest of the present mansion, probably near the slave quarters. This likely original homesite is located fifty meters east of the Madison family cemetery and fifty meters from a possible well. Archaeological surveys in 1987 recovered tin-glazed earthenware, black lead-glazed earthenware, and hand-wrought nails, all of which suggest an eighteenth-century occupation. It was the only site in that estate-wide survey to yield these two types of earthenware. Subsequent excavations have revealed "a root cellar, a well and a very large quantity of artifacts, both architectural and domestic," though no definitive foundation, probably because the structures were impermanent earthfast (or post-in-the-ground) buildings. A series of annual excavations in the 1990s conducted by James Madison University archaeological field schools has revealed a second root cellar as well as a kitchen cellar and perhaps the rear yard of the original house. About 240 meters to the north of the homesite there is an unmarked graveyard, which oral tradition maintains is the slave burying ground. It is nearly enclosed by "a low earthen mound (approximately 50 to 80 centimeters high)." The nineteenth-century slave quarters were located primarily in the Walnut Grove area immediately to the east (and down the hill) from the present mansion, though a second slave Quarter may have existed on the northern boundary of the plantation.[32]

The apparent finding of two root cellars at the 1726 homesite is particularly interesting. In eighteenth-century Virginia, such storage pits, usually rectangular or square and dug into the dirt floor, are strongly associated with slave/African American sites. Though used sporadically by whites in the seventeenth century, such features in the eighteenth and early nineteenth centuries so clearly correlate with African American occupancy that archaeologists generally "use the presence of [root pit] cellars as a marker for identifying slave quarters."[33]

The core of this community, which had worked hard over the course of six to ten years at the arduous task of clearing the fields and preparing the land for tobacco and corn as well as constructing the buildings (including the main dwelling) and probably some fencing and perhaps digging a well for water, may well have claimed some degree of autonomy or informal authority, as they were the first on the land. One can only imagine the disruption or perhaps the set of practical negotiations attendant on the arrival of the master, his family, and their personal slaves in the Mt. Pleasant Quarter in the spring of 1732. Within six months of his arrival, however, Madison would be dead, poisoned by those slaves.

In making that move, Madison joined not just the nascent community of Mt. Pleasant but a larger neighborhood of slaves. Likely linked by shared African ethnicity (or at least similar African ethnic backgrounds) as well as shared experiences (even as shipmates), the people on the various slave Quarters in the district comprised a neighborhood. The slave community was not bounded by plantations but extended across the landscape and encompassed the slaves of masters who themselves came from the same neighborhood along the Mattaponi River.

For the slaves, this meant that they lived in a larger community composed of dispersed compounds in which people commonly expected to travel and visit (and marry) beyond their own immediate settlement. The proverbial slave or Negro grapevine—that conduit of information passed from person to person, which never ceased to amaze white folks with its speed and accuracy—presupposed personal contact. In the eighteenth century, as observers often remarked, slaves in the central Piedmont of Virginia generally had their freedom at night, which was known as "Negro daytime," as long as they were back and accounted for (and at work) by daybreak. In short, from the perspective of the slave community, this was a world of an extended regional neighborhood and a regime of rules, not rulers (though the masters governed, to be sure).[34]

As we have seen, in the 1720s, the slave trade to Virginia was dominated by Bristol merchants and their local colonial agents such as John Baylor, who brought large numbers of Africans from a single general culture area, that of Igboland. Most of these Africans would have wound up on the new western quarters. In these key years, well-connected King and Queen and Spotsylvania County planters and others gained access to large amounts of land in the central Piedmont and seated patents by buying Africans and sending them to settle these new farms, thus leading to the formation of large new counties in the backcountry (Caroline in 1727, Orange in 1734). The slave populations on many of these farms would have comprised loosely constituted groups rather than crowds of cultural strangers; thus, they likely shared specific sets of cultural skills and expectations.[35] Although the physical landscape was quite different, and the cold winter weather would certainly have represented a drastic change, some basic things like the technology of work and even the staple crops may have been familiar. And these African slaves would have been surrounded by related communities of other slaves, also recently imported Africans and their children, as well as some Creoles.

In the 1720s and 1730s, the lands in the district around Mt. Pleasant were patented by three loose groups of planters. The first (Harry and Robert Beverley, Benjamin Winslow, and Henry Willis) were from the Rappahannock and engrossed some 20,000 acres in the Mt. Pleasant vicinity; half were directly to the north and west of Madison, and half were to the south of Chew. However, the original intent of the Rappahannock men was clearly speculative, as only Winslow took up a seat on his land.[36] The second group was actually one man, Colonel John Taliaferro (1687–1744), who originally was from James City County in the Lower Peninsula between the James and York Rivers (via Spotsylvania in the 1720s). Taliaferro patented a huge tract of 16,000 acres generally east of the Taylors, where he seated his family on various parcels.[37] The members of the third group (Baylor, Taylor, Madison, Chew, and Todd) were all from the same twenty–mile stretch on the left bank of the Mattaponi in the upper York River region. Their holdings comprised some 35,000 acres (or roughly one-quarter of Taylor's 1723 great survey). This group was the most important and provided the core of the extended community of slaves, which remained largely intact over three or four generations until the beginning of the nineteenth century.[38]

In 1726–30, when the York River group members were seating their patents to clear the title to their tens of thousands of acres, twenty-five slave ships entered the York River carrying some 5,000 Africans to be sold. Because these planter-merchants were in the top tier of their county but were only in the third tier of power throughout the colony, they would have depended heavily on their investment in slaves to meet the legal requirement for clearing the patent titles. And again, the historical association with Calabar is obvious: 75 percent (3,800 slaves) of the Africans taken to the York River markets in those key years came from the Bight of Biafra, with about 3,000 of them likely Igbo. Assuming that the vast majority of the saltwater slaves were purchased to be sent to clear the western patent lands, which had been engrossed by a small handful of well-placed planter-merchants, the concentration of Calabars in the upland areas seems even more probable.

Initially, these enslaved arrivals were relatively isolated on dispersed subfarms, or compounds, with between five and ten adults per Quarter and a white overseer. In such outlying Quarters, with only one white overseer (who likely was relatively impoverished himself),

TABLE 5.7

Slave Tithables, Montpelier District: Combined List, 1738–1739

Owner	Overseer	Number of Slave Tithables
[a] George Taylor	William Harvey	6
[a] James Taylor	Henry Thornton (1738)/ Mark Thornton (1739)	7
[a] John Baylor	Robert Bohanon (Boannan/Bohanugh)	17
Zachary Taylor		10
[a] Thomas Beale	James Cowherd (Coward/Choward)	6
[a] Frances Madison (1st Qtr.)[b]	Edmund Powell (1738)/ Ambrose Powell (1739)	8
[a] Frances Madison (2d Qtr.)	Erasmus Taylor[c]	7
[a] Captain Todd	John Botts	9
[a] Madame Todd (2d Qtr.)	J. Botts/John Lucas	19
[a] Henry Willis	John Burch	9
[a] Thomas Edmundson	John McCoy (Mackcoy)	5
James Barbour		8
[a] Thomas Scott	not given	9
Thomas Chew		10
[a] Benjamin Winslow	Tod Daultin	7
Erasmus Taylor (1739)		3
[a] John Taliaferro	William Clark	7
[a] John Scott	not given	3
Anthony Head		3
Richard Winslow		3

156

Source: Adapted from Little, *Orange County,* 14, 19; lists of tithables constables
William Bell (1738) and Elijah Daniel (1739) have been combined, with
the higher count used here.

Notes: Tithable slaves were males and females over age sixteen (in general,
half of the enslaved population).

[a] Absentee-owned and/or quarters run principally by an overseer.

[b] "Home House" (Montpelier) quarter. the overseer in.

[c] Erasmus Taylor, Frances Madison's younger brother, is listed as the overseer
at the Black Level tract in 1738. No overseer's name is given for Black Level
in 1739, when Taylor was running his own farm with three adult slaves.

slaves had to do more for themselves. If most of them were African,
that would have meant applying African knowledge and skills to
Creole surroundings.[39] Moreover, this frontier condition could per-
sist for a decade or longer. In the Montpelier district, it is striking
how many of the planting farms in the late 1730s were still absentee
owned and thus run by lone white overseers. For example, in
1738–39, two-thirds of the twenty-one Quarters (settlements) in the
district were absentee owned and/or run principally by an overseer.
And as might be expected, these were the settlements with the most
slaves. In the late 1730s, therefore, as many as 120 enslaved adults,
more than 75 percent of the total, lived at absentee-owned settlements. The vast majority of these slaves would have been African,
and perhaps three-quarters of the Africans would have been from
Calabar (see table 5.7). Slaves in these settlements would have been
particularly dependent on their own skills and knowledge, by necessity, and would have formed a mosaic of black majorities.

Of the approximately 156 adult slaves (or about 300 slaves total)
on these neighboring Piedmont Virginia settlements in the late 1730s,
it is highly likely that between 100 and 120 adults had come from
the same region of West Africa. Furthermore, the Baylor settlements
adjacent to Montpelier, which were the most likely to be dominated

by Calabars and were always absentee owned, were the largest in the neighborhood. Along with the rapidly growing Madison settlements, with their known Calabar connection, the slaves in these two sets of adjacent Quarters likely formed the geographic and cultural core of the initial extended slave community in the district immediately around Montpelier. Two generations later, by 1782, the thirty-four largest slave owners/planters in this district held at a minimum 820 slaves; the holdings of the Taylor-Baylor-Madison core numbered at least 400 slaves, nearly half of the recorded neighborhood slave population.[40] In Orange County in 1782–85, Colonel James Madison was the largest single slave owner, with a minimum of 88 enslaved people under his direct control.

By this third generation, a large proportion of the slaves in this section of the county, or the district of the Little Mountains/Blue Run, would have been related, either by marriage or descent and perhaps by nongenealogical identification (fictive kinship). In other places, it is clear that survivors of the same middle passage from Africa—shipmates—thought of themselves as kin, and one must wonder whether this relationship continued among their children. The rise of the abroad-spouse custom in Virginia, which was well known (and indeed largely respected by masters) in Orange County as elsewhere, would have encouraged multiple layers of cross-cutting connections among neighboring plantations. By the third (or fourth) generation, networks of kinship among the slaves may have extended broadly across a geographical section as well as deeply within related communities. In any case, the slaves' world clearly was not limited by plantation boundaries but should be seen in terms of regional landscapes of family connections, including those of the families of the masters.

An example is the connections between the Madison and Willis families and their slaves. In July 1719, Henry Willis (1692–1740) purchased from John Baylor six newly arrived Africans from Calabar, part of a shipment of 185 slaves on the *Berkley Galley*.[41] Within a decade, Willis had patented 10,000 acres adjacent to the

Madison/Chew tract and immediately sold one-third of it (later called Black Level) to Ambrose Madison. When Orange County was formed in 1734, Willis was named the first clerk of the court, and in the mid-1740s, his son, John (1724–ca. 1750), married Ambrose's daughter, Elizabeth (1725–73). John Willis also helped his brother-in-law, James Madison Sr., establish himself as a planter by sending slaves to build a peach coop for Madison's new brandy-distilling business. Willis also provided hogsheads (oversized barrels to transport finished tobacco) and plank boards for Madison and leased to him the services of his slave blacksmith. By 1749–50, the Willises owned 39 slaves, most of them either African born or first-generation Creoles. In 1752, two-thirds of those slaves came under Madison's legal control when be became guardian of his young niece, Mary, following her father's death. Madison controlled those slaves through 1763 and deployed them on his Quarters between 1752 and 1757.[42]

In effect there was a chain migration of interconnected planter families from one broad area (the upper York River) to the other (the Rapidan River). Just as Madison at his new location was surrounded by his relations, particularly the Taylors and Chews, and some of his most prominent former neighbors (William Todd, the Taliaferros, and Battailes), the slaves were surrounded by other Africans and some Creoles bought by the same loosely associated group of planters and brought from the same general areas.

The slave population on the several subfarms that made up Montpelier was always one of the largest in the county. At first composed largely of recently imported Africans, no doubt mostly from Calabar, but also including some Creoles, the community developed rapidly through natural increase, in part as a result of creating connections of kin with the other Quarters in the region. The large numbers of slave children born throughout the eighteenth century and the lack of any evidence that the Madisons ever purchased further Africans suggest that the slaves in the charter generation quickly created adaptive kinship structures—probably extended families—and a viable community of survivors.

CHAPTER SIX

The Madisons' Slave Community:
The Charter Generation

In early 1825, during his last journey through America, the Marquis de Lafayette made a formal visit to see the retired president at Montpelier. Lafayette stayed for four days, during which he spent some time among the slaves in the Walnut Grove quarter, accompanied by Dolley Madison. Among the slaves he met were Granny Milly, reportedly over a hundred years old, and her daughter and granddaughter, who was about seventy, all of whom lived in one cabin. Granny Milly had learned to speak French from the former gardener Beazée (Bizet) sometime after 1802 and in general was "one of the children's favorites among the old black folk." She may also have been able to read, as her prized keepsake was a bound copy of *Telemachus*, which she kept in a chest in her cabin and would pull out for special occasions. She apparently struck up a friendship with Lafayette and showed her book to him.[1]

It is interesting that the most valuable possession of this aged woman, born perhaps in the 1720s, was a Greek myth about the son of Odysseus and Penelope, who helped his father slay his mother's suitors. Given the charter event at Montpelier, to which Granny Milly was old enough to testify, regardless of whether she could actually read, displaying the book may have served as a *lieu de mémoire* and therefore reflected a requisite "will to remember."[2]

As the French theoretician Pierre Nora argues, the most fundamental purpose of such "sites of memory" is to "stop time, to block the work of forgetting, to establish a state of things, to immortalize death."[3] It is in the nature of such associations that people tend to memorialize sites, rather than specifically events; as Nora suggests, "Memory attaches itself to sites, whereas history attaches itself to events."[4]

With the transformation of the slave Quarter, which was moved from the old Mt. Pleasant site to Walnut Grove down the hill from the present mansion sometime in the 1750s or 1760s, perhaps with the unintended consequence of encouraging a "forgetting" of the earlier events at the Mt. Pleasant homestead, by the 1820s elders such as Granny Milly kept the memories alive. These "old heads" themselves quite possibly served as living *lieux des mémoire*, especially for a community dependent on oral traditions for "stopping time" and remembering the past. Granny Milly apparently was not among the actual charter generation at Mt. Pleasant in the 1720s and 1730s, however. She likely came as an adult in the dowry of five to seven adult slaves provided to James Madison Sr. at the time of his 1749 marriage to Nelly Conway (1731–1829). But Granny Milly would have personally known some of the charter generation. Moreover, this obviously intelligent and vital survivor, who may have learned a second (or perhaps a third) language in her eighties, was a living link who could "stop time" and "immortalize death" for the young slave children who favored her as well as for the rest of the extended community of Madison-owned slaves.

Over the middle decades of the eighteenth century, the Madison slave population had increased steadily. The community of slaves experienced a relative stability over three or four generations. In the seventy-five years after 1725, in part because of to the long life of James Madison Sr., who inherited the balance of the people and lands of Montpelier in 1744 and died in February 1801, the slaves faced only occasional separations, although they must have been painful when they did occur. Slave separations usually took place when the colonel gave a slave to one of his children or when he leased a slave's labor for a one-year period. Many slaves, therefore, continued to live within a couple of hours walk of the home community at Montpelier.

This also was a relatively large community. From the 1770s or perhaps even the late 1760s, as many as 100 people lived under Madison's control on three working Quarters in Orange County. Between about 1773 and 1801, Madison owned a total of about 150 slaves, and in the early 1780s he was the largest single slave owner in the county, with 88 enslaved people; in the mid-1780s, his sons owned a further 70 or so slaves.[5] During the last decade of the eighteenth century, a minimum of 75–100 enslaved people lived at Montpelier: between 1793 and 1801, Madison was assessed county levies for an average of 75 slaves over the age of twelve, most of whom would have been living at the home plantation.[6]

From its formation in the 1720s to its dissolution in the 1850s, the Madison slave community comprised five or six generations.[7] The charter generation of the 1720s and 1730s confronted the challenge of seasoning, or adapting physically, socially, psychologically, and spiritually to the new environment and regime of chattel slavery as well as settling the land. These Atlantic Africans fought the terror of their masters with their own form of struggle *in terrorum* and forged a world where they achieved some degree of autonomy within the "divide and conquer" strategy of the master class. In part, they did so by drawing on ancestral cultural resources to make sense of their new world.

They were succeeded by a creolizing generation (1740s–60s) that saw the growth of a locally born population even as Africans continued as a significant presence. At Montpelier, this generation was consolidated into a larger community at the Home House quarter while their master deployed a revolving or shifting labor regime that meant they tended to stay at different quarters over the years.

The third, or creolized, generation was the high point of the slave community, at least in terms of numbers and of their productivity as workers. Between the 1770s and the 1790s, the slaves produced great wealth for the Madison family, yet this third generation experienced the first significant separations, though often the people sent away from the home community continued to live relatively nearby.

The fourth generation was a time of dark clouds gathering, of generalized worrying, which I will call the "worriment" generation (1800s–1820s). The enslaved people could well have worried about the fact that although they had fulfilled their end of the "working misunderstanding" with the master—that is, trading productive labor for certain rights (including the right to be kept together)—time was catching up with them. Finally, the ruination generation (1830s–50s) saw mass separations through sale and distress and even manumission, leading to the complete dissolution of a community of people whose roots traced back over a full century at Montpelier.

The charter generation of Atlantic Africans and their children, numbering twenty-nine slaves in 1733, actually came from three basic sources. The first was the ten Africans, most probably Calabars (and specifically Igbo), whom Ambrose Madison purchased out of the transatlantic slave trade in 1720–25 or so. Though one or two of these saltwater slaves likely died within the first several years, they formed the core of the Madison slaveholding. But Ambrose also probably received about four adults when he married Frances Taylor in 1721. Furthermore, when Ambrose's father, John Maddison, a "ship carpenter" and junior member of the Commission of the Peace (county court) in King and Queen, died in 1724–25, his 3,000 acres in King and Queen and Caroline Counties were divided among his three sons (Ambrose, Henry, and John III). This inheritance probably also included several slaves.[8] Ambrose tallied up all the debts owed to him by his planter associates in the old Mantapike neighborhood of King and Queen in 1725 and apparently moved later that year with his new family to the Caroline County land that he had inherited, no doubt taking along his personal slaves, at the same time that he invested in his new patent lands further upcountry with the recently purchased Africans. When Madison moved to his Mt. Pleasant quarter in 1732, he would have taken these family slaves with him.

But in the 1730s (and early 1740s), planters in the central Piedmont counties along the tributaries to the York and Rappahannock Rivers continued directly to import Africans, as is evidenced by the routine "age adjudgments" of recently imported African children. Because slaves were taxed per capita based on age (those over age sixteen during the colonial era), planters brought recently imported children into court to have their ages adjudged and recorded for tax purposes. Each age adjudgment required the enslaved child to be walked into court to have his or her age determined by the planter-justices' direct observation. Though this must have been a terrifying experience for children who had survived many other traumas, including enslavement and the middle passage, the ordeal also must have impressed them with the power of the white planters in assembly as a court of law. These records also suggest the outlines of continuing importations of Africans.

In the contiguous central Piedmont counties of Caroline, Spotsylvania, and Orange, more than 350 African children had their ages officially adjudged between 1732 and 1746, an average of 25 per year.[9] In 1736 in Orange County, Madison's neighbor, James Barbour, brought in 4 boys and 1 girl. The names of some of the adjudged children also hint at their origins in Africa. There was a boy named Ebo and another named Juba (1733, 1735 Caroline) as well as a boy named Angolo and another named Mingo (1734, 1742 Spotsylvania), which suggest Central African origins, and other children with afriphonetic names such as Singo (boy), Bimbo (girl), Luckum (girl), Cuffey (boy), and Tem (girl) (Caroline County).

The fact that Juba was nearly always a male name in Virginia is significant. In both eighteenth-century Jamaica and South Carolina, Juba was nearly always a female name, presumably derived from the Akan (Coromantee) day name system and meaning "female born on Monday."[10] The use of Juba as a male name in some parts of colonial North America once puzzled historians, who assumed that the term was used exclusively by Coromantee peoples. Newbell Niles Puckett, for example, thought that the two free black men named Juba in a payroll list of a Connecticut regiment in the Revolutionary War was strange, writing that "either the meaning or the traditional gender of this name had been forgotten by this time."[11]

Among Igbo peoples, however, *júbà* is the root of at least two common traditional names for males as well as the patronym of one well-known Igbo historian.[12] In the various dialects of the Igbo language, *juba* (or *jiuba*) is a typically compound word, from *ji* (yam) and *úba* (canoe), literally meaning "yam barn," which signifies wealth or fortune.[13] Therefore, the use of Juba as a name for males in the Chesapeake (and later the Upper South) follows lexical and semantic fields in Igbo and signifies wealth. The name Juba was widely distributed in colonial Virginia and can be documented in court order books throughout Piedmont counties, including Caroline (1735), Spotsylvania (1747, 1758, 1761, 1771), Orange (1761), Amelia (1755), and Louisa (1760s, 1773).[14] By the nineteenth century, the word *júbà* contained other meanings in the Upper South, including a particular "African" style of song-and-dance ("patting juba," "juba jumping") which produced, in racist parody, the central minstrel figure named Juba. In Tidewater North Carolina, around Edenton, as late as about 1840, slaves chanted "Juba!" as an aggressive refrain in the part of Jonkonnu (a distinctive Christmastime masquerade) in which they demanded money from their masters and other white folks.[15] As a term likely brought by Igbo slaves and found in various usages in areas where Africans from Calabar were numerous, including Orange County, it is significant that *Juba* was not used in areas where the Igbo presence was much less important or at least not as visible.[16] Its use to name boys and men could have constituted a *lieu de mémoire* not just for Africans generally but for Igbo in particular.

Other typically Igbo or Calabar names were known among slaves close to the Madisons' community. At least two late-eighteenth and early-nineteenth-century groups of slaves who had close connections with Madison-owned enslaved people and who likely were kinfolk or at least included related families included adult women named Anica (Ànéka).[17] Another nearby plantation also included a slave named Annica in 1782.[18] The name Nnéka, meaning roughly "Big Mother" or colloquially "Big Mama" (lit. "Mother is greater"), traditionally was common among women in Igboland. The root is *nné* (Ànné, "mother") and is documented rather widely in colonial and early national Virginia. A late example is Annika Cumba, the slave mother of a well-known Albemarle County fiddle player, Jesse Scott (1781–1862), who had connections to Thomas Jefferson's slaves.[19]

Another female name with likely Igbo origins was Annaca/Annaky, which appears in eighteenth-century records for Orange County as well as among Jefferson's slaves.[20] In 1782, a close neighbor of the Madisons, Mary Bell, owned a male slave with yet another African-derived name, Quaw, which was a morpheme typical of Nri-Awka and eastern Igbo as well as so-called Moko (Ibibio and related Cross River peoples) or Kwa Ibo, all of whom were brought out of Calabar.[21] Other slaves in 1782, such as Mimah (Ambrose Madison), Doctor (Joseph Smith), and Truelove (James Madison Sr., Catlett Conway) may have had Africanesque names, either literally or as calques, that served as nominal *lieux de mémoire* to underscore shared historical experiences and connections.

The charter generation of Madison-owned slaves clearly faced a number of severe challenges. Yet they also would have been able to take advantage of growing opportunities to understand their shared predicament in Igboesque ways and to establish connections with people of other Quarters and plantations. In Igboland, as in Virginia, the basic farming tool was the hoe. But other tools, such as axes, shovels, and "beaks, or pointed iron, to dig with," also were used in the Calabar hinterland in the mid–eighteenth century. Furthermore, it is likely that Igbo slaves already knew how to cultivate maize and tobacco, both of which were reportedly grown in north-central Igboland in "vast quantities" in the 1750s. Tobacco was also widely grown around 1700 along the Senegal and Gambia Rivers in Upper Guinea and was well known to the region's major long-distance traders, the Mandingo.[22] In both regions, women and children as well as men farmed the land, though usually not the same crops, with men specializing in produce for long-distance trade and "men's plants," and women in garden vegetables and subsistence crops.

By the early 1730s, the hardest work of clearing the land at the Mt. Pleasant quarter may have been largely over. Ambrose Madison's probate inventory of 1733 includes a wide range of tools, mostly implements for carpentry and for cultivating. There were no axes, for example, or heavy hoes. The most common farming tools, in fact, were thirteen "New Weeding hows," which suggests that the primary fieldwork was cultivation rather than the clearing of new fields. That Madison was preparing for a major construction effort is signaled by the large number of nails, including 16,000 ten-penny nails and 1,200 eight-penny nails.[23] It seems likely that, at the time of his death, Madison had been preparing to establish a new Quarter at his Black Level tract, on the other side of Thomas Chew's half of the original patent.

After his death, Madison's slaves were divided almost equally between these two Quarters. In 1738, there were eight adult slaves at the Home House quarter (Mt. Pleasant) under an overseer named Edmund Powell. In that same year, Frances Madison had six adult slaves at the Black Level farm, under her youngest brother, Erasmus Taylor (1715–94). If the Black Level quarter was established in about 1733, as seems likely, and Erasmus had stepped up to help his widowed sister as overseer at the new settlement, then he would have just turned eighteen. By 1739, when Erasmus was twenty-five, he ran his own farm with three adult slaves, and Frances Madison still had about half her slaves (six adults) at Black Level, with the other seven adults at the Home House quarter, now under Ambrose Powell.[24]

The division of the slaves into two moieties in two Quarters continued through the 1740s, when James Madison Sr. came into his inheritance and began to centralize his slaveholdings at his home plantation, Montpelier. Though Ambrose Madison had originally had two Quarters, with the second one called Todds Folly in 1726, it was only a minimal settlement.[25] It appears that after his murder, the slaves were divided, with half sent south of the mountain to the Black Level quarter under a very young overseer and the other kept at the Home House (Mt. Pleasant) quarter under an experienced overseer.

If this was a "divide and conquer" strategy, however, it would have had the unintended effect of contributing to a basic settlement pattern that would have seemed vaguely familiar to Igbo people. Indeed, the general settlement pattern in Virginia in the first half of the eighteenth century, when Igbo dominated among saltwater slaves, featured a group of cabins constituting a Quarter, and several Quarters making a plantation, which was situated in a "room" or precinct (a neighborhood of connected plantations), several of which made up a section or district, of which several composed a county or even a country. This organization would not have been unfamiliar to "Eboe" slaves.

Though it is naive to think that the ways historical Igbo organized themselves in terms of genealogical descent and across the physical landscape in the eighteenth century was exactly the same as in the early twentieth century, early colonial ethnographies (pre–World War II) are useful in suggesting likely customary patterns of organization and settlement, or generalized models, that varied over time and space. For Igboland, all early ethnographies agree that the concept of "dual division," the segmentary organization of people into related sections, or "the division of villages and communities into 'upper' and 'lower'" parts, was characteristic and expressed a deep cultural principle of Igbo peoples.[26] The other outstanding principle of historical Igbo culture is localism. In fact, Igbo historically maintained a dual concept of belonging, with a genealogical and a territorial element.[27] This worldview was articulated in a kind of concentric, segmentary, or localistic social construction in which people tended to live among (or next to) others with whom they claimed a shared descent. This meant that the further away a person or group lived, the less likely they were to be related. As table 6.1 shows, a generalized scheme of Igbo descent/settlement patterns suggests how genealogical and territorial "belonging" (collective identity) were connected.

In the era of primary settlement in Virginia, planters generally established subfarms with 5 to 8 adult slaves on each quarter. In the eighteenth century, middling and larger planters nearly always had plantations that comprised two or more Quarters, and most slaves were owned in larger slaveholding. In Orange County in 1782, the first year for which complete statistics are available, although three-quarters of slaveholders owned 9 or fewer slaves, two-thirds of enslaved people in the county were owned in groups of 10 or more, and one-third were owned in groups of 20 or more. The owners of the largest slaveholdings (20 or more), however, represented only 7 percent of all masters.[28] In other words, roughly a quarter of slave-owning whites owned two-thirds of the slaves. In 1782 and perhaps as early as the 1760s, the roughly thirty-four middling and large slave-owning planters in the district around Montpelier, with their 820 slaves (at minimum), owned an average of about 25 slaves each (see appendix E).[29]

The district touching on Madison's room, which comprised the Little Mountains–Blue Run area, contained more than 1,400 slaves

TABLE 6.1

Generalized Comparative Genealogical/Territorial Social Organization

Descent Group	Settlement Type	Igbo Term
Family	Household	*Ónùnne*
Extended family	Compound/ homestead	*Ëbo*—úmùnna[a]
Kindred	Hamlet	*Ŏnùma, orógbê* (quarter)—úmùnna
Minimal lineage	Village	*Nkpóro* (pron. ènquóro)—úmùnna
Maximal lineage	Village group	*Òbódo*
Clan	-land	-*ála*/-*áma* (e.g., *Isu-ama*)
People	World	*Ndi*-, or *umu*- (tribe)[b]

Source: Based on a close reading and comparison of Talbot, *Peoples;* Meek, *Law and Authority.* Forde and Jones, *Ibo and Ibibio-Speaking Peoples,* 15, emphasizes only the importance of the "localized patrilineage" (*úmùnná*).

Notes:

[a] A segmentary conception of the localized patrilineage in which exogamy is enforced and which contained the extended family, the kindred, and the minimal lineage but also could extend even to the maximal lineage.

[b] Such a level of abstraction as to be almost mythological; for example, Ndigbo (Igbo people) or Umuchukwu (God's children; lit., descendants of Supreme Deity, colloquially "God boys") (see Leonard, "Notes," 191).

and was the "blackest" part of the county. Of the eleven enumeration rooms (or precincts) in Orange County, James Madison's neighborhood had the greatest number of slaves (more than 500) and the largest average slaveholding (15 slaves).[30]

For Eboe slaves in this eighteenth-century world, the exigencies of chattel slavery would have competed with a dual landscape of belonging, one based on genealogical descent and direct (real and/or fictive) kin relations, and the other based on residence and physical settlement. Such a segmentary topography would have been useful, particularly for African-born slaves and very likely their children, in creating some order out of the chaos of their lives. A generalized organizational system may be discerned in Virginia that in fact resembles a slightly modified Igbo-type scheme, which I term "Igboesque." Table 6.2 suggests that the slaves developed a segmentary means of organizing their relations across both descent and territory.

Such a generalized organizational scheme, which perforce is merely speculative but is perhaps illustrative of an historical Igboesque reality, may be plausible because it also closely mirrors the rather similar (at least structurally) definitional topography that obtained among whites. Though these landscapes were similar in structure, the black landscape of belonging evokes a revised Igbo (Igboesque) imagined cartography, or field of meaning. Of course, Igbo slaves could not simply transfer or carry over ancestral cultural artifacts in their totality to this new *topocosmos*—that is, they could not simply re-create the complex village-level forms of social organization in which they had grown up and from which they had been torn in their new land. But an Igboesque logic of belonging seemed to operate among slaves in Virginia; that its beat was the counterpoint to the logic of the whites should not obscure the distinctive source of its harmony.

The realities of slavery within this regional system of dispersed settlement may well have led Eboe to collapse the concepts of the extended family and the compound into the Quarter while maintaining the sense of the plantation and/or slaveholding as a kind of minimal lineage or localized patrilineage, especially as the white ethos of planter paternalism appropriated the idiom of descent

TABLE 6.2

Eighteenth-Century Settlement Pattern/Speculative Organizational Topography

Descent Group	Black Landscape (or Settlement Type)	White Landscape	Igbo Equivalent
Family[a]	Household[b]	Cabin	Ónùnne
Extended family	Group/kindred	Quarter	Ŏnùma/ëbo/ógbê
Minimal lineage[c]	Plantation	Family[d]	Nkpóro/úmùnna
Maximal lineage	Neighborhood	Room/precinct[e]	Òbódo
Clan	Land/district	(House)/section	-ála/-áma
Tribe	Region	County	Ndi-/umu-
Country	Eboe	Country/river	Igbo
Race	Negro	White	Human

Notes:

[a] Mother and children, though at times the father, too.

[b] Or the "minimum family."

[c] Principal master, or home place.

[d] Or slaveholding.

[e] For the routine use of *room* to designate the enumeration precinct, each of which had its own constable, who basically enumerated the surrounding neighbors, and which generally coincided with the militia precincts (each headed by at least one captain) of roughly fifty households, see OCOB, 2:133; Little, *Orange County.*

(family) to characterize the whole of the master's slaves. By the early nineteenth century slaves, established a clear preference and had forged an accepted plantation custom of marrying outside of one's group, plantation, or even holding, thereby creating kin and other social connections in the wider neighborhood. The marked tendency toward exogamy (abroad spouses) and the consequent ability to live abroad is striking. As James Madison Jr. wrote in an 1823 letter, "The slaves prefer wives on a different plantation; as affording occasions & pretexts for going abroad."[31] The level at which marriage was preferred outside the group—that is, the plantation level— is also analogous to Igbo degrees of exogamy, to the definition of the *úmùnna* as the localized patrilineage of the master's slave family.

In Igboland, where people with localistic and segmentary conceptions of belonging created connections in overlapping ways among and between the various nearby groups, the people created an impressive system of paths and roads through the bush, connecting the clearings, farms, hamlets, villages, and village groups within what one Africanist ethnographer has termed "a network of magnificent roads."[32] The rapid development of Orange County, Virginia, in the 1730s and 1740s also wrought an impressive network of roads or formal paths. Ambrose Madison had petitioned for a number of roads, and Frances Madison petitioned in 1739 for a road around the plantation. James Madison Sr. also petitioned for roads in his time.[33] As early as 1739, the local paths and roads were becoming so complex as to be confusing. In that year, the justices of Orange County were compelled to issue an order requiring the various supervisors of roads throughout the county to erect legible signs or stones at crossroads and to have "inscriptions thereon in Large Letters directing to the most noted place to which each of the said Joyning roads Leads."[34]

In general, these roads or improved paths established districts. Adult slaves on the plantations by which the roads were laid were compelled to work on building and maintaining the routes and consequently would have had further opportunities to interact and to think of themselves as constituting a land.[35] The extensive formal path/road system also would have encouraged people, enslaved as well as free, to travel outside their Quarters. For slaves this would have meant largely at night, when roads would be especially useful, and on Sundays.

The charter generation of Atlantic Africans and their first children at Montpelier, as elsewhere, found themselves in situations that encouraged the development of a sense of both local and regional belonging, or a layered sense of community, in spite of the degrading circumstances of slavery. There was a notable Eboe presence, and presumably influence, in these groups of enslaved Africans. Therefore, some large proportion of the slaves may well have drawn on Igbo cultural resources, such as segmentary localism and dual division, to make sense of their new lives as they adapted to the continuing challenges of living and laboring, of being and doing, of strategic submission and tactical resistance, all within the briar patch of slavery.

In general, the plantation world was essentially divided into two largely separate spheres, that of the whites and that of the slaves. Throughout the British Atlantic, whites learned to call blacks "niggers" and slaves learned to call their masters (and other whites) "buckra." The widespread use of the latter term reflected the ubiquity of Igbo peoples in the Anglophone diaspora, or, for slaves of other ethnicities, the utility of Igboesque ways of defining whites. Although derived from the Ibibio *mbákara* (*mb-* plural; *-kara* to encircle, rule, abuse), slaves everywhere in Anglophone America used the term to denote white folks.[36] Igbo people brought the term into English as *buckra* and perhaps provided the subtext of seeing the white man as "he who surrounds or governs" or as a "demon, powerful and superior being." As a slave saying from South Carolina in the 1770s put it, "Da buccary no be good fatru" (That white man is not good, to be sure).[37]

How did Igboized slaves perceive the *buckra?* One scholar has provocatively suggested that, in Jamaica at least, many African slaves "defined slaveowners as sorcerers" because of the slaves' common conviction that sorcery had played a role in their original enslavement. There is good evidence to support such a supposition, at least in terms of the initial interpretation that many West Africans had of Europeans as spirits and jujus.[38] For example, John Jea, who was born in 1733 in Old Calabar and was taken to New York as a slave, remembered that he and his parents "were often led away with the idea that our masters were our gods; and at other times we placed our ideas on the sun, moon, and stars, looking unto them, as if they could save us."[39]

In general, however, many of the slaves may have seen the *buckra* in Igboesque terms—that is, as *èzè* (masters) or as little kings. As a missionary in Onitsha in the 1850s explained, "*Eze* literally means 'Master,' and is applied to kings and to those who are in an important office."[40] Just as *eze* were spiritually and materially powerful beings who could lord it over the people yet were subject to the customs (*omenani*) of the place, so slaves saw their masters as cruel and powerful yet bound by customary law (plantation customs). Furthermore, slaves everywhere routinely addressed not just their owners but all *buckra* with the ritual salutation of some variation of *master*—"massa," "mossa," "marster," or "marse." Igboized slaves may well have appropriated familiar ancestral concepts to make sense of their masters' formal powers over the slaves, even as they were coerced into signifying their own subordination in the diaspora.

CHAPTER SEVEN

A Montpelier Community of Slaves:
The Creolizing Generation

In murdering Old Master Ambrose in 1732, the slaves had directly confronted Madison's hegemony, and they did so as Atlantic Africans. They likely drew on the lethal expertise of the larger (probably Igbo or, more precisely, Eboe) community of fellow slaves or of adepts among them. They then "remembered" this charter event through the mnemonic of recycled names from the charter generation when naming their own Creole descendants. Madison's murder expressed in graphic terms the violence that was an essential part of slavery. It also established the limits both of the master's power and of the slaves' resistance. The longevity of the Montpelier community of Madison-owned slaves, which remained largely intact through 1801, and their apparent deep memory of the first generation, would have carried the import of the plantation's charter event well into the nineteenth century.[1]

In the eighteenth century, the Madison slave population doubled every thirty or so years. From the 15 or so adults in the 1730s, the number of adults (over age sixteen and likely the full-time workers) reached about 35 in the 1760s and topped 60 in the 1790s. Figured another way, the number of slaves of the extended Madison family increased from 29 in 1733 to more than 60 (estimated) in the 1760s to a known minimum of 124 in 1782. At Montpelier itself, the number of working-age slaves increased from 7 or 8 in 1738–39 to 30 in the 1760s to more than 60 in the 1790s. Therefore, about half of the Madison family-owned slaves lived and worked at Montpelier, with the rest distributed on quarters either adjacent to or in close proximity to the home community.

In the creolizing generation (1740s–60s), there was a steady growth in the slave population, partly from local additions to the community and partly from "natural increase." In the 1740s, James Madison Sr. came into his inheritance, and though he actually owned only some of the family's slaves, he effectively controlled the labor of all of them. In 1749, he married Nelly Conway, of Port Conway in Caroline County, and received 5 to 7 adult slaves (10 to 15 total) as a dowry. In the 1750s, he also gained control over a sizable group of slaves owned by his widowed sister but kept in trust for Madison's niece, Mary Willis (b. ca. 1747). He initially put these slaves to work on some of his Montpelier quarters, and they launched a major rebuilding effort on his several farms. Finally, following his mother's death in 1761, James Sr. inherited the balance of his father's slaves and lands, which by then comprised some 4,000 nearly contiguous acres.

It is also clear that planters in the central Piedmont were continuing to import Africans during the creolizing generation. In the thirty years after 1740, approximately 630 recently imported African children were taken before the county justices in Orange, Spotsylvania, and Caroline Counties. In 1754, Madison's cousin, Edmund Taylor, brought in a girl, and James Madison Sr. participated in judging her age.[2] Some of these slaves were likely Igbo, including a boy named Bonny (Caroline 1751) and several male Jubas (Spotsylvania 1747, 1761; Orange 1761). They would have joined groups and communities where some noticeable proportion of the adults also would have been from Calabar. There is no evidence, however, that James Madison Sr. purchased any Africans from the continuing transatlantic slave trade to Virginia; thus, by the 1750s and 1760s, a growing proportion of his slaves would have been born in the colony.

The slave community centered on Montpelier also experienced its first major separation with the division of Ambrose Madison's estate in 1744. Madison had directed that his widow was to control all of his slaves until one of his children should marry, at which time "the hole of the Estate that I have lent to my wife shall be Devided as the law Directs."[3] Entail by primogeniture, where the eldest son received all of the chattel and real property (slaves and land), was still a legal option at this time, but Madison's estate was divided by partible inheritance: his widow, Frances Taylor Madison, received one-third as her dower right, and the rest was divided equally among the children, demonstrating that the usual legal practice apparently was division per stirpes.[4] Indirect evidence suggests that Frances Madison gained ownership of 10 or 11 adult slaves, with each of her children inheriting 7 or 8 working-age slaves.[5] When Elizabeth Madison (1725–73) married John Willis (1724–ca. 1750) in 1744, she triggered the division of her father's estate.[6] Frances Madison kept her share on the main plantation, as did James; Elizabeth's slaves were taken to her new husband's nearby plantation, and the underage Frances (1726–ca. 1776) assigned hers to the guardianship of her nearby uncle, Erasmus Taylor, who likely already was familiar with the slaves.[7] However, all of these slaves were moved to plantations in the immediate vicinity. A more permanent separation of at least 25 slaves came in 1763, at the height of the creolizing generation.

After James Madison Sr.'s brother-in-law, John Willis, died in about 1750, Madison became the trustee of the two-thirds of Willis's slaves and land that were inherited by Willis's only child, Mary—26 slaves and several thousand acres.[8] About half of these enslaved people were of working age, and they roughly doubled the number of slave workers over whom Madison had legal control. Although Elizabeth Willis remarried about 1751, she apparently chose to have her brother serve as the trustee for the substantial number of slaves that technically belonged to her young daughter.

These Willis slaves were important for two reasons. First, they included some of the original settlers of the district, and they and their children probably were connected with the Madison-Baylor-Taylor set of communities. Second, the decade that Madison owned their labor (ca. 1753–63) was a transformative time at Montpelier, and their labor contributed directly to the rebuilding of the plantation. In fact, Madison's guardianship of his young niece's slaves was a boon and represented quite a coup for the relatively young (and clearly ambitious) James Madison Sr. His first child, a son whom he named after himself, had just been born in 1751, and the plantation community was clearly expanding, including the slaves that his wife, Nelly, had recently brought from Port Conway to Montpelier.

Richard Beale, a substantial planter who was Elizabeth Willis's second husband, conceivably could have been named as Mary's guardian. Beale was certainly known to the Madisons: his brother, Taverner (d. 1756), had married James's other sister, Frances. By gaining control over the labor of these slaves, however, Madison again doubled the number of people whose labor he could command. These slaves included two skilled carpenters, who would have been especially useful and perhaps had already contributed their labor to a new gristmill that Madison had built on the other side of his property in 1752–53.

In the mid-1740s, Madison launched his career as a planter. In 1744, James received direct ownership of the outlying Black Level quarter, composed of 750 acres. He hired an overseer, Benjamin Winn, to the run the quarter, with 8 to 10 adult slaves as the labor. And in 1745 Madison sold his first crop of tobacco under his own tobacco mark. In 1747 he hired a new overseer, Jeremiah White, for the Black Level quarter and built a new forty-foot tobacco barn for the farm the following year.⁹ Shortly after James's marriage, Frances transferred another 900 acres of land to her son's direct ownership.

James launched a major rebuilding effort at Montpelier and his outlying farms in the 1750s. Between 1750 and 1752 he built up both the Home House and Black Level quarters, adding dwellings, tobacco barns, and corncribs. In 1750 James had the slaves build two forty foot tobacco barns, one sixteen foot dwelling and four slave cabins at the Home House quarter, which probably represented the requirements of new housing for slaves that had been deployed previously at Black Level. He also added a sixteen foot dwelling and a sixteen-by-twelve-foot corncrib to the quarter at Black Level, where he sent the Conway slaves. In 1751, at the Home House quarter, Madison had the slaves open a new cornfield at some distance from the old one there, and corn production soared. He had a new sixteen-by-twelve-foot corncrib and an eight-foot-square dairy built, installed a house bell that Nelly's brother procured for them from Fredericksburg, and added locks on two doors. Finally, in 1752, perhaps in anticipation of taking over Mary Willis's slaves, Madison again enlarged the Black Level quarter, adding a new tobacco barn, another dwelling, and four more cabins and mended a chimney on the existing dwelling there.¹⁰

By the end of 1752, Madison's two Quarters would have resembled bustling little villages, with clusters of dwellings, barns, and other outbuildings. It is instructive that Madison felt compelled to put new locks on his doors during these years of expansion. Each Quarter would have looked familiar to planters in eighteenth-century Virginia. As one traveler wrote, "A plantation in Virginia has often more the appearance of a small village, by reason of the many separate small buildings, which taken all together would at times hardly go to make up a single roomy and commodious house. Here are living rooms, bed-chambers, guest-chambers, store-rooms, quarters for the slaves, and who knows what else, commonly so many small, separate, badly kept cabins of wood, without glass in the windows, of the structure and solid quality of a house of cards."[11]

This building binge had long-lasting effects on the built landscape of Madison's lands. As late as 1785, he had twice as many buildings on his plantation (thirty-two) than any other planter in the county.[12] These buildings were likely to be have been of impermanent, earthfast (post-in-the-ground) construction and rather flimsy, although because Madison usually employed trained carpenters (free as well as slave) to build his structures, they may have been somewhat better than the average.[13]

In the spring of 1752, Madison set about creating a third Quarter on 350 acres of adjacent land that had been part of the original patent on Chew's side, plus two small tracts that Chew sold to Madison to discharge some debts. This combined 555-acre tract lay on the eastern side of the ridge that divided Madison's lands from Chew's, on a creek that came to be known as Madison Run. Madison built a gristmill on this site and within a year quartered some slaves there. In January 1754 he hired a white man, Samuel Sutton, to run the mill and named the farm the Mill Quarter.[14]

By 1757 Madison had purchased a total of 1,104 acres from Chew, or about two-thirds of the land that Chew had reserved for himself some twenty years earlier. James came into his full inheritance in 1761, at which point he owned about 4,000 acres of contiguous land divided into three basic farms. To the south was Black Level, comprising 750 or so acres and dating to the 1730s. The Home House quarter was centered on the lands near the present-day family cemetery and extending eastward. Representing the balance of Ambrose's part of the original patent, this Quarter consisted in 1747 of about 1,900 acres, about half of it hilly woodland. Madison first gained legal control of the cultivable part (about 900 acres) upon his marriage and rapidly expanded production of corn and tobacco, opening at least one new field in 1751. During the 1750s, he consistently had large crops of tobacco and corn planted,

TABLE 7.1

Total Corn Production, Montpelier Farms, 1745–1756

Year	Bushels
1745	564
1746	567
1747	605
1748	497
1749	644
1750	871
1751	992
1752	1,008
1753	1,291
1754	2,016
1755	753
1756	3,353

Source: James Madison Sr. Memorandum Book (1744–1757).

averaging about 50 acres in tobacco and another 50 in corn each year.[15] After 1752, the new Mill Quarter, at some distance from the Home House and Black Level quarters, was used primarily to produce corn, with tobacco as a secondary crop. From 1753 to 1756, for example, Madison had slaves plant an estimated 3 acres of corn for every acre of tobacco at the Mill Quarter. The dramatic increase in corn production at Montpelier in the 1750s (see table 7.1) reflected Madison's investment in the new gristmill but also probably meant that the slaves received constant rations of cornmeal. The increase also meant that in times of crisis, such as the severe and sustained drought of 1755, which Madison called "a Fatal Year for Croping," the slaves at Montpelier may have suffered less than others.[16]

The major cash crop, however, was tobacco. Tobacco cultivation was labor intensive and required large reserves of land because continual cropping could rapidly deplete the soil. Planters generally needed about 50 acres per worker (hand) to successfully rotate crops with long fallow periods and provide sufficient pasturage for livestock. Each adult worker could produce an estimated 1,000 pounds of tobacco on a total of 3 acres each year, with another 4 acres per hand generally planted in corn.[17]

In the 1740s, Madison's slaves produced an average of 9,500 pounds of tobacco on about 29 acres each year at Black Level. After 1749, access to more slaves tripled the size of his annual tobacco crops. From 1750 to 1752, the slaves at the two Quarters produced an average of more than 28,000 pounds of tobacco per year, and by 1757 the three farms (including the new Mill Quarter) were producing more than 38,500 pounds annually.[18] Thus, in the 1740s and 1750s, the slaves produced something on the order of 260,000 pounds of tobacco (239,000 net). With the overseers' shares amounting to about 38,000 pounds, Madison would have netted a minimum of nearly 200,000 pounds worth an estimated £1,790.[19] In the dozen years after 1745, Madison's personal income from his tobacco crops rose about 650 percent, to an average of £294.85 (1756–57), and by 1757 his income was soaring along with tobacco prices (see tables 7.2 and 7.3).[20]

The wealth created by the slaves came at great cost to them. Perhaps in response to the remembered dangers of keeping all the slaves in one central community, combined with the value of establishing several farms and no doubt the utility of breaking the slaves into smaller workforces for closer supervision, Madison tended toward a labor regime that shifted the slaves among his Quarters. This revolving labor system meant that almost annually he deployed slaves among his farms, presumably forcing the slaves to move to new quarters each time. In effect, the slaves in the 1740s and 1750s learned to stay at different Quarters.

TABLE 7.2

Total Tobacco Production on Montpelier Farms 1745–1757[a]

Year	Overseer	Quarter	Pounds
1745	Benjamin Winn	Black Level	8,629
1746	Benjamin Winn	Black Level	12,803
1747	Jeremiah White	Black Level	9,352
1748	Jeremiah White	Black Level	7,403
1749	Jeremiah White	Black Level	9,648
1750	Thomas Dauhany	Home House	18,252
	William Brockman	Black Level	9,781
1751	Thomas Dauhany	Home House	14,715
	William Brockman	Black Level	10,809
1752	Thomas Dauhany	Home House	20,531
	William Brockman	Black Level	10,626
1753	Thomas Dauhany	Home House	13,491
	William Brockman	Black Level	7,749
	Thomas Dauhany	Mill Quarter	3,964
1754	Thomas Dauhany	Home House	14,171
	William Brockman	Black Level	6,067
	Thomas Dauhany	Mill Quarter	4,906
1755[b]	Thomas Dauhany	Home House	5,765
	William Brockman	Black Level	2,750
	Thomas Dauhany	Mill Quarter	1,510
1756	Thomas Dauhany	Home House	11,912
	William Brockman	Black Level	8,594
	Thomas Dauhany	Mill Quarter	6,972
1757	Thomas Dauhany[c]	Home House	23,981
	William Brockman[d]	Black Level	14,669

Source: James Madison Sr. Memorandum Book (1744–1757).

Notes:
ᵃ These figures represent a minimum, since these crops were the ones in which James Madison Sr. had a legal interest and probably excluded some tobacco produced solely by his mother's slaves, especially before 1750.
ᵇ Drought year.
ᶜ Crop made by Dauhany for Frances and James Madison combined, likely at the Home House. This figure for the main quarter may be representative of the totals produced there from around 1750.
ᵈ May include the Mill Quarter as well as Black Level.

TABLE 7.3

Estimated Net Income from Tobacco, Montpelier, 1745–1757

Year	Net (in pounds)	Average Price	Estimated Total Value (£)
1745	6,119	1.39	35.43
1746	9,561	1.48	58.96
1747	7,259	1.64	49.60
1748	6,049	1.50	37.80
1749	7,190	1.50	44.94
1750	21,551	2.16	193.96
1751	20,227	1.91	160.97
1752	24,588	2.04	209.00
1753	19,366	1.96	158.16
1754	18,515	2.16	166.64
1755	7,664	3.00	95.80
1756	21,401	2.40	214.01
1757	29,085	3.10	375.68

Source: James Madison Sr. Memorandum Book (1744–1757).
Notes: Prices given in pennies per pound, decimalized. Estimated total values are also decimalized.

Madison was willing to move slaves around, perhaps to keep them busy by opening new fields, establishing new Quarters, and doing all the other work beyond tending tobacco and corn. Such a revolving labor system also suggests a continuing attempt to divide and conquer the slaves, though he tended at times to keep some groups together and eventually to consolidate most of his slaves at the Montpelier core.

Immediately after marrying Nelly, Madison brought her Conway slaves from Caroline County and set them up at his Black Level quarter. In the winter of 1749–50, Madison also sent some of his mother's slaves, over whom he had just gained control, to Black Level to help prepare the next year's tobacco crop. For the following seasons, James split up his slaves, keeping some at Black Level to work with Nelly's gang while putting others to work (along with his mother's slaves) clearing and planting a new field at the Home House farm. Madison maintained this division for the 1752 planting season, with the slaves of James and Nelly Madison at Black Level and the slaves of Frances and James Madison at the Home House.[21]

In 1752–53, Madison again separated the slaves at Black Level, sending between 4 and 6 adults to open the new Mill Quarter.[22] In 1754 he sent some of the Willis slaves to the Mill Quarter to supplement his own from Black Level.[23] In the drought year of 1755, the Mill Quarter was staffed solely with the Willis slaves; James Madison kept his wife's slaves at Black Level and reserved his mother's slaves for the Home House. In 1756, however, he once again reorganized his slave labor force. He kept Frances Madison's laborers at home, sent the Conway slaves to the Mill Quarter, and moved about half of the Willis slaves back to Black Level, leaving the other half at the nearby Willis plantation under their longtime overseer, John Connor. In 1757, Madison split up the Willis slaves for good. He sent those who had spent the previous year working at Black Level to a plantation in Spotsylvania County and relocated about half of the others under Connor to restart an old farm on Mine Run (located on the far eastern edge of the county) that John Willis had run in the 1740s.

After 1757, Madison maintained his three Quarters with his own slaves, while the Willis slaves were distributed between at least four widely scattered farms, far from Montpelier.[24] All of this shifting about disrupted the slaves' community life. As the slaves as a whole creolized and confronted the challenges of incorporating outsiders and of increasing production (and profit for the master), they also learned the difference between *living* and *staying* somewhere. Presumably they all lived at Montpelier, though they could be made to stay at one quarter or another.

For the Willis slaves and their relatives in particular, the 1750s were a time of uncertainty and perhaps of heartbreak. After being divided in 1750, with the two-thirds controlled by James Madison moved about during the ensuing years, many were subsequently sent far away from the Montpelier district. When Mary Willis married in 1763, her slaves were all sent to her new husband's plantation in Spotsylvania.[25] After a decade spent mixed with Madison's slaves, those owned by Mary Willis were sent away forever.[26]

As the revenue flowed in and Madison's access to slaves widened, especially in the 1750s, he began to invest directly in Montpelier's Home House quarter, including building a grand new brick Big House and probably a new slave Quarter (Walnut Grove) by about 1760. During the ensuing decade, he consolidated his slaves by moving most of them to the newly rebuilt Montpelier core.

By the mid-1750s, Madison began construction of the Big House at the foot of the nearby wooded mountain and positioned the dwelling to take advantage of the sweeping view westward to the Blue Ridge. An impressive two-story Georgian structure, with two rooms on each side of a central hall and presumably at least four rooms above, this new seat was largely complete by 1760. It was designed to impress and to reflect Colonel Madison's growing prominence in local affairs.[27] By 1767 Madison had become the predominant

planter in the county, and he was commissioned county lieutenant, a
largely ceremonial but highly esteemed military appointment that
made him a full colonel in the militia, which he headed until 1778.
As usual, Madison's commission was largely politically motivated, as
he had held no previous military rank, and affirmed his standing in
the local pecking order. By 1769, Madison had also become a senior
member of the county's most openly self-selected governing board,
the parish vestry. At the vestry meeting held on 1 September 1769,
he was listed third out of the ten members present, behind only the
Reverend Thomas Martin and Madison's uncle, Erasmus Taylor.[28]

Madison apparently developed the new consolidated slave Quarter,
Walnut Grove, located down the hill to the east, at about the same
time. By the latter 1760s, the largely Creole population, though likely
also still including some African-born slaves and certainly their children of the charter generation, was becoming consolidated at the
Home House quarter. Lists of county levies in 1764 and 1769 (see
appendix B) suggest such a trend. In 1764, Madison was assessed
for 29 adult slaves, 25 of them at his Home Quarter. Five years later,
of the 43 adults on whom he paid taxes, 33 were listed as staying
at one Quarter (presumably the Home House), with the other ten
at a different one (Black Level). Thus, whereas a generation earlier
(1738–39) the slaves were divided roughly into two equal groups
with each half on a separate farm, in the latter 1760s, 75–80 percent
stayed at the core Montpelier community.

The slaves' productivity may have reflected an informal bargain
between master and slave in which the enslaved people, now largely
locally born, in effect traded the production of wealth for relative
stability. Though the revolving labor system of the 1740s and 1750s
was an expression of the master's power, the slaves may well have submitted to his authority to the degree that he guaranteed that they
could stay together. In other words, they may have forged a "working misunderstanding" with their master. Though individuals may
have resisted their slavery in various ways, including occasionally

running away, there is no evidence for the kind of overt resistance that characterized the charter generation or even of some of Madison's neighbors' slaves in the late-1760s.

For example, in the summer of 1767, one of John Baylor's slaves, Tom, was tried for breaking into Erasmus Taylor's house and stealing goods valued at five shillings. After being found guilty at a trial over which Colonel Madison presided, Tom was executed on 15 October 1767, "as he is precluded from the Benefit of Clergy having already received it" and the Court did "adjudge that he Suffer Death." Tom forty-five pounds. In March 1770, another of Baylor's slaves, Essex, was found not guilty of the felony of stealing a hog from Richard Beale. Essex had confessed that "he had given the Same to his Wife [and] therefore they are of Opinion that he is Guilty of a Misdemeanor." His life therefore was spared, but he received ten lashes as punishment.[29] There are no records of similar oyer and terminer trials for any of Madison's slaves.

All indications are that James Madison Sr. was someone who demanded respect. And though the balance of the slaves would have had little personal contact with him, since Madison always relied on overseers (and perhaps enslaved headmen or drivers), collectively they may have forged a grand compromise. Madison certainly was not one to give in to actual demands from anyone, much less his slaves, but the shift toward consolidating the people into one large community in the 1760s marked a major change from an earlier "divide and conquer" regime. And Madison's success may have made him more comfortable with a new strategy for controlling his slaves, using a carrot of relative stability and communal residence along with the stick of threatened separation.

An example of Colonel Madison's actions on the county court give some indication of his persona (or at least the one he showed the public). Madison apparently was well aware that by the late 1760s he had gathered together the various reins of influence and power, probably including "pacifying" his slaves. His actions in these years suggest how he had come to expect others, including his peers on the county court, to accommodate his demands. He was not averse to throwing his newfound political weight around, but there were practical limits to his power.

In the summer of 1769, Madison openly asserted his claim to predominance in county affairs. On 25 August, Orange's court reconvened, and the first matter of business was approving the court's recommendation for sheriff. By law, the colony's governor appointed each county's sheriff, a rather troublesome office. Sheriffs were responsible for tax collecting as well as supervising constables and the county jail and administering the orders of the court, including punishments. But by custom the office rotated among the justices themselves in order of seniority, largely because although the post was time-consuming, its holder made money from a regulated share of taxes, fines, and judgments. The court generally submitted three names to the governor, who then routinely appointed the first on the list.[30]

Madison, whom his peers formally recognized as the "first Justice In the Commission," immediately moved that he should be nominated because he was the most senior member of the county's Commission of the Peace. However, another sitting justice, Reuben Daniel, objected, arguing that Madison was in fact not the court's most senior member because the colonel had failed to officially rejoin the commission after his previous term as sheriff had ended in 1757 and therefore had not been a member for almost two years in the late 1750s. Daniel reminded his peers that he had been named to the commission, qualified as a justice, and served for twenty-two months before Madison was requalified. Therefore, Daniel argued, he was the most senior justice and thus was entitled to be sheriff. Furthermore, Daniel pointed out that he was formally next in line to ascend to the office of sheriff, as Daniel had been named second in the nomination sent to the governor in 1767. At this point, Madison rose, not to contest the facts as presented by Daniel but to parry the "last reason Waged by the sd. Daniel"—in effect, disputing Daniel's claim to leadership of the court. Madison explained that he "did not Interfere at the last recommendation of the Sheriff because Richard Thomas Gent[leman]. who was first recommended he thought first Intitled to it as the said Richard had Acted as a Justice Sometime before the said Madison was appointed Sheriff as aforesaid and that therefore in turn he looked on it the sd. Richard should be first recommended."

The court responded to Madison's interference by confirming the validity of Daniel's claim to the office while simultaneously refusing to deny Madison's claim to being first among equals. In an attempt to avoid upsetting the court's hierarchy—and certainly to avoid upsetting Madison—the justices agreed to recommend both Madison and Daniel to the governor, naming Madison before Daniel in the text of the recommendation. In passing the decision to Williamsburg, however, the justices wanted it known that they did not "in any way determine the Preference of the sd. Madison or Daniel from the Order of placing their names But from the State of the Case hereby cited." In the end, Madison won the battle but lost the war, as Governor Botetourt appointed Daniel sheriff in November.[31]

The controversy over the sheriff recommendation defines the boundaries of Madison's public power and the limits of his political influence in 1769. He demanded and received the deference of his peers on the county court, who could not bring themselves directly to oppose his will even as they acknowledged that the facts contradicted Madison's legal position. Madison was not above the law in his county—indeed, he may have been indispensable to the administration and adjudication of law there—but in this case, the local justices had to stretch that law to accommodate Madison's demands. Colonel Madison, however, was only a county-level planter, a local grandee, whose manifest influence did not extend to the cosmopolitan center at Williamsburg. Madison may have been the acknowledged first gentleman of Orange County, but he was not one of the first gentlemen of Virginia as a whole. Though he ruled, Madison could not do so simply by fiat.

CHAPTER EIGHT

The Creole Generations: Peak and Decline

In early July 1836, as the fields ripened and daily thunderstorms washed across the countryside, bringing blackberries and brief respite from the gathering heat, the Montpelier slaves joined other mourners at the Madison graveyard. The "young" master, former president James Madison, had just died in his eighty-fifth year. After a decade or more of deepening economic troubles and having seen the sale of at least twenty-eight slaves in the past two years, the enslaved people at Montpelier must have been worrying about their futures.

One observer at Madison's funeral, his neighbor, James Barbour, described the scene. The slaves, dressed in their finest, were allowed to attend the graveside service. Having walked from the Walnut Grove quarters, they would have seen the wall of mountains looming blue in the distance to the west. Many of the slaves sobbed openly. Gathered at the edge of the crowd, they could hear the final remarks, and others could hear their sighing and weeping. And when the casket was lowered in to the yawning grave, and the minister intoned the final line, "dust to dust," as Barbour remembered, "the hundred slaves gave vent to their lamentations in one violent burst that rent the air."[1]

Though Barbour and the other whites may have attributed this outburst of grief to the loss of "a kind and indulgent master," the slaves may also have been grieving their own impending ruin. Within a decade, the African American community at Montpelier would be broken up, and by 1850 most of the slaves were dispersed. Though a very few—perhaps ten old people—gained their freedom, even they had to leave the state. For the rest, the death of President Madison marked the beginning of the old community's ruination.

Just as the eighteenth century in general was not merely prologue to the antebellum era, so was Montpelier in the 1820s and 1830s not simply a "mature" plantation in comparison to the previous generations.[2] The apogee of the plantation and the peak of the slave community actually occurred between the 1770s and the 1790s (or perhaps from about 1760 to 1810), even with the disruptions of the Revolution. This was the creolized generation that produced great wealth for the Madison family; the grandchildren of the first to arrive, they were rooted in the soil of this land. Their children and grandchildren would face times of particular worry and ruin, yet unlike the third generation, they did so at several removes from their African ancestors.

The third generation of slaves saw the peak of Montpelier as a plantation community. Born in the 1760s and 1770s and coming of age in the 1780s and 1790s, they grew up in a stable and growing slave community centered on the busy Walnut Grove settlement. By the mid-1770s, Montpelier boasted fifteen to eighteen black families totaling more than a hundred slaves and including nearly fifty working-age adults.[3] At one time or another during these decades, James Madison Sr. apparently owned about 150 slaves. In the mid-1780s, Colonel Madison's farms contained more than thirty-two buildings (not including the four dwellings), perhaps half of them slave cabins.[4] Most of those cabins were now clustered in Walnut Grove, which had kitchen gardens, outbuildings, and enclosures and would have resembled a sprawling little village.[5]

From the latter 1760s James Madison Sr. diversified his plantation business operations, a development that gave the slaves increasing opportunities to specialize in particular tasks. As early as 1766,
he established a blacksmith's shop at Montpelier, near the new
mansion. In 1769 Madison ordered four hundred pounds of steel
and four pairs of blacksmith's "rubbers" from Liverpool. In 1770, the
colonel asked his English contacts to send him three hundred more
pounds of steel and 17,000 nails of various sizes.[6] The shop apparently comprised two working blacksmith bellows, with a full set of
tools for each.[7] His main blacksmith, at least by the 1780s, was a
man named Moses, who presumably supervised several other enslaved
blacksmiths or apprentices. Madison also had at least one full-time
slave carpenter and a brandy-distilling operation that dated originally
from the 1740s and used as many as three stills. An 1805 visitor
described Montpelier's extensive craft workshops: "a forge, a turner's
shop, a Carpenter and Wheelwright; all the articles too that were
wanted for Farming or the use of the House were made on the Spot."[8]

Tobacco remained the main cash crop at Montpelier. Though
annual production varied according to the market price, in a peak
year such as 1775, the slaves produced nearly 50,000 pounds of the
valuable commodity, or more than forty hogsheads.[9] In the 1790s,
Madison had three working farms (and a fourth one to house
old slaves). One of his overseers remembered that around 1795,
Madison's "land was much worn but he made as good crops as were
generally made in the neighborhood." And though there were years
in the 1790s when he produced no tobacco or only partial crops,
when they did plant tobacco, the slaves produced about 40,000
pounds annually. At one time, Madison could field a gang of twenty-
seven weeders and a gang of nineteen grubbers (against tobacco
worms).[10]

He had also substantially diversified his planting operations. As
corn, wheat, and hay prices rose after the revolution, Madison invested
in plows, scythes, and other grain-cultivating tools. By the 1790s, his

slaves were producing roughly 1,500 bushels of wheat, about 1,200 barrels of corn, and 100,000 pounds of hay annually.[11] He could field a planting gang of eighteen workers for the corn, fourteen plowers for the wheat and other grains, and as many as twenty-one to harvest wheat and hay.[12] The shift from hoe to plow agriculture increased both the skills required of the slaves and opportunities for them to gain some control over the process of production. The slaves may have negotiated something closer to a task system or at least had greater influence over the pace of planting, cultivating, and harvesting the main crops. The importance of sowed crops by the 1790s also suggests that the physical landscape of Montpelier had been substantially altered, with expansive open fields cleared of stumps and large rocks.

Finally, the need for wood, especially for cooking and for fencing, also employed a number of people. As many as seventeen slaves could be put to chopping wood; assuming that each slave family or cabin would have had its own narrow axe, this number tallies well with the estimated number of slave families at Montpelier. Madison also may have had two slaves who specialized in felling trees—perhaps the carpenter and his assistant.[13]

By the 1780s, there is evidence of emerging status differences among the slaves, at least in the eyes of the master. A number of slaves had gained their owner's favor, including one enslaved overseer, Sawney. Another accomplished slave, William "Billey" Gardner, accompanied James Madison Jr. to Philadelphia in the early 1780s. When James was planning to return to Montpelier, Billey apparently refused to go back, having tasted relative freedom in the city. As James wrote to his father in 1783, "On a view of all circumstances I have judged it most prudent not to force Billey back to Va. even if [it] could be done; and have accordingly taken measures for his final separation from me. I am persuaded his mind is too thoroughly tainted to be a fit companion for fellow slaves in Virga. The laws here do not admit of his being sold for more than 7 years. I do not expect to get near the worth of him; but cannot think of punishing him by transportation merely for coveting that liberty for which we have paid the price of so much blood, and have proclaimed so often to be the right, & worthy the pursuit, of every human being."[14] Gardner received his freedom and by the early 1790s was conducting mercantile business on Madison's behalf in Philadelphia. Gardner's wife, Henrietta, also worked there as Thomas Jefferson's washerwoman from at least 1791 through 1800, earning twenty pounds per year.[15]

In 1787, Colonel Madison listed fifty of his slaves—no doubt the working adults—who received shoes. Ten received special (probably higher quality) "English" shoes, including the overseer, Sawney; the blacksmith, Moses; and the carpenter, Harry. All three of these people also were given the right to choose their new masters upon the colonel's death. Moses apparently chose James Madison Jr., Harry's fate is unknown, and Sawney chose and subsequently outlived Nelly Madison.[16] Such special accomplishment and status may have resulted from accommodation to the demands of the master but may also be seen as a form of resistance that forced master(s) to recognize the individuality and personality of at least some of their slaves.

Other slaves resisted the slavery system more directly, but proximity to the master did not always guarantee submission. Anthony (b. ca. 1769), apparently of mixed race or at least of light complexion, had served the colonel as a "waiting servant." In 1786 Anthony ran away, apparently intending to escape to freedom. James Madison Sr. advertised for Anthony's return in a Richmond newspaper, providing an interesting description of the young man and his clothing: Anthony was "about 17 years old, low, but well made, has very light hair and gray eyes; he carried with a Great Coat, made of white plains, with a small red Cape; a jacket of red plains, and another of white linen, each without sleeves; an Oznaburg coat, two pair of breeches, and a pair of striped overalls, felt hat, shoes, and metal buckles; he has been used to house business, and a waiting servant."[17]

Beginning in the mid-1770s, Colonel Madison gave about a third of his slaves to his children when they came of legal age as advances on their inheritances. But most of these slaves who were separated from the home community remained living nearby. When he died in February 1801, the colonel still directly owned 108 slaves, of whom two-thirds were over age sixteen. But a crisis arose over the division of Madison's estate in 1801–3. Not until the 1820s would the number of slaves at Montpelier again approximate the size of the community at the turn of the nineteenth century.

Madison's death likely launched a period of likely concern for the slaves. This "worriment" generation of the 1800s to the 1820s saw the first substantial separations from the home community of slaves, a continuing dispute over the estate (lasting until the 1830s) among the heirs, and somoe divestment of Madison family properties. Furthermore, the last of the slaves whose memories reached directly back to the charter generation died, as did the slaves' direct connection to the Conway family in the 1820s. Granny Milly, likely a Conway slave born in the 1720s and reputedly 104 years old in 1825, died relatively shortly thereafter, Nelly Conway Madison died in 1829, and Sawney (another likely Conway slave) probably died around 1830, severing the old Conway connection. Finally, in this time of declining economic fortunes, in the 1820s, it must have been especially worrying that former president Madison was becoming a public advocate for the American Colonization Society, which sought to "repatriate" African Americans to Liberia.[18]

The immediate division of the master's estate was put off until the early fall of 1801. Estate sales were held in early September and October and again in late November.[19] The division of the slaves was somewhat contentious, in part because the colonel had advanced more than forty people to his children over the preceding twenty-five years. In early October, James Madison Jr. wrote to

TABLE 8.1

Slaves over Age Sixteen, Montpelier, 1786–1825

Years	Average Number	Most	% Change
1786–92	46	51 (1791–92)	
1793–1801	65	72 (1801)	+41
1802–12	42	48 (1809)	−35
1813–25	50	55 (1815)	+19

Source: Personal Property Tax Lists, Orange County: James Madison Sr., James Madison Jr., Dolley Madison, Nelly Conway Madison.

Thomas Jefferson, "The distribution of the slaves among the Legatees & the subsequent interchanges among them for the accomodation of both have consumed the whole of this week [27 September–3 October]."[20] This must have been a worrisome week for the slaves, with several choosing their own masters and the others awaiting the choices made for them. The slaves were divided into lots, with the widow receiving one-third as her dower right and the five surviving children splitting the rest. The division of the slaves meant that about a third of the enslaved people were separated from the Montpelier community, although disputes among some of the heirs over the exact distribution of the people and other properties dragged on until after President Madison's death.[21] The number of slaves at Montpelier would not rebound to the levels of the 1790s until about 1820 (see tables 8.1 and 8.2).

Overall, about fifty slaves were dispersed to Colonel Madison's children, although James Madison Jr. apparently bought some of the slaves back from his brothers and sisters, credited against his share of the larger estate. About half of these slaves, however, wound up leaving the Montpelier area forever in October 1801,

TABLE 8.2

Slaves over Age Twelve, Montpelier, 1789–1845

Years	Average Number	Most	% Change
1789–1801	71	80 (1801)	
1802–12	47	54 (1812)	−34
1813–22	57	64 (1815)	+21
1823–33	58	63 (1833)	+2
1835–45	45	53 (1840)	−22

Source: Personal Property Tax Lists, Orange County.

when they were sent to Major Isaac and Nelly Hite at Belle Grove plantation in Frederick County, across the Blue Ridge.[22]

The residual slave community that remained at Montpelier amounted to forty-five or fifty adults and their children, or between ninety-five and a hundred slaves in all. The basic workforce actually remained of a similar size, as James and his mother bought most of the farming tools during the estate sales, including all twenty-seven weeding hoes.[23]

The years that followed represented the apex of James Madison Jr.'s political career. He served as secretary of state throughout his close friend Thomas Jefferson's presidential administration (1801–9) and then served two terms as the fourth president of the United States (1809–17). He was away from Montpelier for most of this sixteen-year period but returned there at the close of his presidency. Some of the slaves may have found that his absence provided a further opportunity to gain autonomy in their everyday lives, while others who accompanied the Madisons to Washington gained other kinds of opportunities. The many slaves who remained in Virginia, however, may have seen signs that things were not so well with the master even as he reached the height of his political power and influence.

For example, the children of President Madison's sister, Nelly (1760–1802), seemed to resent the way the colonel's estate had been divided. Their complaint eventually extended to a general one against the administration of the estate by the colonel's third son, William, who did not keep particularly good records of his executorship and may have cooked the books in his own favor. On the one hand, James Madison Sr.'s estate was not complicated: he had paid off all of his debts in his declining years. As the litigants put it in 1803, "the affairs of the estate are not embarrassed by debt or in themselves intricate or perplexed."[24] On the other hand, in the 1770s and 1780s the colonel had advanced forty-two slaves to his children, two of whom predeceased him. The apparent squabbling among some of James Madison Sr.'s children and perhaps some of his grandchildren led Secretary of State Madison to force an 1803 order from the High Court of Chancery in Richmond ratifying the equal distribution of his father's slaves and other property among his mother and surviving siblings.[25] But his sister, Nelly Hite, had died in 1802, and her son apparently continued to feel slighted: he pushed a chancery suit in the Orange County court for many years.

One consequence of the family conflict over the colonel's estate was the sale of a commercial flour mill on the Rapidan River roughly adjacent to where Francis Madison had since the mid-1780s operated a 1,000-acre plantation (with his twenty to twenty-five slaves) at present-day Madison Mills in Madison County.[26] The mill had been a partnership between Colonel Madison and his three surviving sons (James Jr., Francis, and William) and was built around 1795. Colonel Madison also operated a working farm where he kept another group of between twenty and twenty-five slaves.[27] In 1805 the mill was valued at $3,333.33, and in 1808 it was sold to a merchant from Tidewater Maryland for £1,100 (Virginia currency), or $1,945.[28]

The forced sale of the mill on the Rapidan affected the slaves in at least two ways. First, since Colonel Madison's slaves had been distributed in 1801–3, the group at Madison Mills apparently were brought back to Montpelier.[29] Their (re)incorporation into the altered slave community would have necessitated some renegotiation and certainly personal and social flexibility among the slaves. Furthermore, these people (re)joined the slave community as part of a retrenchment as a result of the master's family's court business. James Madison Jr. clearly gave some of these matters his personal attention, at least through about 1818 (and again in 1835), and the house slaves, especially Madison's waiting slaves, were no doubt aware of these things and carried the news to the people in the quarter.

President Madison's declining finances during his retirement years also must have concerned the slaves, if they knew about the situation. The slaves must have viewed as negative developments a series of bad harvests between about 1819 and 1825, the former president's mortgaging of half of his 5,000 acres around Montpelier (beginning in the 1820s), and the sale of three of his outlying farms in the 1820s as well as the well-known profligacy of his stepson and presumptive heir, John Payne Todd.[30] When Madison began winnowing his papers, actually burning some documents in 1827, his actions would not have inspired confidence among the slaves, whose fates were tied directly to their master's financial condition.[31]

Another issue that apparently worried the slaves in this generation was their master's public advocacy of the American Colonization Society. Founded in 1816 with a mission of "returning" freed slaves to the newly established semicolony of Liberia in West Africa, Madison became a public supporter of sending not just freed slaves but all black people "back" to Africa.[32] In fact, he may have sold (or perhaps given) the society his old plantation gristmill on Madison Run.[33] But his slaves, like black people in general, were less than enamored with this idea of repatriation. For example, as late as 1835 (when Madison's health clearly was declining), he told a visitor, Harriet

Martineau, that he knew that his slaves "had a horror of going to Liberia, a horror which he admitted prevailed among the blacks."[34]

The sizable generation of slaves born in the 1820s and 1830s and coming of age in the 1840s and 1850s grew up in a time of ruin.[35] This ruination generation saw the sale of roughly 25 percent of the Montpelier slaves in 1834–35, followed by President Madison's death in 1836, the sale of the mansion in 1842, and the divestment of the remainder of Montpelier in 1844. They would have reached adulthood at a time when the Montpelier slave population was split, with perhaps half leased to the new plantation owner, Henry W. Moncure of Richmond, and most of the other half sold off, apparently dispersed in small numbers by John Payne Todd between 1845 and Dolley Madison's death in 1849. By 1851, only fifteen slaves were left. They were living at Todd's residence, Toddsberth, by the old gristmill on Madison's Run. Forty slaves were staying at Montpelier, now under yet another new owner, Benjamin Thornton of England.[36] At Todd's death in 1852, he manumitted ten elderly slaves and provided each with two hundred dollars for resettlement, as the law required that they leave the Commonwealth.[37] With the exception of a half dozen of Dolley Madison's personal slaves, who also received their freedom, the rest either disappeared into the maw of the interstate slave trade or were dispersed among a number of local plantations and farms.

In 1850, the old core of Montpelier was a ghost of its former self. Under Thornton's ownership in that year, the main farm of some 700 improved acres (and 334 wooded), was worth an estimated $20,000. Yet everything about the operation was reduced: most noticeably, the place produced no tobacco at all and only 350 bushels of wheat. The decline of the plantation quickened through the following decade, and by 1860 there were only twenty slaves left at Montpelier, which had yet another new owner, Thomas J. Carson.[38] On the eve of the Civil War, Montpelier was used as much for pasturage as for anything else. In 1860, Carson's slaves produced only

TABLE 8.3

Comparative Farm Production, Montpelier, ca.1800–1860

	1801	*1850*	*1860*
Slaves	108	40	20
Horses/colts	28	19ᵃ	24ᵃ
Oxen	20	16	9
Cattle/calves	101	25	66
Hogs	253	50	30
Sheep	77	60	57
Tobacco (pounds, finished)	32,696		2,800
Wheat (bushels)	1,500ᵇ	350	2,000

Source: Orange County Will Book, 4:54; U.S. Census, 1850, 1860.

Notes:

ᵃ Includes asses and mules.

ᵇ From deposition of Thomas Melton, 28 January 1835, *Hite v. Madison* (ca. 1798–99), Orange County Circuit Court, Clerk's Office.

2,800 pounds of tobacco, less than 10 percent of the 1800–1801 crop, and very little hay, though 2,000 bushels of wheat were produced on nearly 300 acres. Compared to its apex at the turn of the nineteenth century, however, by the 1850 Montpelier as a plantation had become largely ruined (see table 8.3). In a sort of poetic justice, by the Civil War even Toddsberth was in complete ruin.[39]

After the sale of at least twenty-eight slaves between the fall of 1834 and February 1835, the sense of things unraveling, of falling apart, must have quickened. In September or October 1834, James Madison Jr. sold sixteen slaves to his second cousin, William Taylor, of Pointe Coupée, Louisiana, apparently as the alternative to manumitting them and sending them to Liberia, where the slaves refused to go.[40] Over the winter of 1834–35, Madison sold another dozen slaves, and the number of slaves on which he was taxed dropped from sixty-three in 1833 to forty in 1835.[41] It is no wonder that the slaves at President Madison's funeral vented their anguish. Though perhaps half of the community remained at Montpelier after Dolley left the plantation in the summer of 1844, even they may have been dispersed across the countryside. Therefore it is likely that a great many of the hundred or so Madison-owned enslaved people in 1836 were separated from each other by sales, bequests, and even manumissions (for a select few) during the ensuing decade. The great majority, and perhaps even all, were removed from the old home place of Montpelier. This collapse broke a set of roots centered on the original Mt. Pleasant settlement that dated back more than 125 years and five full generations.

Even as the Madison slaves collectively faced ruination and dispersal, some individuals seemed determined to mark their identification with the extended community that included Montpelier. Some social memories persisted even—or especially—after all of these painful separations.

One example is the slave family of Ralph Jr. (Ralph Philip), his wife Caty (Catharine), and their three children, William, Sarah, and Benjamin. Ralph was born around 1811 and was apparently named after his grandfather. Caty was born about 1822, and by her early twenties the pair had three young children. The entire family was deeded to Payne Todd in 1844, and within two years, the parents claimed full legal names, including the surname Taylor, perhaps derived from their extended kin or even from the group of slaves that President Madison's grandmother had brought with her to Mt. Pleasant.[42]

Another man was Major Height, who "stayed" at Montpelier and worked under Carson in 1867. Because no other male slave was named Major in the immediate Madison slaveholding, it is quite possible either that he had belonged to one of Madison's neighbors and was related to the group sent to the Hites sixty-five years earlier or that he was a descendant of one of the Hite slaves and had made his way back to the old home place after Emancipation.[43]

Nancy Rose Barbour was born in 1798, during the third generation, and lived until about 1902.[44] Her maiden name, Rose, signifies a connection with the slaves given to President Madison's youngest sister, Frances Taylor Madison (1774–1823), who married Dr. Robert Rose in 1800. In approximately 1822, they moved west to Tennessee, presumably with their slaves, and Frances Rose died during the process of resettlement. Nancy probably married her husband, Phil Barbour, about 1820, and the couple apparently lived all of their lives in Orange County. Their thirteen children, none of whom ever learned to read or write, included Conwayaba Ella, whose name evoked historical connections among some of Montpelier's long-time slaves that dated to the mid–eighteenth century, if not earlier, and extended well into the twentieth century along with Conwayaba's life, although she bore no children. Conwayaba married a day laborer named George Anderson (b. ca. 1837) in 1869, at which time they were living on Montpelier, where George was employed. Nancy Barbour outlived her husband and nine of her children, and in May 1900, when she turned 102, she was living with Conwayaba and George Anderson in the village of Orange.

In Orange County in the 1930s, other realities evoked perhaps an even older social memory. At least some black people still believed in conjure. During the Great Depression, one Works Progress Administration researcher who lived in the Mine Run area reported in 1936 on the "queer beliefs" of at least some black people in the Burr Hill area: "There is a Negro in this community who firmly believes that he has been 'conjured,' or in other words someone has put a spell on him. He will name the person who did it. He says that he knows of a person who will remove the spell for five dollars, but he is unable to get to the person or to provide the necessary five dollars. He says he was conjured in his feet and joints. . . . Two favorite ways of 'Conjuring' were by spreading corn meal or by driving small pegs in the ground across one's path. There seems to be no doubt but what some of them have died from mere fright because of this queer belief."[45]

In other parts of Piedmont Virginia into the 1930s, the ontological connections (historical, spiritual, or putative) between conjure and Africa could be quite transparent. For example, in Waterford in Loudoun County, a rather infamous black man named Edward Gaskins (b. ca. 1863) was said to be "touched" and had somewhat of a dangerous reputation. He was the root doctor for the surrounding community and although he was born in Virginia, he always claimed that he had been born in Africa, a claim that people generally believed. He owned a walking stick, and people claimed to remember seeing it "move like a snake," which proved to all that he indeed was African born, at least spiritually.[46]

Today, no one in the little village of Waterford, which has lost its entire black population, personally remembers this man or his world, which on a certain social level flowed dead on from an imagined Africa. Just like at Montpelier, the task of remembering lay with those who relied on oral traditions.

CHAPTER NINE

A Long Memory

In the world of Montpelier, the 1732 murder of Old Master Madison likely was not forgotten by the blacks if indeed it was ever forgiven by the whites. It was, in short, a charter event in the plantation's history. The fact that the slaves found reason to kill their master within about six months of his arrival at the Mt. Pleasant settlement and that the two Madison slaves involved outlived their successful conspiracy makes the event a founding one in the history of the plantation that would come to be known as Montpelier. Ambrose Madison may have come to a "strange death," in the words of one local researcher, but the enslaved Africans and their children would mark this generation, would remember it—indeed, seemed determined to remember it—through the most basic means at their disposal: the naming of their descendants. The striking recycling of the names of members of this Atlantic African charter generation and the possibility of the use of names as *lieux de mémoire* for these two "age sets" (adults and children ca. 1732), as the community of the first arrivals, is not only evocative of Africanity—even Igboesque Africanity[1]—or of the cultural autonomy of the slaves but also serves as a profound act of human remembering.

As historians of slave naming systems have noted, people whose histories were likely to be recounted orally, as among the enslaved generally in North America, used personal names not only as a way to mark the individuality of particular persons but also to connect individuals to communities and their collective histories.[2] For example, as Cheryll Cody has noted regarding an extended slaveholding in South Carolina, which included at least some Igbo slaves, "sharing a kin name was a useful device to connect children with their past and place them in the history of their families and communities."[3]

Of the twenty-nine slaves alive during the conspiracy against Old Master Madison, fifteen were adults (over age sixteen), and fourteen were children: there were ten men, five women, four boys, and ten girls. The great disparity between the numbers of men and women and boys and girls suggests that a number of the men were probably young adults. However, three of the men had names suggesting that they were African born (Bristoll, Spark, Turk), and of the afriphonetic names among the female slaves, all were girls (Cussina, Juda, Letta). Of these six slaves' names, only Juda was recycled in succeeding generations.[4]

The loss of Turk from the pool of slave names is not surprising, as he seems to disappear from the record of Madison slaves and was most likely sold, although he was still at Mt. Pleasant when Madison's inventory was taken in April 1733.[5] Dido, however, apparently lived the rest of her life among the Madison/Montpelier slave community. A Dido was hired out periodically to a neighboring planter between 1766 and 1774. If this was the same Dido, she would have been in her mid- to late fifties, but it is just as possible that this was a second-generation enslaved woman named after the original Dido.[6] There were at least two other Didos in the extended Madison slaveholding. One was a young woman in 1782, owned by Ambrose Madison's son and principal heir, Colonel James Madison; the other Dido was owned by Ambrose's brother-in-law, Thomas Chew before 1781, when she was a productively aged woman.

In 1791, she was sold to Colonel Madison's son, Ambrose, and by 1793 she was the senior female slave in that group.[7] This Ambrose (1755–93), the grandson and namesake of the old master, died unexpectedly not long after purchasing Chew's Dido, which must have called to mind the tragedy of the original Dido and Ambrose for those who were aware of it. In any case, the name Dido was not reused in the nineteenth century.

However, among some 261 discrete slaves known to have been owned by various heirs of the first Ambrose Madison from his death through about 1850, there was a marked preference for the reuse of names from the first generation, especially in the eighteenth century. At least twenty-four names (twelve of adults and twelve of children), or 83 percent, of the first-time generation were recycled (see table 9.1). Children's names were even more likely to be reused: of those alive in 1733, 86 percent of children's names were recycled, compared with 80 percent of adults' names. Parents in the first generation tended to name their children after each other or perhaps after themselves, because the names of these original adults appear to have persisted only in the eighteenth century. The names of some children alive in 1732–33—Betty, Kate (Catey), Nancy, Sarah, Tom, and Violet (almost half of the cohort)—remained active in the mid–nineteenth century or at least can be documented between 1844 and 1869, although it must be noted that these were common English names.

All together, the 75 people with the names of the original group of slaves at Mt. Pleasant make up between a quarter and a third (29 percent) of the sample of 261 slaves in the extended Madison slaveholding over time.[8] Moreover, in the early 1820s there were at least ten very elderly slaves in the Walnut Grove slave quarters on Montpelier; a man and a woman (Granny Milly) born in the 1720s, a man born in the early 1730s, five women and a man born in the 1740s, and a woman born in the 1750s. The household of Granny Milly (age 104), her daughter, and her granddaughter would have

TABLE 9.1

Charter Slave Names among Madison-Owned Slaves

Anthony	1733, 1782, 1782, 1782
Betty	1733, 1782, 1782, 1834
Billy	1733, 1780, 1782, 1782, 1794
Catharina	1733, 1782, 1782
Claris	1733, 1782
Daphne	1733, 1782
Dick	1733, 1782
Dido	1732, 1782, 1782
George	1733, 1773
Hannah	1733, 1782, 1794
Harry	1733, 1766, 1787
Isaac	1733, 1780, 1794
Jack	1733, 1787
Joe	1733, 1772, 1782, 1791
Juda	1733, 1770
Kate	1733, 1765, 1782, 1782, 1844
Lucy	1733, 1782, 1794
Nancy	1733, 1782, 1782, 1869
Nanny	1733, 1782
Peter	1733, 1782, 1791
Sam	1733, 1782, 1791
Sarah	1733, 1801, 1844, 1846
Tom	1733, 1770, 1794, 1844
Violet	1733, 1782, 1845

Notes: Variations and diminutives are included. The slaves were owned by Ambrose Madison/Frances Taylor Madison, James Madison Sr., Nelly Conway Madison, Ambrose Madison II, Francis Madison, William Madison, Nelly Madison Hite, James Madison Jr. and Dolley Madison, John Payne Todd.

been a living museum of collective memories.[9] These people connected the era of President Madison's retirement with the time of his grandfather's murder and its aftermath, and they lived long enough to tell the tale to a fifth generation.

One man, Willoughby, illustrates the potential for many layers of signification and remembering, both in his name and in what little can be inferred about his life. When he was born in about 1785, probably at Montpelier, there were five adult slaves named Willoby on plantations in the immediate vicinity.[10] All but one were owned by masters with close familial connections with Colonel James Madison, but none were owned by a Taylor. One owner, Lawrence Battaile, was Madison's maternal cousin; another, Major John Willis, was married to Madison's niece; a third, Catlett Conway, was Nelly Madison's nephew; and the family of the fourth, Lawrence Taliaferro, had connections with the Conways from Port Conway, Caroline County, dating back to the 1730s.[11] However, in the early 1780s, no Taylor is listed as owning a slave named Willoughby.

Willoughby apparently grew up at Montpelier, weathered the various sales and separations of the 1830s, and was deeded by Dolley Madison to her ne'er-do-well son, John Payne Todd, in 1844. In a mortgage deed in 1845, Willoughby was listed as being born around 1785, which perfectly coincides with his probable birth date.[12] Two years later, aged over sixty, Willoughby was among the remnants of the Madison slaves at Todd's residence, Toddsberth, after Todd had leased about half of his slaves to the new owner of Montpelier, Henry W. Moncure.[13] In 1850, now about sixty-five years old, Willoughby was one of the last eleven slaves, all aged between fifty and seventy-eight, owned by Todd, including one family with the surname of Taylor. An 1846 deed of mortgage by Dolley Madison named this family Ralph Philip Taylor; his wife, Catherine; and their children, William Henry, Sarah, and Benjamin. In 1851, Ralph Taylor's grandfather, Old Ralph, also lived with the family, which suggests that the surname Taylor may have had three or four generations' depth among this group of Madison slaves.[14] When Todd's will was probated in July 1852, only the younger Ralph appears to have been manumitted, although Todd intended for the other family members to receive their freedom. Willoughby also received his freedom, as well as two hundred dollars to resettle with. Like the others, Willoughby apparently left Virginia (or at least Orange County), as per the law on manumitted slaves.[15]

From 1853 through 1867, there is no evidence that a free black man named Willoughby remained in Orange County (his name never appears on the per capita personal property tax lists), which indicates that he likely was forced to leave the county. Following the Civil War and Emancipation, many ex-slaves wandered across the country, often in search of long-lost relatives and old home places. In 1869, one old man named Willoughby Taylor was listed in the annual Orange County tax lists as "migratory." Assuming that *migratory* meant "homeless" and that this man was in fact the one from Montpelier, the name Willoughby Taylor would have had deep connections in the whole section around the old plantation. But in 1869 only five black families lived at Montpelier; a year earlier, only three black families had lived there, including Edward Taylor, though he was gone by 1869. And although Willoughby's contemporary, elderly ex-slave Nancy Barbour (b. 1798), was staying on Montpelier with her daughter Conwayaba's family in that year, the very barrenness of the old plantation, and the fact that no Taylors were left living there, must have seemed forbidding. Here, then, was an octogenarian in the era of freedom, wandering the roads of his old country in search of his people. Too old for work and perhaps denied residence by the current owner of Montpelier, whom he would never have known, Willoughby Taylor continued his desperate search on his own.

Willoughby's last name may suggest a remembered origin among some of the slaves of Montpelier that could have dated at least to the mid–eighteenth century, when the Taylor family dominated the region around Montpelier. It is also possible that some of the Madison slaves maintained the memory that they descended from the adults that Frances Taylor brought to her marriage to Ambrose Madison in the 1720s. Willoughby's first name, however, suggests an even deeper memory, also from the Taylor side of the extended Madison family.

Willoughby was a family name that entered into the Taylor clan in the era of the patriarch James Taylor (1674–1729). His son, Zachary (1707–68), married Elizabeth Lee (b. 1709), namesake of her grandmother, Elizabeth Willoughby (b. ca. 1640).[16] Elizabeth Lee's father died the year she was born, and the usual practice in such cases was for the mother to keep a controlling interest in the residual estate (including slaves and their increase) until Elizabeth either turned twenty-one or married, when she would receive her inheritance, including slaves. It is quite likely that the name Willoughby entered the extended Taylor slave community through Elizabeth's marriage to Zachary Taylor in the second quarter of the eighteenth century. Zachary was Frances Taylor Madison's brother and one of the settlers of the section around Montpelier, so it is possible either that the slaves that Elizabeth Taylor brought to her marriage included a Willoughby or that the masters reused the name from her maternal relations and the slaves subsequently passed it on, including among the slaves of Elizabeth Taylor's nephew, James Madison Sr. Subsequent interconnections among the slaves of the various related plantations trickled the name down the generations.

The name Willoughby itself, however, stretched back to the middle of the seventeenth century. Indeed, the name was made prominent by the Virginia patriarch of that family, Colonel Thomas Willoughby (1632–72) in the era before there were many slaves in the colony.[17] In a society that prized genealogical depth, the deep roots evoked by a name such as Willoughby Taylor, especially when attached to a black man in central Virginia in the mid–nineteenth century and particularly an ex-slave of the extended Taylor-Madison family, could not fail to have meaning. Regardless of whether the slaves knew who the original Willoughbys were, this name remained in the active pool of names.

Like Willoughby Taylor, the great majority of Madison slaves seemed to have surnames that signified their connections to a larger community or at least one that stretched beyond their owner-ship by the Madison family. Surnames are known for very few Madison-owned slaves or former slaves in the nineteenth century, but the only known ones are Barbour, Gardner, Jennings, Taylor, and Stuart.[18] In fact, given the prominence of the Madisons, espe-cially the president, it is surprising that few if any of their slaves took that name as a surname. The only example I have found is one run-away in 1804 who had been forcibly separated from the community and wound up far away in Stafford County. This man, named John, was sold off shortly after the death of Ambrose Madison II in 1793 and was described by his new master in a fugitive slave advertise-ment a decade later as likely to "add Madison to his name, as I pur-chased him from the estate of Ambrose Madison, of Orange County, Virginia, and he frequently made use of that name."[19] Perhaps, like Willoughby, whom John might have known as a young man, he claimed a name that asserted a set of connections with people and a place from which he had been torn.

For some of the slaves, those connections were rooted in a place and people whose histories stretched back well over a century. At this point, however, it is striking how few people after slavery in Orange County incorporated Madison into their name. Perhaps the memory of the forced dispersal and dissolution of the community in the decade after President Madison's death was just too painful to mark.[20]

The four generations after the charter one saw the peak, decline, and finally the dissolution of the slave community at Montpelier. Assuming that Granny Milly's bound copy of *Telemachus,* which in

1825 may have been a *lieu de mémoire* signifying the slaves' collective memory of the circumstances surrounding the community's charter event nearly a century earlier, was itself passed on, eventually it was lost, abandoned, or forgotten as the people were forcibly dispersed. But for a century, through the 1830s, the Montpelier community of slaves endured and at times even thrived.

It is perhaps no accident that President Madison, who in 1801 inherited not just the land and the slaves of Montpelier but the stories that went with them, was ambivalent about both slavery as an institution and the slaves themselves, living out a kind of perpetual passive aggression with the enslaved people.[21] As his slave manservant, Paul Jennings, who said only good things about his former master, recalled in a memoir published in 1865, the congenitally shy Madison frequently asserted, "I never allow a negro to excel me in politeness."[22]

Historians, however, have tended to portray Montpelier as a rural retreat, a pastoral place out of which James Madison grew and to which he retired after his presidency, rather than as the scene of a bustling black community with a particular past. Earlier works tended to evoke Montpelier almost as a stereotype of the Edenic plantation and its "good and faithful servants." Some even stretched further to portray enslaved African Americans as docile, tractable dolts.[23] The only nuanced discussion of slaves and slavery has focused on President Madison's later years and is more concerned with the anguished place of slavery in his intellectual life than with the lived experience of the people Madison owned.[24] Architectural historians necessarily have focused on the construction of the mansion and its alterations over time; social historians emphasize Madison's efforts at agricultural reform in the 1820s and 1830s.[25] Other than the increasing attention paid to documents on internal plantation affairs and slavery in the *Papers of James Madison* since the mid-1980s, the importance of the Montpelier slave community to the story of the Madisons has been largely overlooked.

During the eighteenth century and into the nineteenth, the slaves made Montpelier. In the second quarter of the eighteenth century, enslaved Africans and their immediate descendants cleared the forest and seated the patent on what was then the western edge of colonial settlement. In subsequent decades, the slaves developed the landholdings; cultivated and harvested the tobacco, corn, wheat, and other cash crops; constructed the buildings and altered the landscape; ran the distilling, blacksmithing, and gristmilling operations; managed the Big House and dependencies; and in the process enabled in the most practical ways the rise of the Madison family from local prominence to regional predominance.[26]

As is too often the case, and in part reflecting the difficulties of recovering the histories of "forgotten" people, only a half dozen slaves generally are mentioned in the historiography of the Madisons: Sawney, Billy Gardner, Granny Milly, Paul Jennings, and Sukey. Slaves who had the closest personal connections to the Madisons tend to be the ones about whom historians know anything, and even these people merely get the most cursory historical treatment.[27] For example, the story of Sukey, which Paul Jennings included in his memoir published half a century later and which has often been repeated, represents nearly all that is known about her, at least from conventional sources: she was a house slave at the White House who rather comically lolled out of a window as the British approached Washington to torch it in 1814.[28]

Even Jennings, who crossed the dual divides of freedom and written history, publishing "reminiscences" of his former master, sheds little light on his own experiences. He exists as a sort of literary adjunct to President Madison. The two things for which Jennings is best remembered—shaving Madison every other day for sixteen years and attending him on his deathbed in 1836—are at once quotidian and self-effacing. But Jennings, who was born around 1799, must have been an exceptional person. Apparently of mixed race or light complexioned, he was a fifteen-year-old house slave at the

White House in 1814, and he survived the British raid to wait on the Madisons' at their Octagon House residence. Jennings may have learned the barbering trade during these Washington years, as he apparently took over for someone else in these duties in 1820 or so. When the Montpelier community was dispersed in the 1840s, Jennings stayed with Dolley, again in Washington, where he came to the attention of powerful senator Daniel Webster. In 1845, Webster purchased Jennings, allowing him to work off his purchase price, and at some time prior to the Civil War Jennings became a free man.[29] In 1865, Jennings published a short pamphlet containing his fond memories of James Madison that actually obscures more than it clears.[30]

Some individual life histories may be pieced together, especially those of exceptional individuals whose lives constantly intersected with those of their masters. But even the few who show up regularly in the surviving sources require a great deal of inference to give them agency in the events of their lives.

A good example is Sawney (ca. 1737–ca. 1830), likely a Creole slave born in the Port Conway area of African-born parents who took on increasing responsibilities at Montpelier over the course of his long and productive life.[31] Sawney apparently was the son of a slave bequeathed to Nelly Conway and thus probably grew up on a farm in Caroline County or at Port Conway, where he lived with other slaves on land owned by Nelly's brother, Francis (1722–61).[32] He likely was one of the group of ten or fifteen slaves (half of them adults) that Nelly Conway brought to her September 1749 marriage to James Madison Sr.[33]

Sawney came of age working and living with this same Conway group, members of which were kept together at Madison's Black Level quarter, near Montpelier, at least for the first four crop years (1749–52). Many of the slaves, probably including those with whom Sawney lived, also built dwellings and barns, as Madison had at least eighteen new structures built by 1753. In the fall of 1752, Madison received permission from the county court to build a water mill "on his land on the Run [creek] called Chews Mill Run, and where a Mill belonging to Thomas Chew Gent[leman]. had formerly stood."[34] The following year, the colonel sent half of the slaves at Black Level to run the new gristmill. By 1756, when Sawney was now of full working age (about nineteen), all of the slaves that came with Nelly lived and worked at this Mill Quarter farm. Since Thomas Dauhany, the white overseer for that quarter also served as overseer at the larger Home House quarter, the slaves at the Mill Quarter may have had a black driver.[35] Sawney, therefore, would have started working full time (ca. 1753) in a small gang on an outlying subfarm run by an experienced slave man under the general supervision of a largely absentee white overseer. The master was likely never the most direct influence in Sawney's early life, as the immediate slave community (an extended family of Conway slaves) lived at several removes from James Madison Sr.

Sawney also would have known other slaves on nearby farms in Orange County to whom he was related, either directly by descent or indirectly through the owners' familial relations. These included the twenty-five to thirty people (including fourteen adults in 1737) living on a Quarter owned by Nelly's widowed mother, Rebecca Catlett Conway (d. 1760).[36] In the 1750s and 1760s, now a full adult, Sawney probably had other relations on the farms owned by Erasmus Taylor (twenty adults in 1753), Francis Conway II (fifteen adults in 1756), and William Moore (eleven adults in 1764) as well as the people whom he had joined at Montpelier.[37]

In 1769, Colonel Madison chose Sawney to accompany young James Jr. to the College of New Jersey (Princeton) and serve as James's manservant.[38] Just as important, Sawney was responsible for safely transporting his young master back and forth between Virginia and New Jersey. Now over thirty years old, Sawney had primary responsibility for the slightly built and shy teenager: the slave either had impressed the colonel or had become friends with James Jr.

This slave, who most likely was not a part of the central slave community at the Home House quarter, at least in the 1750s, had come to the attention of the master and received a special responsibility.

Sawney apparently acquitted himself well, as he received added responsibilities in the ensuing decades. By 1782, Sawney was one of the most important enslaved people at Montpelier. In the 1782 enumeration, he was listed second among the men, following only the blacksmith, Moses.[39] By that year, Sawney, now in his forties, was one of the plantation overseers, responsible for supervising one of the four Quarters, possibly the Mill Quarter or another one bounding the main plantation on the south. He was even allowed to harvest tobacco on his own account and sell it to Colonel Madison. Sawney's quarter produced at least five hogsheads of tobacco, or about 6,350 pounds gross (5,700 pounds ready for market). About 725 pounds were "Sawney's . . . own crop," credited to him and then used to pay one of the white overseers, James Coleman. The hogsheads of tobacco were carried from "Sawney's to Rocketts" (the tobacco warehouse in Richmond) and were inscribed with a tobacco mark that signified that Nelly Madison's slaves had produced the crop under Sawney.[40]

By the early 1780s, his influence among the slaves in general was probably substantial. For example, there are nine slaves named Sawney in the enumeration lists for 1782, with eight of the nine on plantations in the several rooms around Montpelier—that is, in central and western Orange County. And five were slaves of families with close connections to the Madisons.[41] In the mid-1780s, Sawney was one of the select slaves to receive "English" shoes rather than the cheaper and coarser type of shoes distributed to the rest of the working-age slaves.[42] It also seems likely that he at times lived in an actual house, which would have meant windows and perhaps stone chimneys and even glass and which also was much larger than the usual one-room, dirt-floored slave cabin. In 1785, when there were three full-time white overseers and Sawney was the fourth overseer,

Colonel Madison had four "dwelling houses" on his plantation, or set of subfarms. Assuming that one was the Big House, the others probably were reserved for overseers.[43] However, in 1782, only one white overseer was named, and in 1783, one of the three overseers was the colonel's son, William. Since Sawney continued to work as an overseer at least through the mid-1790s, he may have received use of the house at his farm.[44] Sawney apparently ran his Quarter for so many years that the farm became known colloquially as Sawney's.[45]

By 1807, when Sawney was about seventy years old, he was a favorite slave of Nelly Madison, who specifically willed him the right to choose his own master upon her death.[46] By the 1810s or 1820s, Sawney lived in the central Walnut Grove quarter and was mostly retired. He "raised yams, cabbages, and chickens whose eggs Miss Dolley [Madison] bought."[47] In the 1820s, then, he and his owner, two ninety-year-olds, shared a general history that reached back to the mid–eighteenth century, though on opposite sides of the great divide between free and slave, master and servant, white and black. Sawney outlived his mistress and died in the early 1830s, perhaps the last of the old Conway group at Montpelier.[48]

Slaves such as Sawney filled responsible positions in James Madison Jr.'s life from his youth in the 1760s through his adulthood in the 1790s. It is noteworthy, however, that in regarding the evils of slavery, President Madison worried greatly about an eternal mutual dislike between whites and blacks, even if slavery ended, as a result of "reciprocal antipathies" that would always risk a "danger of collisions" between the two races. By 1819, he advocated the colonization of African Americans "back" to Liberia, a prospect that "horrified" his slaves in the 1830s.[49] Even in Madison's constitutional thinking, it is noteworthy that he tended to address the dangers to republican virtue of aristocracy posed by slavery and the tyranny of the majority (numeric or structural). One can only speculate to what degree his later philosophical and political thinking on slavery and African

Americans and the problem of white supremacy (or black inferiority, as he might have put it) in general in the American republic were influenced by his upbringing in and then oversight of a plantation community whose charter event occurred when the African slaves had killed the old master, his grandfather, the patriarch of Montpelier—perhaps with good reason.

Ironically, this event and its local, regional, and Atlantic associations as well as its historical significance for a particular place and time, has until recently remained hidden. Modern observers could perhaps overlook the failure on the part of pre–World War II Madison hagiographers and even more disciplined historians such as Irving Brant (though he in particular delved in great detail into other events of the 1720s and 1730s in the settling of Montpelier) to comb the county records and see Ambrose Madison's death for what it was. The general impression is that Ambrose simply died young, an impression that has been repeated by more recent Madison biographers. Even a recent if specifically local history account that glosses Madison's murder as a "strange death" resolutely does not pursue the implications of the African slaves using poison to kill the old master within six months of his permanent arrival in their settlement.[50]

Since 1984, however, the Montpelier estate, including the original 1720s–30s homesite, has been the flagship property of the National Trust for Historic Preservation, which has been attempting assiduously to develop the place into a national historic site to commemorate President Madison. But unlike the plantations of his presidential contemporaries—Mt. Vernon and Monticello—or later presidential plantations such as Andrew Jackson's Hermitage in Tennessee and other sites such as Colonial Williamsburg's Carter's Grove, the National Trust has only just begun to integrate the historical slave community into its larger interpretive program. Its public tours and overall historical interpretation still downplay the story of the murder of the plantation's patriarch. Rather than seizing the opportunity the tell the story of the essential violence that under-girded the system of slavery in Virginia, as elsewhere; of the many modalities of slave resistance; of the known African connections of the earliest enslaved people at Montpelier; and simply of the human drama, the National Trust has tended to bury this charter event in the plantation's history.[51]

Recovering the past at public history sites defined as having national significance especially demands the willingness to see and tell all of the story and to embrace complexity and contingency and irony in doing so. Unlike other presidential plantations, however, there is a known "ethnic" African connection among the enslaved population at Montpelier or at least a connection with a particular region in Atlantic Africa. This connection and its significance for the history of the plantation community remains largely unexplored.[52]

CHAPTER TEN

Historical Creolization in Virginia

In the Virginia Piedmont in the second quarter of the eighteenth century, Igbo forced migrants were the first arrivals. They set the basic patterns of material, social, and ideological culture of enslaved communities to which succeeding waves of saltwater (Central African especially) and Creole (Tidewater) slaves acculturated. In other British Atlantic areas, such as Jamaica and the Lesser Antilles, especially after 1750, Igbo arrived as latecomers who then Igboized already existing institutions and cultural patterns. In both cases, people made do with what they had at hand to fashion what they needed to sustain themselves, to forge connections among and between each other, and to make sense of their new worlds. This process of historical creolization in the Chesapeake was one of bricolage, of mixing and matching, of adapting and adopting a combination of new and old ways of doing things and of being people, and it resulted in an Igboesque regional "common tradition."[1]

On some eighteenth-century Virginia plantations and slaveholdings, the Igbo presence was palpable. One such set of communities were the slaves of planter-merchant Francis Jerdone (1720–71), who came to Virginia around 1740 and quickly set about acquiring credit, land, and slaves, settling recently patented land in Louisa

County. By the 1760s, he owned sixty-seven adult slaves on four plantations totaling more than 8,000 acres in Louisa, Spotsylvania, and Albemarle Counties plus perhaps others in Charles City and New Kent Counties.[2] The slaves' names suggest that a number of Igbo people were enslaved at these Quarters. In the 1760s, there were two slave men named Calabar, a woman named Eboe Sarah, a man named Juba, a man called Breechy (an afriphonetic name relatively common in the Piedmont and perhaps derived from the same Eboan/Igbo root as the honorific title *mbreechi*),[3] and a woman named Cumba, whose husband was Sambo.

Other slaves who might have been Igbo on the Jerdone plantations included a man named Moody and another named Doctor (d. 1785). Most importantly, there was no adult named Mingo or variations of Angola/Congo, but there was an Anakey in 1796 as well as a second Juba in 1827 among the slaves of Jerdone's son, also named Francis.[4] It is interesting that Eboe Sarah's husband was "Old Will the Cooper" and that a slave man in an Igbo-influenced area would be called Doctor. Other records suggest that these may have represented specialties of Igbo slaves in colonial North America. For example, in the colonial South Carolina fugitive slave advertisements analyzed by Daniel Littlefield, three of the four Igbo in those records were coopers and the fourth was listed as a "kind of doctor" (and was the only person so listed).[5]

These Jerdone-owned Igbo or Igboized slaves were distributed evenly through the various Jerdone plantations. In 1768, Eboe Sarah and her daughter, Virginia Sarah, were in Albemarle (with twenty-four other adults). Breechy and Coomba (and Sambo) were at the Spotsylvania Quarter, and the two Calabars (and Doctor) were at Jerdone's home plantation in Louisa, with Juba on a second Quarter in that county.

The way that these adults named their children is also intriguing, suggesting that the slaves with the most afriphonetic names had strong affective ties with each other and that Igbo principles may have guided some of the other slaves' naming choices. One slave man (presumably Native American) named Indian Ben, had a wife named Beck (which Newbell Niles Puckett indicates may have been a female "African" name during the eighteenth-century));[6] in 1779, the same year that the adult Breechy died, they named their newborn son Breeche. Ben and Beck apparently lived on a different Quarter than Breechy and Beck, so naming a child for him could have been simply a necronymic act. But given the importance of the ideology of reincarnation, which all accounts of historical Igbo philosophy emphasize was bound up with child naming, historians may be able to see such moments in a new context. In a different vein that suggests a possible African-derived internal kinship structure, whereas Coomba and Sambo named a son Moody (b. 1760), Moody and Margery named a daughter Coomba (b. 1771). Finally, Barnet (b. 1769), a son of "Sarah at Ivy Creek" (probably Virginia Sarah), was convicted in 1810 of "attempting poison" (which often meant administering folk medicine or basically engaging in conjure or sorcery) and was transported out of the state. At about the same time, a woman named her newborn son Barnet (b. 1809).[7] And the boy named for this transported grandson of Eboe Sarah came of age in a community that included an older man named Juba (1827).

Igbo cultural dominance in the Chesapeake was not a foregone conclusion, given the known presence of other Africans in the region. Central Africans seemed to have been the major secondary group, and because of the use of political terms such as Congo (likely derived from *manikongo*) and Angola (*ngola*) as toponyms and personal names, they seem to stick out. If, in fact, Mingo was a Central African name, then the twenty-four Mingos in colonial records (representing twice the number of Jubas, for example) could suggest that in a population of 100,000 people, as many as 2,500 men and boys at any one time drew on an alternate ancestral nomenclature for their slave names. Since most Central Africans were brought in a second wave of slave imports in the 1740s and 1750s, they may have had to acculturate to already Igboized slave communities. And not only were Igbo the first arrivals in much of what became the Black Belt, but the high proportion of Igbo women in the colony may have given them disproportionate influence in the socialization of Creole children.

It is probable that Igboized slave communities incorporated some material, social, and ideological artifacts of Central African peoples, especially when they paralleled those of Igbo. On a larger scale, since Congo and Angola also were important in the slave trade to the Carolina low country (1720s–30s and 1790s–1807) and in the Spanish trade to New Orleans (1780s–1808), we should expect to see "Bantuisms" in antebellum southern life.[8] But in the Upper South, what is most noteworthy is the relative lack of such markers of a Central African presence—for example, Kongolese political marronage, use of manioc or of the term *-gombo* for okra, slave "king/queen" festivals, and the term *wanga* for charm. Instead, for the Upper South one sees creolized Igboisms like decentralized authority (rules not rulers), yams as a staple, the term *okra* for the vegetable, slave Jonkonnu, and the term *mojo* for charm.[9]

The other two major groups, Mande/FulBe and Akan, seem to have been rapidly absorbed into the Igboesque Creole culture. Slaves readily and everywhere ate pork, and nowhere in Virginia does the term *Mandingo* occur, for example. Since Muslim Africans in general probably made up no more than 10 percent of slaves taken to North America and even less to the Chesapeake, the lack of African-Islamic elements in American slave culture should come as no surprise. The supposed Akan influence in the Upper South requires reconsideration, especially since the fourteen-day Akan day name system, which in Jamaica in the nineteenth century operated as a single onomastic set (and may have done so in colonial South Carolina as well), either collapsed in colonial Virginia and quickly disappeared or was subsumed by a different Creole Afro-Virginian system.[10] By the nineteenth century, furthermore, when Juba became a stock stereotype of American minstrelsy, that character was always male.[11]

Igbo as well as other Africans in early Virginia had to adapt to a new physical landscape that differed substantially from Igboland. Virginia was hotter in the peak summer months, with temperatures rising to over 100 degrees Fahrenheit, and was of course much colder during the winter. The radical seasonality of the New World would have seemed strange to people from subtropical lands relatively close to the Equator where the temperature usually stayed in the 80s and where the two "seasons" were those of the dry Harmattan from November through February (of the Western calendar), when hot dusty air blows south from the Sahara, and the perhaps hotter wet rainy season that prevailed through much of the rest of the year. Furthermore, Igbo in Virginia might would have found odd the fact that creeks and rivers flowed to the east, the direction of the sunrise, whereas in Igboland the major rivers flowed from north to south, or across the sun's daily path.[12] In Igboland, clayey soils tended to be found in low-lying areas, with sandy soils in the uplands, whereas the opposite was the case in Virginia. Finally, even though large parts of historical Igboland were "derived savanna," or dry woodland, rather than the lush rainforest of myth, the mostly pine or deciduous forests in the interior of the Chesapeake would have seemed quite new and different.[13]

Given these differences, however, a number of physical realities of the Virginia landscape would have seemed quite familiar to diasporic Igbo, especially those in the Piedmont region. Much of the interior of both Igboland and Virginia had, in the words of a Nigerian archaeologist describing the Anambra Valley of northern Igboland, "a gently rolling topography."[14] Mosquitoes and malaria were common to both regions as well. In Virginia, for example, some slaves considered yams to be a prophylaxis against malaria: Uncle John Spencer (b. 1857) remembered that the slaves in King George County "used to cultivate a lot of sweet potatoes because they kept off malaria."[15]

In the Virginia summer, as throughout much of the year in Igboland, the land was alive with cicadas, fireflies, and tree frogs. On the Calabar coast in the 1820s and 1830s, at least two Europeans commented on the chirping of "the land Crabs" (cicadas?) and the swarms of fireflies. When walking through Bonny in 1825, R. M. Jackson noticed that "my ears were absolutely stunned by the chirping of the land Crabs existing here in vast numbers, whilst myriads of fire flies flitting before us plainly showed the grass from which they sprang." On the Niger River at the town of Eboe (Aboh), R. A. K. Oldfield remarked that "at night, the atmosphere was loaded with millions of fire-flies, illuminating it as far as the eye could reach."[16] The author of a 1922 collection of African American folk rhymes commented on two rhymes with idiosyncratic language that he termed "Guinea or Ebo Rhymes," both of them about frogs (and one specifically about tree frogs).[17]

Much of the flora and fauna would have been new to Igbo exiles. There were no hippopotamuses, crocodiles, parrots, monkeys, duikers (bush antelopes), among other familiar animals, nor were there the many varieties of ferns and broad-leafed ground plants of Igboland. The important towering *iroko* tree (*Chlorophora excelsa*), used to make dugout canoes in riverine Igboland and a sign of ritual permanence, did not appear in the Chesapeake.[18] But the towering tulip poplar tree (*Liriodendron tulipifera*) in Virginia was called the "Canoe tree" in the third quarter of the eighteenth century, and Native Americans used its roots as a medicine for malaria.[19] As early as the 1730s, Anglo-Virginians generally used the wood of this tree for a number of things, as William Byrd noted around 1737: "beautiful troughs, sticks, as well as walls in houses, roof shingles, chests for all needs, likewise for millwork, since it is very tough and lasting." Apparently its association with canoes came later, perhaps with Africans.[20]

Other plants and animals would have been familiar. In Eboan Africa, Igbo raised pigs, poultry, bush bullocks (*muturu*), dwarf sheep, and goats; in Virginia they had hogs, "Guinea keet," and in the eighteenth century often sheep (raised for wool and for mutton for masters' tables). In Igboland, people fished creeks and lagoons for crabs, prawns, crayfish, catfish (*Clarias*), and tilapia as well as sardines, oysters, and perch, and land tortoises were well known. In Virginia, slaves nearer the Chesapeake Bay gathered crabs and oysters while Afro-Virginians in general would find turtles (terrapins), crayfish, catfish, perch, herring, and other edible creatures in the many creeks and rivers. Deer would have substituted for duikers, and rats, hawks, and vultures (buzzards) lived in Virginia as well as in Igboland.[21] Clearly then, and contrary to the assertion that Africans in the New World faced "an almost completely strange environment," Igbo would have found many things in Virginia at least partly familiar.[22]

Moreover, tobacco, cotton, and perhaps maize were grown in Igboland in the mid–eighteenth and early nineteenth centuries, as attested by Equiano as well as by early Niger River explorers. Equiano noted that "our vegetables are mostly plantains, eadas [cocoyams], yams, beans, and Indian corn"; perhaps exaggerating, he claimed that in Igboland, people had "plenty of Indian corn, and vast quantities of cotton and tobacco." In the 1830s, Oldfield noted that on the middle reaches of the Niger, "Indian corn . . . is much cultivated," and when traveling up the river, he commented on "several fields of corn" he saw growing.[23] In Virginia, where slaves grew tobacco and corn using mostly iron hoes or other primary tools and cultivated yams (and other familiar domestic cultigens) in their Quarters, Igbo would have had to shift emphasis from their old staple to the *buckra*'s new ones but still would have been operating within a basically familiar agricultural system.

The ubiquitous West African oil palm (*Elais guineensis*) and kola nut palms of Igboland, however, did not exist in Virginia. The lack of oil palms, and thus of palm wine (*mimbo*) and eating oil (for *fufu*) meant a major shift, but perhaps the abundance of berries in Virginia (including blackberries and what some people in the Piedmont called "wine berries") as well as persimmons (a favorite food of opossums that people processed into persimmon beer) and fermented fruits (apples, peaches), would have made up the difference for palm wine, at least for drinking purposes.[24] Lard would have sufficed for frying foods, and gravy or melted butter would have worked for mashed potatoes instead of the pungent castorlike palm oil for pounded *fufu*.[25]

The technology of slave work in the first half of eighteenth-century Virginia, with its hoe-based agriculture and cultivation of corn and tobacco in hills rather than in drilled rows, would have made sense to Igbo exiles. In fact, because tobacco was such a troublesome crop, requiring great care in planting, weeding, worming, tending, cutting, stripping, curing, and pressing into large barrels for shipment, the skills of Igbo farmers, women included, may well have been as important to the tremendous expansion of tobacco and corn production in the eighteenth-century Chesapeake as the skills of other Africans were to the development of rice agriculture in colonial South Carolina. The eventual shift to plow-based Piedmont agriculture and the diversification into wheat in the second half of the century followed the physical creolization of the slave population. Those succeeding generations, however, continued to draw on Igbo material, social, and ideological resources to adapt to slavery in the region.

Igbo exiles and their Afro-Virginian descendants had to rely on ancestral material resources because their masters, the *buckra*, were so niggardly in their provisions. Slave owners stinted the slaves, throwing the people back onto their own resourcefulness for sustenance. In the eighteenth and nineteenth centuries, masters provided slaves with only the barest necessities. Weekly or monthly rations consisted of salt fish and/or pork, corn or cornmeal, and salt and perhaps molasses. The largest plantation holders usually doled out salted herrings as well as smoked pork and corn, which the slaves pounded and mixed with beans and boiled into hominy.[26]

The eighteenth-century inclusion of salted fish, usually herring, is interesting. Equiano, for example, wrote that in his Eboan community, "dried fish . . . we esteemed a great rarity, as our waters were only brooks and springs." Igbo also had made vegetable salt out of "wood ashes" and may have expected salt from their masters in Virginia.[27] By the early nineteenth century, the common custom in Virginia was to give slaves cornmeal, bacon, salt, and molasses.[28] In the nineteenth century, moreover, a colloquial Virginia term for flour was *ingany*, a word that intriguingly resembles the nineteenth-century Igbo word for millet, *inyari*.[29]

Slaves augmented their meager food rations by hunting wild game and growing their own staple vegetables while using the corn or meal supplied to make either bread or mush or both. As might be expected in a society where the night was "negur day-time," slaves primarily hunted nocturnal animals such as raccoons and opossums.[30] The basic diet, and the use of one-pot stews, remained largely consistent over the course of a century and a half. Hugh Jones wrote in 1724 that in Virginia, corn (maize) was "of great Increase and most general Use; for with this is made good Bread, Cakes, Mush, and Hommony for the Negroes, which with good Pork and Potatoes (red and white, very nice and different from ours) with other Roots and Pulse, are their general Food."[31] This basic outline of the Afro-Virginian diet, along with such slave specialties as "'possum and sweet potatoes, ham hock cooked with cabbage or turnip greens, hoe cake and watermelon," also remained the norm throughout much of the nineteenth century.[32] James L. Smith wrote that when he was a child in the 1810s and 1820s, corn was ground in a hand mill and then boiled; when ready, "the pot was swung from the fire and the children squatted around it, with oyster shells for spoons. Sweet potatoes, oysters and crabs varied the diet."[33]

Most importantly, slaves in Virginia relied on a number of garden cultigens, nearly all of which were West African plants that people commonly grew in Igboland. Scholars have identified a number of these "southern" garden cultigens as indigenous to West Africa. In Virginia, however, where Igbo were the first to arrive, many of these food crops were Igboisms.[34]

Some of these plants—greens or kale (cabbages and mustard leaves) (*Brassica sp.*), black-eyed peas (cowpeas) (*Vigna unguicuilata*), gourds (*Lagenaria leucantha*), okra (*Hibiscus esculentum*), spinach (*Spinacia oleracea*), squash (*Cucurbita sp.*), watercress (*Nasturtium officinale*), and watermelon (*Cucumis lanatus*, var., *Citrullus vulgaris*)— were native to West Africa. Others—including sweet potatoes or yams (*Ipomoea batatas*), Indian corn or maize (*Zea Mays*), pumpkins (*Cucurbita pepo*), cymbling (simlin squash) (*Cucurbita verrucosa*) and squash (*Cucurbita melopipo*), and peanuts/groundnuts (*Arachis hypogaea*) as well as tobacco (*Nicotiana sp.*) and perhaps tomatoes (*Lycopersicum esculentum*) and "sweet potato pumpkin" (*Cucurbita moschata*)—were indigenous to the Americas but had been incorporated by people in Igboland probably by the early or mid–seventeenth century. Other West African food crops in the era of the slave trade, though not necessarily grown in Virginia, included yams (*Dioscorea sp.*), eggplant (*Solanum melongena*) (called Guinea squash in Virginia around 1800 and not eaten by whites), plantain (*Musa paradisiaca*), rice (*Oryza glaberrima*), millet (*Panicum miliaceum*), cassava/manioc (*Manihot utilissima*), and Melegueta pepper (*Aframomum melegueta*).[35]

Igbo slaves in Virginia, however, tended to grow kitchen or subsistence crops that they already knew, especially sweet potatoes, black-eyed peas, greens, squash, pumpkins, okra, and watermelon as well as gourds, groundnuts, and Guinea squash.[36] Instead of Melegueta pepper, the slaves grew cayenne pepper (*Capsicum annuum*) and added beans (brownish-black colored "horse beans") (*Faba vulgaris*), pigeon peas (*Cajanus indicus*), and other pulses (*Vigna sp.*) but did not grow classic European vegetables such as English garden peas (*Pisum satvium*) or asparagus (*Asparagus officinalis*) that were staples of Anglo-Virginian diets.[37] As late as the 1850s in Spotsylvania and Louisa Counties, at least according to Uncle Bacchus White

(b. 1852), black folks "never did eat 'pargus and green peas 'till after de war, nuver liked dem."[38]

More significantly for our purposes, moreover, Afro-Virginians did not come to rely on cassava. This basic staple of peoples to the interior of the Angola coast in the long eighteenth century (who had incorporated the native American root crop long before) would have flourished in Virginia.[39] Manioc did not become a staple of Afro-Virginian foodways because the people who came later adapted to the foodways of those who were already there and who had established not only the system of plantation customs but much of the folk food crop system.

In effect, Igbo in Virginia substituted yams for their old primary staple (*Dioscorea*) but maintained nearly all the secondary subsistence crops of their ancestral village agriculture except for cocoyams and plantains (and tropical fruits such as pawpaws/papayas). The loss of plantains and bananas seems to have been made up with maize and meal. Okra, associated with fertility as well as with proverbial knowledge in some parts of Igboland, and black-eyed peas (which in Virginia and indeed the entire South still brings good luck if eaten on New Year's Day), and squashes and watermelons and gourds and "greens" and others quickly reappeared and continued as staples of Afro-Virginian slave foodways.[40]

Many slaves in eighteenth-century Virginia made their own low-fired ceramic cooking pots and eating bowls, now termed colonoware.[41] These colonowares were previously assumed to be imports from local American Indian groups, but evidence now indicates that slaves applied African conceptions and techniques of potting to make the ceramics.[42] At one late-eighteenth- and early-nineteenth-century site, Pohoke and Portici in Prince William County, archaeologists found sherds enough to define a minimum of twenty-four vessels (and more than 50 percent of the everyday wares recovered at the Pohoke site). Most of these items were used by slaves in the eighteenth-century phase of the site's occupation and then thrown away in the 1820s and 1830s.[43] Kathleen A. Parker and Jacqueline L. Hernigle clearly identify the eighteenth-century unglazed, burnished, low-fired earthenware they found at the Prince William site as "African colonoware."[44] Rather than assuming, as for example Leland Ferguson did in his otherwise fine book on early African American archaeology, *Uncommon Ground* (1992), that Indians or others made the finer examples of colonoware, with slaves making lower-quality yet often highly burnished items in conscious imitation of the creamwares and stonewares that whites used at the time, Parker and Hernigle assume that the potters used African-based skills to make the pots (even if the shapes were evocative of European forms).[45]

Parker and Hernigle give an excellent description of the potting skill required to make African colonoware:

Colonoware recovered from both [Pohoke and Portici], excluding the tobacco pipes, was coiled. This manufacturing technique involves placing hand-rolled, snake-like, strands of clay, one on top of another, in a circular column. The first strand, or coil, is placed on a flat piece of clay which forms the base of the vessel or object constructed. Clay coils are added horizontally until the desired height of the object is achieved. The coils are then pressed or smoothed together with the potter's hand or tools such as pebbles, a wooden disk or spatula, or a mushroom-shaped clay or wooden pottery trowel. This smoothing produces a finished appearance and reinforces the vessel by blending the coils together.

The interior and exterior vessel surfaces of the colonoware are smoothed. Many of the vessels have been burnished, or polished, with sticks, bones, or pebbles. The vessel exteriors exhibit unintentional, irregular, discolorations known as fire-clouding. These marks suggest the objects were fired in open-air kilns. Most vessel interiors have been intentionally blackened with soot or charcoal. No tempering agent is visible in any of the pottery fragments.[46]

The coiling technique, the extensive smoothing and rounding of both the inside and outside of the pots, and the appearance of fine burnishing as well as the outdoor kiln firing of the wares and perhaps the desire of a flat bottom and/or tripod bases (like English pipkins) seem quite Igbo-like.

The making of pottery was a woman's craft in historical Igboland, and they often sold their product at market.[47] In 1911, British government anthropologist Northcote Thomas recorded the potting system of an old woman near Awka who was a traditional potter. The similarities to what has been found in late-eighteenth-century north-central Virginia are remarkable.

> I observed the whole process of pot-making at Nofia. The following objects were provided:—a flat dish as a rest for the broken neck of a calabash, on which the pot had to rest. A piece of calabash used for rounding the sides of the interior, a leaf of *bokokba* for smoothing the mouth, a stick called obala for smoothing the sides, a pot of water with *odala* leaf in it, and a smoother for the mouth called *akeleka* and, at a later stage, *ola* bark and a mineral called [*nchala*] for producing a varnish.
>
> Two pots were made, one a soup pot standing about six or eight inches high with a neck to it, the other a flat open pot for grinding pepper in. The first process was to wet the clay and work it. When this was done it was picked over so that no stones might be in it; then a handful of clay was taken and rolled out in the hand; this roll was held in the right hand and flattened out in the left until a nearly flat disc was produced about twice as big as the bottom of the pot was eventually to be; the sides of this were raised and additional rolls of clay put on [coiled].
>
> When it was high enough for the neck to be put on, the outside was smoothed with *obala*, then the vertical neck was put on and smoothed also. Next it was bent over and smoothed with a leaf and then the belly of the pot was enlarged with a piece of calabash. After this the narrowed neck was again smoothed with *obala;* the bottom of the pot

was thinned out with the hand, a rim was cut out in the neck with *akeleka,* and a calabash was taken to level the bottom and to effect final smoothing. The process was virtually the same in the case of an open pot [they are put out to dry for three days before the final burning].

Before the final burning the pots were rough dried with a light fire of grass; for the final baking the midrib of palm trees and light wood was used. When the fire died down the pots were picked out with the aid of a stick, and while they were still hot a decoction of fresh *ola* bark was applied with the aid of a palm tree fibre. This causes the pot to become glossy and reddish in colour. If fire were applied after the *ola* decoction has been put upon the pot, the colour becomes black.[48]

Except for the uses of specialized plants and leaves and local mineral "decoctions," some of which may have had juju as well as functional purposes and which might have been quite easily re-created or substituted in Virginia's physical environment, the description of precolonial Igbo potting technology fits quite well with what is known of eighteenth-century Virginia colonoware, thereby further supporting the thesis that slaves made the pottery.

Furthermore, flat bottoms and tripod bases need not signify a European aesthetic. Although some sources mention the use of wood wares (bowls largely) in the early nineteenth century, Equiano mentioned the "manufacture" of "earthen vessels, of which we have many kinds." One early-nineteenth-century description of Niger Igbo cooking, in which pots were placed directly above the fire on a stand made of other "broken jars," presupposes both a flat bottom and the usefulness of a tripod base for the stewing that was the mainstay of foodways.[49] Allen wrote that Igbo people on the Niger cooked mostly stews over an open-hearth fire: "The apparatus used for cooking is very simple. Three broken jars are placed upside down, to support the vessel containing the viands, and the fire is made between them. Very little skill, however, is required in the preparation of food."[50]

Gourds (calabashes) were another important Igbo material cultural item that continued in Virginia. In Igboland, they were used as cups and bowls and drinking ladles, as were gourds in Virginia. And whereas in the antebellum era many Afro-Virginian slaves stopped making colonoware as they acquired access to old creamware that the *buckra* were giving up in favor of tinware as well as access other wares, slaves continued to use gourds and dippers (even after Emancipation) in their daily life. One woman born in 1858 said that the people then "had a heap of goars whar you use in back times to drink cool water out of." Another Virginia woman, born in 1863, said, "You know people use to raise goards fer dippers, an' de goards grew on vines in ev'ybody's garden."[51]

Other aspects of Afro-Virginian material culture signify an Igbo connection. Dugout canoes, ideally made out of the canoe tree, evoke the canoes of riverine and coastal Igboland, especially compared to the reputedly short canoes found in the Carolina low country.[52] The use of tulip poplars in Afro-Virginia is especially interesting given that at about the same time in western Jamaica, the most Igboized part of that island, blacks there chose a single tree, the towering Cotten tree (*Eriodendron*) for their large dugout canoes.[53]

The style of fences that at least some slaves used in the years before the Revolution, in which they pounded in earthfast posts and then wove in cedar branches to make a kind of wattle fence, was not only unlike the stereotypic Anglo-Virginian split-rail worm fences but also resembled the kind of woven mat and/or brush fences constructed in historical Igboland. Philip Vickers Fithian described one such wattle fence in 1774: "they drive into the Ground Chesnut stakes about two feet apart in a strait Row, & then twist in the Boughs of Savin [juniper/cedar] which grows in great plenty here."[54]

The ubiquity of blue glass beads in Upper South slave sites may also be an Igboism. The color blue was a lucky one in general, and in mid-eighteenth-century Eboan Africa (at least Equiano's part of it) blue was "our favorite color." The people dyed their clothes a bright blue (apparently not indigo), which they extracted from "a berry, and is brighter and richer than any I have seen in Europe."[55] On the coast, trade beads (mostly acori but also other blue ones) had been a part of the Calabar slave trade since as early as the 1660s.[56]

Other historical Igbo crafts, such as blacksmithing and wood-working, may have found expression in early Virginia. Although no carved doors or panels such as those for which Igbo woodcrafters were noted in the late nineteenth and twentieth centuries have been found in Virginia, southern black craftsmen sometimes fashioned ornate wooden canes, often with serpent motifs. Other objects, such as an eighteenth-century wrought iron sculpture recovered in Alexandria, Virginia, and presently held in a private collection (and apparently last exhibited in the 1960s), may evoke an Eboan aesthetic. Although John Michael Vlach sees that sculpture as "a powerful work" whose execution seems "to suggest the primal essence of human form," to me it evokes more the kinds of figurines made from wood or clay that inhabited southern Igbo *mbari* (ritual-art) structures or even Igbo *ikenga*.[57] The verticality and semirepresentationalism of the standing-figure sculpture are characteristic of much folk Igbo sculpture, with its elongated figurines, especially in contrast to the squat bronzes of Benin and the hyperrealistic terra-cotta heads of Yorubaland.

This evidence on slave foodways and potting, the material culture of work, and perhaps such things as the aesthetic appeal of blue beads as well as artwork like the Standing Figure sculpture suggest that the old assertion about how forms of African technology and economic life "had but a relatively slight chance of survival" is in serious need of revision.[58] In fact, much Igbo or Igboized material culture was retained in that of the slaves in early Virginia.

Slaves also drew on ancestral Eboan social-cultural resources in adapting to slavery in Virginia. Initially spread out in relatively small clusters of ten to thirty people in Quarters and then often regrouped a generation or two later as successful masters rebuilt their plantations and established larger centralized slave villages (rows), the people drew on familiar Igbo concepts of dual division, nested social relations, and exogamy to develop Igboized "plantation customs" that in the eighteenth century, at least, became generalized and facilitated visiting among settlements by way of manifold paths.

Throughout Igboland, largely patrilineal groupings of kindreds (*umunne*), for whom the descent was bilateral and the kinship idiom predominated, also organized themselves in two socially defined halves, what ethnographers call "moieties." Dual division meant that any grouping, whether kindreds in a clan, clans in a village, or villages in a village group, had a rival but related grouping of people.[59] The historical Igbo social-political world was one of concentric circles of relations at diminishing degrees of consanguinity. A kindred was part of a clan (*ebo*), at least two clans made up a town/village (*ogbe*), and at least two towns made up a place/district (*ala*). Such a nested sense of social relations could also have described the world in which slaves perceived themselves: first part of a Quarter, at least two of which made up a farm, two or more of which comprised a plantation, which was often part of a *buckra*'s holdings. In the mid–eighteenth century, Anglo-Virginian planters who could afford to do so shifted slaves around among and between their plantations, farms, and Quarters.[60] Such ruthless planter capitalism may have unintentionally encouraged rather than disrupted the development of slave community life in the Chesapeake.[61]

Afro-Virginians also forged a number of plantation customs that facilitated the creation and reproduction of slave social relations. Exogamy, or marrying out of the group, was the rule in historical Igboland (as indeed throughout Atlantic Africa). In eighteenth-century Virginia, slaves may have applied this concept to Quarters so that people married between settlements, and the localism suggests an Igboized version of the concept rather than, for example, the applying of exogamous rules to the whole plantation or to a particular master's entire slave population.

In the nineteenth century, such "abroad" spouses comprised the slave common tradition in Virginia, which whites thought was a function of slaves' desire for an excuse to go off the plantation. As discussed earlier, James Madison wrote to Jedidiah Morse in 1823 that slaves "prefer wives on a different plantation; as affording occasions & pretexts for going abroad." At about the same time, a traveler in the region remarked that those slaves "who are married generally choose their wives on a distant plantation, because it gives them an excuse for being out at night." Tom Epps (b. 1848), an ex-slave raised in Prince George County, remembered that slaves "always wanted to marry a gal on 'nother plantation cause dey could git a pass to go visit 'em on Saddy nights. . . . All de courtin' and marryin' was done at night. Dey would live at de same place dey live befo' dey marry."[62]

The slaves also drew on generalized West African (or perhaps Igbo) conceptions of extended kinship to further and deepen the social ties among people. In Igboland, there was a diminished emphasis on the concept of the autonomous individual. The minimal social grouping, the *umunne,* was a set of people in related families. In Virginia, slaves reworked the ancestral tradition of extended kinship into a common one of fictive kinship. Caroline Hunter (b. 1847) remembered that during slavery, "it seemed lak yo' chillun b'long to ev'ybody but you." Slaves addressed each other in familial terms—brother, sister, aunt, and uncle.[63] There also are examples in the literature of elderly relations calling strangers as well as grandchildren "daughter" or "son."[64] In 1759, Andrew Burnaby witnessed a poignant accidental reunion of a grandmother and her fourteen-year-old grandson, whom she called her child, in Spotsylvania County: "an old woman . . . who proved to be the boy's grandmother, accidentally cast her eyes on him; she viewed him with great attention for some time; then screamed out, saying that it was her child, and flung herself down upon the ground. She lay there some seconds; rose up, looked on him again in an ecstasy of joy, and fell upon his neck and kissed him."[65]

Slaves in the eighteenth century seemed to have raised their children in ways characteristic of Igboland. In Virginia, numerous white travelers commented on how many enslaved children and youths wore little or no clothing, with many apparently accustomed to wearing nothing at all, as was the case in Igboland.[66] Some whites interpreted the loose nature of both slave and West African clothing as a preference for being nearly nude; thus, there was an element of ethnocentric definition of nudity. As in Igboland, however, many young Afro-Virginian slaves wore few or no clothes up to puberty.[67]

This social artifact of childhood nudity, presumably largely in the summer, continued in the nineteenth century. Henry C. Knight (1824) commented on the "little ones, which in summer wear nothing more than a remnant of a shirt, and not infrequently go literally nude." One ex-slave woman born in the 1830s in North Carolina and raised in Orange County, across the Virginia line, wore no clothes at all until she hit puberty at age fourteen. She told an interviewer, "I went naked as your hand till I was fourteen years old. I was naked like that when my nature come to me."[68] It is tempting to see such social nudity of children and some youth solely as a function of masters' failure to supply enough clothes to cover their slaves. It is also possible that pedonudity had an internal African-oriented social logic, especially since many slave women were made to weave and could have dressed their children if necessary.

Another social fact of slave child rearing, often seen in terms of white strategies of control rather than in terms of early African American cultural logic, was the apparently general custom of not marking slave birthdays. Throughout the ex-slave and fugitive narratives of the nineteenth century, people commented that they did not know their ages. As early as the 1770s, as Fithian's encounter with Dadda Gumby at Nomini Hall illustrates, some Afro-Virginians did not know their children's exact ages or dates of birth. This phenomenon has been interpreted as a manifestation of a pan-African concept of cyclical time that contrasts with modern linear time and perhaps as reflecting ancestral African institutions such as age grades and age sets.[69]

The ancestral Eboan tradition included cyclical and seasonal time concepts as well as age grades, in which the year (as Equiano explained) was dated from when "the sun crosses the line." More important, however, was the belief that each child born was the reincarnation of some previous person, usually a remembered ancestor. The many Igbo women in early Virginia would have had to reckon with reincarnation whenever they gave birth. It makes sense to believe that individual birth dates were not important because conceptions of totally unique individuality may not have made sense to the people then; therefore, birthdays were not celebrated as discrete events. The importance of the group and of reincarnation in the ancestral Igbo tradition found expression in the common Afro-Virginian tradition of not marking children's birth dates. Fannie Berry (b. 1841) related that "As ol' folks use to tell us, 'You ain't got no business knowing yo' age.' 'Go away from here,' my mother use to tell us when we asked 'bout our age. 'Lemme be. All I know,' she would say, 'you are ol' enough to smell yourself.' Ha, ha. Baby! Is you writing dat down?"[70]

Igbo conceptions of the relation between work and playtime may also have carried over to Virginia. Afro-Virginians created the concept of "negur day-time" in the eighteenth century and continued it in the nineteenth century, with some slaves calling midnight "low twelve."[71] They also may have applied the Igbo concept of the four-day *izu*. Traditionally, one day was a feast day, so that slaves "deserved" (and eventually got) not just the one Sabbath day off of the English week but something approximating the two days off of an eight-day *izu ukwu*—a half day on Saturday and all day Sunday, or possibly Saturday afternoon to Monday dawn each Christian week.

Chesapeake planters in the early eighteenth century initially had cut out the old English servants' custom of a half day of work on Saturday as part of the shift from indentured to enslaved labor in the region. Lois G. Carr and Russell R. Menard argue that this new system of labor management and other measures increased the annual average number of workdays from 286 with indentured servants in the late seventeenth century to 312 with slaves in the eighteenth century.[72]

Plantation customs in the eighteenth century varied as to the days that slaves got to work for themselves or to spend "playing." In the 1720s, when such customs were in flux, some planters allowed "all Saturday, some half Saturday and Sunday; others allow only Sunday." By the 1770s, many slaves, such as those at the farm in Albemarle County where Thomas Anbury was paroled during the revolution and those at Robert Carter's Nomini Hall, had Saturdays (and presumably Sundays). As Fithian wrote, generally "here by five o-Clock on Saturday every Face (especially the Negroes) looks festive & cheerful." Nicholas Cresswell, however, noted that in 1774, Sundays were "the only days these poor creatures have to themselves, they generally meet together and amuse themselves with Dancing to the Banjo."[73]

By the nineteenth century, however, the common custom in Virginia was for slaves to have both a half day Saturday and all day Sunday. One ex-slave, born in 1849, remembered that "Saddy only worked half-day, an' dem slaves would sho' carry on 'cause dey was gonna celebrate dat night."[74] Sundays everywhere was a rest day, but Afro-Virginian slaves from the mid–eighteenth through mid–nineteenth century often used the day not to rest but to play.

As early as the 1750s, white preachers exhorted masters to keep their slaves, in the words of Samuel Davies, "from rambling about on the Lord's Day . . . and do not connive at their working upon it for themselves." For whites, Sunday was the Sabbath, but for many Afro-Virginians it was a feast day. In 1770, one writer noted that the slaves in Virginia spent that day "either in the ridiculous Recreations usual with them in their own Country, or in labouring on that Day to provide themselves with an Necessaries or Conveniences of Life."

About 1800, Old Dick at Pohoke Plantation in Prince William County told a white visitor that on Sundays "the negroes were at liberty to visit their neighbors." Henry Bibb in Kentucky recognized that many slaves had their own way of celebrating the day of rest, when those "who make no profession of religion, resort to the woods in large numbers on that day to gamble, fight, get drunk, and break the Sabbath." In Virginia at the same time, another ex-slave remembered that he was often lonely on Sundays "because the field hands were away that day; the boys would be away frolicking at some place they had chosen."[75]

What did these people do? The most common activities were group ones such as gaming, dancing, "rasslin," and hanging out and drinking—when not tending to their "necessary Labour, on Saturday and Sunday."[76]

Much of early Afro-Virginian dance and music was performed in a distinctively African way. Igbo instruments like box drums and a banjolike stringed instrument were common in Virginia and North Carolina. The word *banjo* itself signifies Igbo, as in *ba-njo* (being bad), and it is curious that in Jamaican Creole *banja* means "to play the fool."[77] The banjo, as Thomas Jefferson noted, was an instrument "brought hither from Africa," and many Central African peoples called their version of a stringed gourd by variations of *mbanza*. Equiano also remembered that slaves in his area had "many musical instruments, particularly drums of different kinds, a piece of music which resembles a guitar, and another much like a stickado." In the early twentieth century, an anthropologist among the Igbo also noted, in the racist idiom of the time, that "the most interesting of the Ibo instruments is the 'ubaw-akwala,' a sort of primitive guitar—or is it the original of the nigger banjo."[78]

The term *banjo/banjer*, however, apparently was first used in the Chesapeake. It became the common word for this instrument between 1754 and the 1780s, whereas in the West Indies the term *banza* predominated until a general shift to *banja/bonja* after about 1810.

Slaves on the North Carolina plantation where Harriet Jacobs grew up also used a drum made of a "box, covered with sheepskin [and] called the gumbo box"; Igbo slaves on a Jamaican plantation at about the same time relied largely on a similar box drum that they called "Gambys (Eboe drums)."[79] In 1774, Edward Long described such "goombah" drums in the West Indies as "a hollow block of wood, covered with sheepskin stripped of its hair."[80]

One of the most distinctive forms of antebellum African American slave dancing, juba, had become an important part of the slave common tradition by the nineteenth century. Juba was a type of rhythmic jump-step dance that only black folks did. Dancers often patted their legs, arms, and chest (perhaps what subsequently came to be called doing the hambone) or "patting juba."[81] There are a number of references to juba and patting juba in the antebellum published primary literature, although none in eighteenth-century sources.[82] Although Winifred Vass has assigned a Kongo or "Bantu" origin to the word, it was also associated with another Upper South slave artifact, Jonkonnu, which also likely was a creolized Igboism.[83] Juba and patting juba seem to have been products of the elimination of drums (such as the eighteenth-century "qua qua" in Virginia) from the nineteenth century common tradition.

Jonkonnu, known by various names including John Canoe and John Koonering, was common in slave societies throughout the British Americas.[84] A Christmastime slave masquerade with a distinctive cow-horned masker who demanded gifts from the powerful and sometimes wielded a whip, Jonkonnu was like an African men's masking society transported to the New World.[85] Not known or at least not mentioned before the third quarter of the eighteenth century, Jonkonnu became a highly visible aspect of Afro-Caribbean societies at roughly the same time as 500,000 to 750,000 Igbo peoples flooded onto Caribbean sugar islands—after 1750.[86] The masquerade has also been identified in 1820s Suffolk Virginia as well as

early-nineteenth-century North Carolina and perhaps late-nine-
teenth-century Rappahannock County, Virginia.[87]

Generally given a Gold Coast provenance, this slave social fact
was most likely an artifact of Igbo people in the Diaspora.[88] The
association of Jonkonnu with "gambys" and with cow-horn and other
animal masks as well as with distinctive peaked-hat masks nearly
identical to mid-twentieth-century Kalabari masks, plus the tempo-
ral association of the Afro-Caribbean version with the period of
greatest Igbo importation (1760s–1820s), point toward Igboland as
the source of the African American performances.[89]

Njokku, the "yam-spirit cult," was an important institution in historical Igboland (cognate terms included *njoku, onjoku,* and *ifejioku*),
and there was also the yam-associated *okonko,* or Igbo secret society
equivalent of Efik *ekpe.* Nineteenth-century sources attest to animal
and ragman maskers in Bonny and Elem Kalabari, and these read
much like both "root Jonkonnu" and twentieth-century northern
Igbo *omabe* and *odo* masquerades.[90] It seems that diasporic Igbo
combined elements from both essentially shared traditions into a
Creole institution. In effect, moreover, the Jonkonnu troupe may
have served as an all-male slave "secret society" much like a masking
version of *okonko.* Jonkonnu clearly was a male preserve, with a
leader who wielded a whip or stick in association with fierce animal-
masked others. What slaves got was an annual visitation by *njokku* in
mmuo (fearsome masking); those who participated as maskers gained
honor and prestige within the slave community.[91] African American
Jonkonnu was a creolism but not randomly so.

Although there are no known descriptions of Jonkonnu in the
eighteenth-century Chesapeake, slaves in colonial Virginia also had
a holiday at Christmas, ranging from one day to a week, in which
they engaged in some sort of reveling. If Jonkonnu was a creolized
reinterpretation of the Igbo *njokku* or a diasporic expression of
okonko clubs, which celebrated the new year as well as the yam-spirit
(which seems much more plausible than the other attempts to

explain the phenomenon in terms of a minor trade chief on the Gold Coast during the 1720s), the continuing reliance of Igbo in Virginia on yams would suggest that those Christmas revels may have been an early form of Jonkonnu. Also, the southern Igbo men's clubs, *okonko*, could have provided a secondary model for organizing such masking performances.[92]

Another social resource was the use of buttons as gaming pieces and perhaps as a form of money as well as for amulets. Archaeologists of slavery in the Chesapeake have been puzzled by large numbers of buttons routinely found in the root cellars of slave sites. At one plantation in Prince William County, ninety-seven buttons (mostly metal and bone) were found; at Monticello, one building on Mulberry Row yielded forty such buttons.[93] William Kelso has suggested that these caches of button represent the by-product of slave quilt making.[94] It is also possible that these buttons were counters or game pieces for a complicated betting game known as *okwe* (similar to mancala) that people all over Igboland (and throughout West Africa) played.[95]

There is also a distinct possibility that eighteenth-century Afro-Virginian slaves used buttons as a form of money. In general, buttons in the colonial era were used by men, as most women's clothing used clasps and hooks, and were often made of metal or bone. Slaves may have appropriated buttons as a form of currency; it fell out of circulation by the early nineteenth century, when even slaves got access to small coinage. The buttons left in root cellars had not been discarded so much as stored, like any other devalued money. Exploring the Niger River north of Aboh during the 1830s, Oldfield "purchased several bunches of plantains for a button each: blue cut beads were also in great demand here."[96]

Is it an accident that in the archaeology of slave sites in the Upper South, blue beads and buttons (and cowries) also are associated with each other and with root cellars dug to store yams? Or did the Afro-Virginian descendants of Igboized slaves see buttons as money in a local exchange system and blue beads as valuable (and perhaps powerful)?

Buttons in colonial Afro-Virginia therefore were most likely the creolized analog of cowries in large parts of historical Igboland. In general, the Atlantic African "cowrie zone" in the eighteenth century included interior Mande (Bambara) and central and northern Igboland (Nri-Awka, Ika/Anioma) as well as the Slave Coast in general and Angola but did not include Gold Coast and Windward Coast areas or coastal Senegambia.[97] Equiano, however, mentioned that in one of the areas to which he was taken on his initial passage to the coast, where the language and the customs of the people were the same as in his home village, their money "consisted of little white shells, the size of the finger nail."[98]

Cowrie shells (both *Cypraea moneta* and *C. annulus*) have been found in slave contexts throughout Virginia, from Yorktown to Williamsburg to Monticello, usually in sites occupied in the colonial era and especially from those dating between the 1720s and 1770s.[99] Although exceedingly rare on archaeological sites elsewhere, with not a single shell found in archaeological excavations in the Carolina low country,[100] nearly two hundred cowries have been recovered from thirteen sites in eighteenth-century Virginia. About three-quarters of these cowries were found at a single site in Yorktown, where they were mixed into sand and gravel to form the surface of a walkway between the main house, kitchen, and a well; they may have represented excess ballast from slave ships.[101] At least twenty-six cowries from ten sites, however, were found in domestic slave contexts, including root cellars (Monticello, Williamsburg); the single cowrie found at one site in Williamsburg was in a layer that also included "colonoware, a pierced coin, and a smokey quartz crystal," while at another Williamsburg site the cowrie was in a well.[102]

How African slaves used these cowries in Virginia is not clear. They may have been used as amulets or as part of divination kits. For example, in one slave burial in Barbados, archaeologists found a necklace of "European-made glass beads, drilled dog teeth, fish vertebrae, and a carnelian bead," and seven cowries.[103] It is likely that cowries had multiple uses, including serving as protective charms, personal adornments, status markers, part of divining kits, gaming pieces, and even tokens doled out by *buckra* to reward good behavior.[104] They could have served as tiny *lieux de mòmoire,* or constant reminders of African background.

If Igbo in Virginia drew on ancestral material culture to make ends meet and on social-cultural resources to make connections, they drew on ideological resources to make sense of their new world. Most Igbo arrived in the Chesapeake in the summer or early fall and, finding that they could forge an autonomous life in the nighttime, must have paid attention to the stars, as the Calabar-born John Jea suggested. In precolonial Igboland, the only two constellations that anthropologists found Igbo people commonly knew were what Igbo called Yam Barn (Orion) and Hen with Her Chickens (the Pleiades).[105] When these people first confronted the onset of cold weather in their new world, they would have noticed that Yam Barn and Hen with Her Chickens had followed them (as Orion and Pleiades rose in the east in the autumn night sky) on the same path as the moon. Igbo slaves likely drew on ancestral ideological resources to make sense of their new worlds and in the process Igboized slave religious common traditions throughout the British Americas.

As we have seen, in Virginia as in Igboland, doctoring or conjuration could also mean administering poisons. As Philip Schwarz has noted in his study of slave trials in Virginia, colonial prosecutions for "poisoning" were unusually common in Piedmont counties.[106] In such prosecutions—and, indeed, probably in the case of Ambrose Madison in 1732—men often provided the "poisonous medicines" to other slaves to administer to third parties. The substances were often put in food or in water or milk pails. Whites eventually learned to differentiate between malicious poisoning, which they almost always punished with death, and benevolent "administration" of such secret medicines. Both were illegal after 1748, but the latter usually brought a whipping while the former most often brought execution.

The famous case of Eve, mentioned earlier, an enslaved woman in Orange County who was burned to death for poisoning her master in 1745, is particularly instructive.[107] Eve was executed so brutally not only because she was the victim, as Schwarz noted, "of common law, her status as a slave, and her identity as a woman," although these condemnations played into many such prosecutions and executions, including hers. Nor was she burned at the stake simply for overturning the master-slave relationship by wielding of "the demonstrably powerful weapon of poison." In Eve's case, her master did not die.[108]

Eve was condemned to a most terrible death not solely for attempting to poison her master, an action that often brought hanging, but because she did so by poisoning his milk. Mountague drank it unknowingly and then "languished," apparently near death, for several months. Whereas whites saw milk as "the *ova* and *mala* of Virginia" and taken at every meal, the vast majority of slaves in early Virginia were lactose intolerant. It has been suggested that in nineteenth-century Virginia, "lactose intolerance for black adults might have reached as high as 100 percent."[109] The only two major African ethnic groups that are known to have been 100 percent lactose intolerant (at least in the mid–twentieth century) were Igbo and Yoruba.[110] Eve and others like her chose to poison the precise staple food that they did not take, thereby avoiding harm to unintended victims, even if they did not understand exactly why they did not drink milk but instead trusted in the efficacy of lived experience. This represents a powerful example of historical creolization in Afro-Virginia.

In the nineteenth century, descendants of these enslaved people believed it was good luck to sit under a sycamore tree. This image of the sycamore as a totem of good luck provides a powerful metaphor for the process of historical creolization, or how Africans became

Afro-Virginians. Sycamore trees are peculiar for a number of reasons. They are the broadest-leafed of the deciduous trees. They grow
near water and provide the best shade on hot summer days. The base
looks much like any other tree, with rough dark brown bark. But as
the tree grows it changes form, becoming smooth and white as it
reaches for the sky. Yet the roots feed the whole tree through the
rough base, up against which one sits in repose. Though some of the
youngest tips will have turned white and smooth at the top, the dark
rough base remains indispensable, weathering storms and floods
and the searing heat, a stolid ancestral trunk out of which comes
something ever new yet always and forever nourished by the old.

CONCLUSION

A Thread of Evidence

As we have seen, in the second quarter of the eighteenth century, Ambrose Madison and his peers and neighbors bought Igbo, usually in small groups including both sexes and often to settle newly claimed land in the Piedmont. In 1732, a conspiracy among these Atlantic Africans resulted in the murder of their master. But in the spring of 1733, the two Madison-owned slaves directly involved in the conspiracy, Turk and Dido, were still living at Montpelier. Other planters, like Henry Willis and Madison's cousin, Larkin Chew, who also had bought three pairs and two pairs, respectively, of Igbo slaves during the 1719–20 slave-buying season through Colonel John Baylor of Walkerton, would have faced similar situations, as did Frances Taylor Madison, Ambrose's widow, and her overseers on these upcountry quarters. For the masters, the burning question was how to deal with communities of slaves composed largely of "bad" Africans.[1] Rather than, as Thomas Jefferson would later put it, holding the wolf by the ears, many planters in this earlier generation were left holding the bag (and, of course, a whip).

Some fifty years later, in 1782, however, there was still a Dido living at James Madison's Montpelier. And as late as the 1820s a half dozen slaves aged between eighty and one hundred lived at Walnut

Grove (the slaves' village at Montpelier), who would have been nearly direct links not just with the dispatching of Old Master but with the knowledge of the old Guinea folk as well. In the middle decades of the nineteenth century, this hundred-year-old community was forcibly broken up and dispersed. Though some descendants still used names to express their connections with kin and land—as metaphorical sites of memory—old Granny Milly's bound copy of *Telemachus* disappeared or was lost to the vagaries of time.

To tell this set of interrelated stories, I have moved from the general to the particular to the regional. The transatlantic slave trade was much less random and much more patterned than historians have previously assumed, and I argue that populations of displaced Africans were more like loosely constituted groups than crowds of cultural strangers. Throughout the diaspora, we can see charter generations of particular groups of Atlantic Africans. For Virginia, especially the broad Piedmont region, the main historical connection was with the hinterland of the Bight of Biafra.

A series of broad transformations throughout the Anglophone Atlantic world—from the emergence of Bristol merchants in the slave trade to the decline of the Nri civilization and the consequent rise of Bonny as a slave trade port on the Calabar coast to the concentration of Igbo in shipments to Virginia and the settlement of the central Piedmont—date to the second quarter of the eighteenth century. By surveying the basic economic, political, and cultural backgrounds of Igbo peoples, we can begin to grasp the various knowledges, skills, and expectations that they brought with them into their new world of chattel slavery. The fact that the slaves at Montpelier used poison to murder their master, with all that this esoteric knowledge implies about the culture of the slaves in Virginia as elsewhere in the diaspora, is the fulcrum that connected the history of this enslaved community to their forebears in what is now eastern Nigeria.

In trying to recapture the agency of Igbo in this one part of the African diaspora, it is important to remember that creolization, the process of adapting to new physical and social conditions and the basic process of cultural change, was in fact a historical process. Atlantic Africans continued to influence these new communities in concrete ways. In the terrible conditions of chattel slavery, people struggled to remember and used people, places, and things as sites of memory for doing so. At Montpelier, we can see this process work itself out over three generations; however, even in the nineteenth century, there were aged people whose memories stretched back to the charter generation.

The enslaved people at James Madison's Montpelier in fact were part of a larger community. Slaves struggled to create connections of kith and kin across the physical and social landscapes of slavery. Many members of the charter generation were brought to this region as part of a larger chain migration, and their children and grandchildren created a complex web of relations within this plantation district. Not only did the patterns of migration bring many Igbo peoples to this region, but the structure of settlement would have encouraged a kind of mental topography that may be termed Igboesque. Masters such as Colonel James Madison Sr. apparently consciously separated and rotated their slave laborers in the 1730s and 1740s, perhaps reflecting a strategy designed to divide and conquer them. The slaves themselves learned to stay at their assigned Quarters but they likely lived throughout the district. They established a parallel world in which black people were a mosaic of mini-majorities. The descendants of the Igboesque charter generation claimed a deep connection with the land and neighborhood of Montpelier—and presumably with its stories.

The limited data on the larger slave community suggest that people used names both as sites of memory and to preserve collective memories. I have presented a number of individual sketches of mostly Madison-owned slaves as well as a sort of composite or collective biography of the largely Igbo-influenced slave culture in the region. The fact that the murder at Montpelier occurred on the land of what is now a major national historic site presents an extra challenge. The documented Calabar/Igbo connection among the slaves at this presidential plantation presents a unique opportunity to incorporate particular African histories into the interpretive framework of this public history site. Whereas in the 1980s Mt. Vernon pioneered the presentation of architectural authenticity and in the 1990s Monticello pioneered the incorporation of African American history into the center of its historical interpretations, in the early twenty-first century, Montpelier presents the challenge of bridging particular African and American histories.

It is virtually certain that patriarch Ambrose Madison knew that he was dealing in and with Igbo slaves. And as a nation, the Igbo have a story to tell. The Montpelier Foundation and the National Trust for Historic Preservation currently are investing impressive resources into the reconstruction of the Madison era at this presidential plantation. As befitting the homeplace of the father of the U.S. Constitution, part of their plan is the expansion of an advanced institute for the study of democracy. It is noteworthy that one of the most celebrated sayings of the Igbo, "Igbo enwegh eze" (the Igbo have no king) directly evokes the deep principle of village democracy that marks Eboan political culture.

If nothing else, the murder at Montpelier must evoke the culture of violence that undergirded chattel slavery. Again, the Montpelier Foundation has an opportunity to weave the essential violence of slavery into the social history of this plantation community. The eighteenth century was not simply the present set two hundred years ago; it was a different world. A fully rounded interpretation that includes the particular African pasts of many of the slaves and the multiple legacies of the slave trade in Atlantic context will fill a glaring lacuna in Virginia's early social history. This is the central challenge in understanding this murder at Montpelier.

In 1909, the by-then middle-aged scholar and activist W. E. B. Du Bois (1868–1963), who himself would bridge the Reconstruction and civil rights eras by dint of his long life, reflected on the apparent fact that black Americans could not "trace an unbroken social history from Africa."[2] At about the same time, his archrival, Booker T. Washington, born a slave in Virginia, also noted this profound discontinuity, though in personal terms. He wrote in 1901 that although he knew he had kin (a grandmother, uncles and aunts, and cousins), he had "no knowledge as to what most of them are."[3]

Unlike Washington, however, Du Bois insisted that there indeed remained a historical "nexus" between Africa and America. In a call that still reverberates today, he urged the sustained study of historical evidence, especially of the relatively voiceless "folk," that might reveal "the broken thread of African and American social history."[4] Even with Melville Herskovits's heroic efforts in the 1930s[5] (hamstrung as he was by the limited basic data on the African provenances of American black populations) and the return to these fundamental questions in the closing decades of the twentieth century, particular groups of Africans still remain largely invisible in early North American history. But the evidence for the relevance of particular African peoples in specific times and places, not just in Virginia but throughout the Atlantic world, increasingly demands attention and sustained inquiry.

One such thread may be picked up at James Madison's plantation. Though the descendant community has dispersed and research into the historical experiences of their enslaved ancestors is barely in its infancy, the murder of Ambrose Madison by Atlantic Africans in 1732 remains the charter event in the history of Montpelier. It also challenges us to recover the historical presence of particular groups of Africans in North America, including Igbo in Virginia.

APPENDIX A: New Virginia Slave Trade Statistics, 1676–1775

In the first quarter of the eighteenth century, the Virginia market was particularly important in the slave trade from the Bight of Biafra but then declined

TABLE A.1

Estimated Numbers Embarked from the Bight of Biafra and to Virginia, 1676–1775

Years	# Biafrans Embarked	# Landed Biafrans (Known)[a]	# Landed in Virginia	% Biafrans Landed (Known)	% Igbo[b]	% Est. Igbo Landed in Virginia
1676–1700	33,869	16,410	1,131	6.9	6.5	4.5
1701–25	28,772	14,670	6,720	45.8	8.0	36.7
1726–50	64,082	41,093	9,407	22.9	8.0	18.3
1751–75	266,472	194,682	4,865	2.5	8.0	2.0
1676–1775	**393,195**	**266,855**	**22,123**	**8.3**	**7.9**	**6.6**
1701–50	**92,854**	**55,763**	**16,127**	**28.9**	**8.0**	**23.1**

Source: Derived from Eltist et al., *Transatlantic Slave Trade:* twenty-five-year period; Where slaves embarked = Bight of Biafra.

Notes:

[a] Number estimated to have landed (disembarked) throughout the Americas whose destination was known.

[b] Global estimate of percentage of Igbo among Biafrans embarked (and therefore also among Biafrans disembarked) from Chambers, "Significance of Igbo," 109–10.

over the course of the century. Between 1701 and 1750, the Virginia market accounted for about 30 percent of Africans taken from the Bight of Biafra; about a quarter of those Africans were Igbo. An analysis of quinquennia (1716–45) makes the point even more dramatically. For a relatively short time, the long generation of the 1710s–40s, when the great expansion occurred, the Virginia market was the major one for slaves from the Bight of Biafra, suggesting the reach into the Nri-Awka/Isuama heartland. The tidal wave that followed, which put great strains on Nri and other peoples in north-central Igboland, was directed to Jamaica and the Lesser Antilles (especially the anglophone islands of Dominica, Grenada, Barbados, St. Kitts, and St. Domingue); together, these six islands accounted for 73.7 percent of Biafrans landed (347,302 out of 471,583).

Of the total number landed in Virginia 1676–1775 (about 83,500), an estimated 37,266 were from the Bight of Biafra (44.6 percent); of those Biafrans,

TABLE A.2

Estimated Numbers from the Bight of Biafra Landed (Disembarked) in Virginia, 1676–1775

Years	# Africans to Virginia (Embarked)	# Africans Landed (Known)[a]	# Biafrans Landed	% of Africans (Known)	% Igbo of Africans Landed[b]	# Total Landed Africans
1676–1700	5,304	3,809	1,400	36.8	23.9	4,471
1701–25	26,166	15,261	8,373	54.9	43.9	21,351
1726–50	42,267	19,883	11,626	58.5	46.8	35,108
1751–75	27,249	23,111	6,270	27.1	21.7	22,627
1676–1700	**100,986**	**62,064**	**27,669**	**44.6**	**35.3**	**83,467**
1701–50	**68,433**	**35,144**	**19,999**	**56.9**	**45.5**	**56,369**

Source: Derived from Eltist et al., *Transatlantic Slave Trade:* twenty-five-year period; Where slaves embarked = Bight of Biafra.
Notes:
[a] Number of Africans landed in Virginia with a known coastal provenance.
[b] With a known coastal provenance. Estimated share of Igbo among Biafrans is 65 percent (1676–1700) and 80 percent (1701–75) (Chambers, "Significance of Igbo," 109–10).

some 29,500 were likely Igbo. Furthermore, of the total number landed between 1701 and 1750 (or 56,370) an estimated 32,074 were from the Bight of Biafra (56.9 percent), and of those Biafrans, some 25,659 were likely Igbo. Therefore, of the estimated 30,000 or so Igbo likely landed in Virginia in the century after 1676, 87 percent arrived between 1701 and 1750. This was a huge wave of Biafrans in general and of Igbo in particular.

Between 1716 and 1740, a majority of Africans from the Bight of Biafra were sent to Virginia. Of the roughly 31,000 Biafrans embarked, about 10,600 were known to have been sent to Virginia (representing more than 55 percent of those with known destinations); about 44 percent of Igbo sent into the diaspora would have wound up in Virginia. Thus, an estimated total of 17,114 Biafrans sent to Virginia. From the perspective of the Bight of Biafra, Virginia in this era was the major or most likely market, the destination for a majority of

TABLE A.3

Slave-Trade Numbers from the Bight of Biafra, 1716–40, by Quinquennia

Years	# Biafrans Embarked	# Biafrans Embarked (Known)[a]	# to Virginia (Disembarked)	% Landed (Known)	% Igbo Landed in Virginia	Next Ranked
1716–20	6,975	4,548	2,819	62.0	49.6	(672)[b]
1721–25	2,747	2,156	1,926	89.3	71.5	(230)[c]
1726–30	9,591	5,863	2,619	44.7	35.7	(1613)[d]
1731–35	6,838	3,234	2,134	66.0	52.8	(611)[e]
1736–40	4,797	3,382	1,101	32.6	26.0	(1136)[e]
1716–40	30,948	19,183	10,599	55.3	44.2	

Source: Derived from Eltist et al., *Transatlantic Slave Trade.*

Notes:

[a] With known destination in the Americas.

[b] Martinique.

[c] Barbados.

[d] Jamaica.

[e] South Carolina.

Biafran Africans. They were approximately six times more likely to be sent to Virginia than to the other two major markets, Jamaica and South Carolina.

Some 65,000 Africans were sent to Virginia between 1716 and 1755; of these, some 53,570 survived the voyage, and of these, some 37,500 (70 percent) had their coastal provenance given (known). Some 57 percent of those shipped out of Africa were from the Bight of Biafra, and roughly 45.5 percent likely were Igbo. From the perspective of Virginia, the wave from the Bight of Biafra and thus the era of Igbo dominance occurred from approximately 1716 to 1755 and resulted in some 30,500 Biafran Africans (25,000 of them Igbo) arriving in Virginia in one long generation. This Biafra-Virginia nexus was especially concentrated in 1716–30 and 1741–50, when Biafrans were 62 percent and 75 percent of imports, respectively, or about two-thirds of those cohorts combined.

TABLE A.4

Slave-Trade Numbers of Africans Sent to Virginia, 1716–55, by Quinquennia

Years	#Africans Embarked	#Africans Embarked (Known)	#from Biafra	% of Africans[a]	Est. # of Igbo[b]
1716–20	7,444	5,533	3,473	62.8	2,778
1721–25	5,909	4,766	2,463	51.7	1,970
1726–30	10,104	4,552	3,238	71.1	2,590
1731–35	9,634	5,464	2,636	48.2	2,109
1736–40	10,726	3,935	1,360	34.6	1,088
1741–45	6,165	1,696	1,404	82.8	1,123
1746–50	5,638	4,236	2,988	70.5	2,390
1751–55	9,322	7,314	3,741	51.1	2,993
1716–55	64,942	37,496	21,303	56.8	17,041

Source: Derived from Eltist et al., *Transatlantic Slave Trade.*
Notes:
[a] Percentage of Africans with a known coastal provenance.
[b] as per 80 percent of the number from Biafra.

An estimated 30,600 Biafrans were actually landed, 24,500 of them likely Igbo. Consequently, as a general statement, it can be estimated that about 25,000 Igbo, and perhaps 5,000 Moko (Ibibio/Efik, including Andoni and Okrika) landed in Virginia between about 1716 and 1755.

TABLE A.5

Estimated Number of Biafran Africans and Igbo Landed, 1716–55

Years	# Total Africans	# Total Biafrans	# Total Igbo
1716–20	6,126	3,847	3,075
1721–25	4,902	2,534	2,025
1726–30	8,316	5,913	4,732
1731–35	8,069	3,889	3,115
1736–40	8,919	3,086	2,471
1741–45	5,037	4,171	3,335
1746–50	4,677	3,297	2,638
1751–55	7,520	3,843	3,076
1716–55	**53,566**	**30,580**	**24,467**

Minimum Number of Slaves Owned by Madison Family

| Year | Number of Slaves[a] | | Total | Remarks |
	Age 16+	Age 12+		
1720–21	2			Women from "Calabar" (Nigeria)
1725	8			Africans clearing patent lands 1725–26
1733	15		29	at Mt. Pleasant (Montpelier)
1738	14			2 quarters; Edmund Powell, Home House overseer (8); Erasmus Taylor, Black Level overseer (6)
1739	13			Home House (7); Edmund Powell, Black Level overseer, (6)[b]
1745	18			Home House (7)
1746	18			
1747	19			
1748	17			
1749	20			JMS marries NM

(Continued)

Year	Number of Slaves[a]		Total	Remarks
	Age 16+	Age 12+		
1750	18			Home House, Black Level quarters
1751	17			
1752	20			
1753	27			JMS constable for tithables
1755	18			JMJ & FTM only
1756	13			JMJ & FTM only
1757	17			
1758	17			JMJ & FTM only[c]
1762	33			crossed out
1764	29			Home House (25), quarter (4).
1765	39			hired out 6 hands
1766	42			hired out 6 hands
1767	30			JMS; hired out 1 hand
1769	43			Two quarters, 33 and 10[d]
1777	48			Revolutionary War assessments
1778	46			Revolutionary War assessments[e]
1779	46			Revolutionary War assessments
1780	49			Revolutionary War assessments
1782			124	JMS, JMJ, AMII[f]
1783			107	JMS, AMII
1784			84	JMS only
1785			81	JMS only
1786	39	43		JMS only
1787	50		86	JMS, JMJ[g]

(*Continued*)

Year	Number of Slaves[a]		Total	Remarks
	Age 16+	Age 12+		
1788	43	51		JMS, JMJ
1789	56	71		JMS, JMJ, AMII
1790	58	76		JMS, JMJ, AMII
1791	60	78		JMS, JMJ, AMII
1792	62	78		JMS, JMJ, AMII
1793	78	92		JMS, JMJ, AMII
1794	74	89		JMS, JMJ, MWM
1795	75	92		JMS, JMJ, MWM
1796	80	94		JMS, JMJ, MWM
1797	80	92		JMS, JMJ, MWM
1798	72	83		JMS, JMJ, NCM
1799	77	85		JMS, JMJ, NCM
1800	75	82		JMS, JMJ, NCM
1801	86	94	108 (JMS only)	JMS (108), JMJ, NCM
1802	52	56		JMJ, NCM, NM[h]
1803	49	58		JMJ, NCM, NM
1804	56	62		JMJ, NCM, NM
1805	41	53		JMJ (23), NM
1806	45	49		JMJ (27), NM
1807	39	42		JMJ (23), NM
1808	———	———		JMJ elected president
1809	48	54		JMJ (27), NM
1810	43	47		JMJ (35), NM
1811	43	47		JMJ (35), NM
1812	41	45		JMJ (33), NM
1813	51	56		JMJ (43), NM
1814	50	56		JMJ (44), NM
1815	55	64		JMJ (48), NM
1816		59		JMJ (51), NM
1817	52	59		JMJ (45), NM

(*Continued*)

Year	Number of Slaves[a]		Total	Remarks
	Age 16+	Age 12+		
1818	54	59		JMJ (49), NM
1819	52	60		JMJ (45), NM
1820	53	58	112 (1820 U.S. Census)	JMJ (48), NM
1821		48		JMJ (43), NM
1822		49		JMJ (44), NM
1823		50		JMJ (46), NM
1824	44	50		JMJ (41), NM
1825	45	50		JMJ (41), NM[i]
1827		61		JMJ (57), NM
1828		61		JMJ (57), NM
1829		61		JMJ
1830		61	97 (1830 U.S. Census)	JMJ
1831		61		
1832		61		
1833		63		
1834				JMJ sells 16 adult slaves to William Taylor
1835		40		12 more adult slaves sold; Harriet Martineau visits Montpelier
1836		38		JMJ dies 28 June
1837		44		DM
1838		44		DM
1839		47		DM
1840		53	105 (1840 U.S. Census)	DM
1841	44	52		DM[j]
1842	36	43		DM sells core of Montpelier, remains in occupancy until 1844

(*Continued*)

Year	Number of Slaves[a]		Total	Remarks
	Age 16+	Age 12+		
1843	36	39		
1844	36	39	53	DM sells remaining Montpelier lands
1845		40		JPT (20), H. W. Moncure[k]
1846		30		JPT (12), H. W. Moncure
1847		33		JPT (12), H. W. Moncure
1848		23		JPT (6), H. W. Moncure
1849		4		JPT
1850		5	11 (1850 U.S. Census)	JPT

Notes:

[a] The age cutoff for these categories varies but reflects the sources and generally refers to tithables. For 1736–1815, 1817–20, 1824–25, and 1841–44, the number is of males and females aged sixteen and up; for 1816, 1821–23, and 1827–40, it is the number of males and females aged twelve and up; for the 1820 U.S. Census, the number is males and females aged fourteen and up; for the 1830 and 1840 U.S. Census, the number is males and females aged ten and up.

[b] For 1725–39, an average with about eleven adult slaves (aged sixteen and up).

[c] For 1745–58, an average of about eighteen adult slaves.

[d] For the 1760s, an average of thirty-six adult slaves.

[e] Madison also paid taxes on 4,548 acres of land.

[f] Using the epistemic figure of eighty-eight total slaves for James Sr., nine for James Jr., and twenty-seven for Ambrose (1755–93) on a neighboring plantation (U.S. Census Bureau, *Heads of Families*, 39, 49; PPT 1782). The figures for 1782–85 and 1787 are epistemic; see also Scott, *History*, appendix B, p. 236.

[g] The figure for sixteen and up from 1787 shoe list, Madison Account Books and Miscellaneous Papers. The total is epistemic, as James Sr. was taxed for thirty-eight over age sixteen and thirty-four under sixteen, and James Jr. was taxed for six over sixteen and eight under sixteen.

[h] The division of Colonel Madison's estate, which sent as many as twenty-seven slaves to his daughter, Nelly Hite, at Belle Grove, Frederick County, clearly diminished the number in the core Montpelier slave community.

[i] For 1802–25, an average of forty-six adult slaves (aged sixteen and over).

[j] Slaves listed 1841–54 are aged sixteen and up.

[k] Todd apparently leased about half his slaves to Moncure. These are tithables aged sixteen and up.

Estimated Number of Slaves at Montpelier, 1738–1850

Year	No. Tithes[a]	Known Totals	Remarks
1738	8		6 at Black Level
1739	7		6 at Black Level
1745	7		11 at Black Level
1750–52[b]	15		
1764	25		4 at Black Level
1769	33		10 at Black Level
1777[c]	48		
1778	46		
1779	46		
1780	49		JMS advances 9 slaves (5 adults, 4 children) to AMII at Woodley
1782		97	JMS, JMJ
1783		79	JMS gives 27 slaves (11 adults, 16 children) to JMJ, William Madison, and Nelly Hite
1784[c]		112	
1785		81	
1786	39	73	JMS only
1787	46	84	JMS, JMJ
1788	43		JMS, JMJ
1789	45		JMS, JMJ
1790	49		JMS, JMJ
1791	51		JMS, JMJ

(Continued)

Year	No. Tithes[a]	Known Totals	Remarks
1792	51		JMS, JMJ
1793	62		JMS, JMJ
1794	62		JMS, JMJ
1795[d]	63		JMS, JMJ
1796	67		JMS, JMJ
1797	65		JMS, JMJ
1798	61		JMS, JMJ
1799	66		JMS, JMJ
1800	63		JMS, JMJ
1801[e]	72	108	JMS, JMJ
1802[f]	41		
1803	39		JMJ, NM
1804	42		JMJ, NM
1805	41		JMJ, NM
1806	45		JMJ, NM
1807	39		JMJ, NM
1809	48		JMJ, NM
1810[g]	43		JMJ, NM
1811	43		JMJ, NM
1812	41		JMJ, NM
1813	51		JMJ, NM
1814	48		JMJ, NM
1815	55		JMJ, NM
1820	53	112	JMJ, NM
1824	44		JMJ, NM
1825	45		JMJ, NM
1827[h]	61		JMJ, NM
1828	61		JMJ, NM
1829	61		
1830	61	97	
1831	61		
1832	61		

(*Continued*)

Year	No. Tithes[a]	Known Totals	Remarks
1833	63		
1834	————		JMJ sells 16 adult slaves to William Taylor
1835	40		12 more adult slaves sold
1836	38		
1837	44		DM
1838	44		DM
1839	47		DM
1840	53	105	DM
1841	52		DM
1842	43		DM; DM sells core of Montpelier, remains in occupancy until 1844
1843	50		DM, H. W. Moncure
1844	53		DM sells remaining Montpelier lands, deeds 41 slaves to JPT, moves to Washington, D.C. with remaining 6 slaves
1845	42		JPT, H. W. Moncure
1846	20		H. W. Moncure
1847	23		
1848	18		
1849–51[i]	0	40	

Notes:

[a] For 1738–1825, slaves aged sixteen and over; for 1827–51, slaves aged twelve and over.

[b] Based on crop production. In 1745–49, he deployed between eight and ten adult slaves at the Black Level quarter; upon his marriage to Nelly Conway in 1749, he received approximately eight adult slaves, sending half to Black Level and in roughly 1753 half to establish a third farm at the Mill Quarter. In 1753 he was assessed for a total of twenty-seven tithables on his three farms (Home House, Black Level, Mill Quarter); his two overseers were William Brockman and Thomas Dauhany ("Making of Montpelier," 81–83, based on Crop Memoranda, JMMB). In 1745–49, James Sr. had an estimated eight to ten adult slaves at Black Level; in 1753–56, he had an estimated five to seven adult slaves at the new Mill Quarter.

cFigures for 1777–80 are from parish and county levies paid by Colonel Madison for Revolutionary War assessments and are listed in his hand; in 1778, Madison paid taxes on 4,548 acres of land (Madison Account Book and Miscellaneous Papers). In 1773, Madison had advanced six slaves (four adults and two children) to his son, Francis (Hite v. Madison, Orange County Circuit Court, Clerk's Office).

cColonel Madison purchased a 1,500 acre tract on the Rapidan River in Culpeper (now Madison) County; he gave 1,000 acres to his son, Francis, and established a separate farm on the other third. In 1784, Francis had a total of twenty-one slaves; Colonel Madison had twenty-eight slaves on the other tract (*Hite v. Madison*, Orange County Circuit Court, Clerk's Office; Fothergill and Naugle, *Virginia Tax Payers*, 79). Therefore, in 1784, Colonel Madison owned a total of 112 slaves, of whom 84 were Orange County, and 28 in Culpeper County.

dColonel Madison, in equal partnership with his sons, James Jr., Francis, and William, established a commercial flour mill (subsequently known as Madison Mills) at Barnet's Ford on the Rapidan, on the Culpeper (now Madison) County side of the river. The plans were launched in 1794, although the mill may not have begun operating until 1796. Following the deaths of Francis in 1800 and of Colonel Madison in 1801, the division of shares became so complicated that it was deemed best to sell the venture. In 1805 the mill and its 16.5 acre site were valued at $3,333.33 (£1,885 in Virginia currency), and in 1808 the property was sold to David Smith of Cecil County, Maryland, for £1,100 Virginia currency (or $1,945) (*Hite v. Madison*, Orange County Circuit Court, Clerk's Office; Hackett et al., *Papers*, 2:125–26 n.1). From the steady growth in the number of Colonel Madison's tithables in Orange County, it appears that he staffed the Madison Mill venture with his slaves already in Culpeper (Madison) County; the overseer of that farm in 1800–1801 was Thomas Melton (*Hite v. Madison*). The Madison Mill site was on Francis's property, as evidenced by a 1794 letter from James Jr. to his father that stated, "I retain the conviction I brought from home in favr. of the Mill at my brothers. . . . I am so much disposed to forward the plan of the Mill which I view as particularly favorable to the interest of my brothers as well as myself, that If a pursuit of it depends materially on my contribution, I shall not hesitate to make the sacrifice" (Hunt, *Writings*, 2:214–15).

eColonel Madison died on 27 February 1801. A listing of all his property was drawn up on 10 March 1801, with equal one-sixth shares of the slaves, including those who had been advanced but died between the drawing up of Madison's will in 1787 and his death, to be divided among the heirs. A formal inventory of his estate was made on 1 September and included 108 slaves, sixty-four hoes (twenty-seven weeding, nineteen grubbing, eighteen hilling) (which approximated his number of adult slaves in the 1790s), seventeen narrow axes, sixteen wheat-cutting tools (nine scythes and seven cradles), three blacksmith's bellows (of which two were in working order), three brandy stills (and pewter coils), nearly 32,700 pounds of tobacco, and £283.79 (decimalized) in cash (of which apparently £200 was in gold coin) (Brugger et al., *Papers*, 1:11, 123–24, 359; *Hite v. Madison*, Orange County Circuit Court, Clerk's Office). The estate sale was held on 9 September: James bought, among other items, fifty-four hoes (twenty-seven weeding, fifteen grubbing, twelve hilling); his mother, Nelly, bought the nine scythes and seven cradles (Hackett et al., *Papers*, 2:155 n.3; *Hite v. Madison*). Colonel Madison's heirs apparently agreed that between about 1773 and 1801, he controlled or owned a total of 150 slaves, including those he had "advanced" before writing his will in 1787, and that a one-sixth share meant 25 slaves, or a valuation of £1,650 per share (for a total valuation of £9,900 or about £10,000, or roughly ten times the value of the commercial flour mill on the Rapidan); between about 1773 and 1801, Colonel Madison had dispersed 52 slaves, or about one-third of his total slaveholdings. Eighteen of the slaves went to heirs close to Montpelier (James Jr. and Ambrose), nine went to heirs within about a three-hour walk (Francis and William), and 25 went far away (to Nelly Hite in the Shenandoah Valley) (*Hite v. Madison*). The final division of the slaves and the negotiations among the several legatees at the end of September 1801 took a full week to accomplish (Hackett et al., *Papers*, 2:154).

[f]James inherited the 1,800 acre tract of Montpelier as well as a 475-acre tract on the Rapidan River in Culpeper (Madison) County. Before his death, James Sr. had clearly controlled James Jr.'s slaves. Colonel Madison conditioned his bequest of the 475 acres on James Jr. making "no charge or claim against me hereafter for the use of profits I received or had of his negroes which I had then in possession for which I have already made him ample amends in money and lands heretofore given" (*Hite v. Madison*, Orange County Circuit Court, Clerk's Office).

[g]In 1810, Nelly apparently gave title to seventeen or eighteen slaves, all at Montpelier, to her son, James Jr. (PPT; in 1809, she was assessed for twenty-five slaves over age twelve [twenty-one over age sixteen], and James was assessed for twenty-nine over age twelve [twenty-seven over age sixteen]; and 1810, Nelly paid taxes on eight slaves [all over age sixteen], and James paid taxes on thirty-nine tithable slaves [thirty-five over age sixteen]). By her November 1807 will, Nelly Madison reserved the right of eight of her slaves (Simon, Peter, Sawney, Sam, Tabby, Violett, Mary, and Pamela) to choose their own master, and she reaffirmed this right in two subsequent codicils (1808, 1817) (OCWB 1829). In around 1817 she sold her slave, Harry (probably a tradesman), to James for six hundred dollars. Her will was probated 25 March 1829. The slaves apparently were allowed to make their choice of master in around 1826, and they all chose to stay at Montpelier.

[h]In 1826 or 1827, Nelly Madison apparently transferred title to her slaves to her son, James Jr.: in those years, she was assessed for only four slaves. She died on 11 February 1829.

[i] Montpelier was purchased in 1849 by Benjamin Thornton of England. He was assessed for no tithables in 1849–51; however, the 1850 U.S. Census listed forty slaves under his name. It is likely that a rump group of forty slaves resided at Montpelier in 1850.

Abbreviations Used

AMII	Ambrose Madison II (1755–93)
DM	Dolley Madison (1768–1849, widow of JMJ)
FTM	Frances Taylor Madison (1700–1761)
JMJ	James Madison Jr. (1751–1836)
JMS	James Madison Sr. (1723–1801)
JPT	John Payne Todd (1792–1852)
MWM	Mary W. Madison (widow of AMII)
NCM	Nelly Conway Madison (daughter of AMII)
NM	Nelly Madison (1731–1829; widow of JMS)

Name	Year First Mentioned	Owner at First Mention	Sex	Age at First Mention	Remarks
Aaron	1773	FM	M	adult	gift from JMS
Abby	1782	JMS	F	child	PPT 1782, 33d;[a] shoe size 5 (Abigail)[b]
Abner	1787	JMS	M	adult	shoe size 10
Abraham	1787	WM	M	adult	gift from JMS
Abraham	1801	JMS	M	adult	sent to Hites, valued at £15
Abraham	1844	DM	M	adult	b. ca.1827; deeded to JPT, 1844; age given as 18, 1850 (OCDB 42:331)
Abram	1782	JMS	M	adult	PPT 1782, 22d
Abram	1852	JPT	M	adult	freed by JPT with $200 to resettle with, 1852
Agathy	1782	JMS	F	child	PPT 1785, 3d
Aggy	1782	AMII	F	child	PPT 1782, 13th; 1794 INV (Agnus), valued at £45
Aleck	1852	JPT	M	adult	freed by JPT with $200 to resettle with, 1852
Alexander	1787	JMJ	M	child	son of Dinar; gift from JMS; 1846 at Toddsberth

(Continued)

Name	Year First Mentioned	Owner at First Mention	Sex	Age at First Mention	Remarks
Alice	1787	JMS	F	adult	shoe size 7
Alice	1787	JMJ	F	child	daughter of Dinar; gift from JMS
Amey	1773	FM	F	child	b. ca.1771; gift from JMS; considered adult by 1787
Amey	1787	JMJ	F	child	daughter of Dinar; gift from JMS; inherited by DM; deeded to JPT, 1844; valued at $150, 1852; freed by JPT with $200 to resettle with, 1852
Amy	1782	AMII	F	child	PPT 1782, 14th (last female); 1794 INV valued at £40
Anna	1787	JMS	F	adult	shoe size 8; 1801 sent to Hites, valued at £80
Anthoney	1733	AM	M	child	at Mt. Pleasant; 1733 INV the youngest boy listed; prob. "Old Anthony" who was married (by 1780) to Betty; possibly "old black Toney" in 1817 ([Paulding], "Unpublished Sketch," 435)
Anthony	1782	JMS	M	adult	b. ca.1769; mulatto waiting servant; runaway, 1782; PPT 1782, 10th
Anthony	1782	JMS	M	adult	PPT 1782, 24th
Becca	1844	DM	F	adult	deeded to JPT, 1844
Beck	1766	JMS	F	adult	hired out by JMS (also in 1769, 1772); PPT 1782, 7th; shoe size 6

(Continued)

Name	Year First Mentioned	Owner at First Mention	Sex	Age at First Mention	Remarks
Beck	1780	AMII	F	child	gift from JMS; daughter of Celia; PPT 1782, 10th; an adult with child, James, together valued at £55, 1794
Ben	1782	JMS	M	adult	PPT 1782, 1st
Ben	1782	JMS	M	adult	"L. Ben" (Little Ben); PPT 1782, 12th; shoe size 8
Ben	1794	AMII	M	adult	1794 INV, 1st male, valued at £20
Ben Sr.	1844	DM	M	adult	b. ca.1800; deeded to JPT 1844; age 45, 1845; freed by JPT with $200 to resettle with, 1852
Benjamin	1846	DM	M	child	Benjamin Taylor; son of Ralph and Catharine Taylor; with DM in D.C.
Betty	1733	AM	F	child	at Mt. Pleasant; hired out with children by JMS John Cave, 1765, 1770, 1774; married to Old Anthony by 1780; PPT 1782, 5th; shoe size 5
Betty	1782	JMS	F	adult	PPT 1782, 6th; shoe size 9
Betty	1782	JMS	F	child	PPT 1782, 31st
Betty	1834	JMJ	F	child	sold with 15 others to William Taylor; Taylor refused to accept her
Bill	1794	AMII	M	adult	1794 INV valued at £40
Billey	1780	JMJ	M	adult	Billey Gardner (d.1795); gift from JMS; son of Old

(Continued)

Name	Year First Mentioned	Owner at First Mention	Sex	Age at First Mention	Remarks
					Anthony and Betty; went with James Madison Jr. to Philadelphia, 1780; married Henrietta, Thomas Jefferson's washerwoman; listed under JMJ in Williamsburg, 1782; JMJ manumits in 1783; Henrietta works for Jefferson for £20 per year, 1791; "merchant's agent" who traded on Madison's behalf, 1793
Billy	1733	AM	M	child	at Mt. Pleasant
Billy	1782	JMS	M	adult	PPT 1782, 31st; 1787 English shoe size 11
Billy	1782	AMII	M	adult	PPT 1782, 13th and last male in adult cohort (prob. teenager); PPT 1783, 9th; 1794 INV valued at £45
Blar	1784	JMS	M	adult	PPT 1784, 11th
Bristoll	1733	AM	M	adult	at Mt. Pleasant; 1733 INV, 3d
Caleb	1786	JMS	M	child	PPT 1786, prob. infant
Captain	1782	JMS	M	adult	PPT 1782, 19th
Casloe	1752	JMS	F	adult	mother of Davy; 1782 PPT superannuated; 1801 PPT superannuated
Casloe	1780	AMII	F	child	daughter of Celia; gift from JMS ca.1780; PPT 1782, 12th; 1794 INV valued at £45

(Continued)

Name	Year First Mentioned	Owner at First Mention	Sex	Age at First Mention	Remarks
Cate	1765	JMS	F	adult	d. ca.1774; hired out by JMS to John Cave, 1769
Cate	1782	AMII	F	adult	PPT 1782, 4th; PPT 1783, 4th
Catharina	1782	AMII	F	adult	AMII PPT 1782, 7th; gift from JMS; d. ca. 1787
Catharine	1844	DM	F	adult	Catherine Taylor (Caty), b. ca. 1822; deeded to JPT, 1844; wife of Old Ralph Taylor and with DM in D.C., 1846; freed by JPT with $200 to resettle with, 1852
Catherine	1782	JMS	F	child	PPT 1782, 34th
Catterenea	1733	AM	F	child	Catharina; at Mt. Pleasant
Celia	1768	JMS	F	adult	hired out by JMS 1771, 1773; given to AMII with children (Savina, Patty, Beck, Casloe), 1780; PPT 1782, 2d; PPT 1783, 2d; 1794 INV valued at £30
Charity	1782	JMS	F	child	PPT 1782, 28th
Charity	1794	AMII	F	child	daughter of Esther; 1794 INV
Charles	1782	JMS	M	adult	PPT 1782, 21st; shoe size 10
Charles	1844	DM	M	adult	b. ca.1814; deeded to JPT, 1844
Charlotte	1782	JMS	F	child	b. ca. 1770; PPT 1782, 27th; PPT 1785, last adult; by 1787 an adult, shoe size 6.
Charlotte	1844	DM	F	adult	b. ca. 1824; deeded to JPT, 1844

(Continued)

Name	Year First Mentioned	Owner at First Mention	Sex	Age at First Mention	Remarks
Claris	1733	AM	F	adult	(Clarissa?); at Mt. Pleasant; 1733 INV, 4th
Clarissa	1782	JMS	F	child	PPT 1782, 40th
Cress	1773	JMS	F	adult	Creass; hired out 1773; shoe size 9
Cussina	1733	AM	F	child	at Mt. Pleasant
Cyrus	1782	JMS	M	adult	PPT 1782, "exempted" (superannuated)
Dainger-field	1794	AMII	M	child	1794 INV, valued at £40 (prob. ca. 15 years old); free black man named Dangerfield Walker lives at Montpelier, 1868 (Carson PPT 1868, p. 284, no. 16)
Daniel	1782	JMS	M	child	PPT 1782, 26th
Daphne	1733	AM	F	adult	Daffney; at Mt. Pleasant; 1733 INV, 3d
Daphne	1782	JMS	F	adult	PPT 1782, 1st (female)
David	1794	AMII	M	adult	1794 INV, 4th
Davy	1752	JMS	M	child	b. 3 July 1752, son of Casloe; given to JMJ ca. 1785; in JMS PPT 1782–85; PPT 1782, 7th
Davy	1782	AMII	M	adult	PPT 1782–83, 7th (prob. teenager)
Delphia	1782	JMS	F	adult	PPT 1782, 25th
Demas	1782	JMS	M	child	son of Eliza; PPT 1782, 32d; given to Nelly Hite, 1783
Dianna	1782	JMS	F	child	daughter of Eliza; PPT 1782, 32d; given to Nelly Hite, 1783

(Continued)

Name	Year First Mentioned	Owner at First Mention	Sex	Age at First Mention	Remarks
Dick	1733	AM	M	adult	at Mt. Pleasant; 1733 INV, 10th
Dick	1782	JMS	M	child	PPT 1783, prob. infant
Dido	1732	AM	F	adult	at Mt. Pleasant; convicted conspirator in Ambrose Madison's death; 1733 INV, 5th and last adult female, prob. teenager; apparently hired out to John Cave, 1766, 1770, 1774
Dido	1782	JMS	F	adult	PPT 1782, 20th; shoe size 7
Dido	1782	AMII	F	adult	owned by Thomas Chew (d. 1781), valued at £50; sold to Ambrose for £51, 1791; 1794 INV, 1st female listed, valued at £40
Dinah	1787	JMS	F	child	daughter of Dinar; given to JMJ
Dinar	1787	JMS	F	adult	given to JMJ with 6 children
Dolly	1782	JMS	F	child	PPT 1782, 39th
Dorcas	1784	JMS	F	child	PPT 1784, 2d
Dudley	1794	AMII	M	child	son of Hannah, 1794 INV
Edmund	1782	JMS	M	adult	PPT 1782, 18th
Edom	1782	JMS	M	child	PPT 1782, 35th; shoe size 5
Edward	1868	JMJ?	M	adult	Edward Taylor residing on/employed at Montpelier, 1868 (Carson PPT 1868, p. 270, no. 27)
Eli	1794	AMII	M	child	son of Hannah; 1794 INV
Elijah	1782	AMII	M	adult	PPT 1782, 12th; PPT 1783, 8th; 1794 INV valued at £40

(Continued)

Name	Year First Mentioned	Owner at First Mention	Sex	Age at First Mention	Remarks
Eliza	1767	JMS	F	adult	hired out, 1767, 1771, 1773; PPT 1782, 14th; given with children Joanna, Dianna, Demas, Pinder, Webster to Nelly Hite
Eliza	1785	JMS	F	child	PPT 1785, very young child
Ellen	1844	DM	F	adult	deeded to JPT, 1844; 1846 OCDB deed of trust
Ellick	1844	DM	M	adult	deeded to JPT, 1844
Esther	1782	AMII	F	adult	PPT 1782, 8th; 1794 INV, with daughter Charity valued at £55
Eve	1782	JMS	F	adult	PPT 1782, 21st; shoe size 6
Ezekiel	1782	JMS	M	child	PPT 1782, 34th; shoe size 4
Fanny	1784	JMS	F	child	PPT 1784, prob. an infant; 1844 DM deeded to JPT
Frank	1783	AMII	M	adult	PPT 1783, 4th; 1794 INV, valued at £25
Frank	1801	JMS	M	adult	sent to Hite's, valued at £90
Gabriel	1844	DM	M	adult	b. ca.1800; deeded to JPT, 1844; age 50, 1850; 1852 valued at $100; freed by JPT with $200 to resettle with, 1852
George	1733	AM	M	adult	at Mt. Pleasant; 1733 INV, 6th
George	1773	FM	M	child	son of Nell; gift from JMS
Gideon	1773	FM	M	adult	gift from JMS
Gilbert	1782	JMS	M	child	PPT 1782, 29th
Giles	1782	JMS	M	adult	PPT 1782, 25th; shoe size 8
Guy	1782	JMS	M	adult	PPT 1782, 17th

(Continued)

Name	Year First Mentioned	Owner at First Mention	Sex	Age at First Mention	Remarks
Guy	1852	JPT	M	adult	valued at $150; freed by JPT with $200 to resettle with, 1852
Hannah	1733	AM	F	child	at Mt. Pleasant; 1733 INV, youngest girl; hired out by JMS 1772; given to FM, 1773
Hannah	1782	AMII	F	adult	PPT 1782, 5th; PPT 1783, 5th; 1794 INV, valued with son Dudley at £45
Hannah	1794	AMII	F	adult	valued with son Eli at £40
Hanover	1786	JMS	M	child	PPT 1786, prob. an infant
Harriett	1844	DM	F	adult	b. ca. 1819; deeded to JPT, 1844; aged ca. 26, 1845
Harry	1733	AM	M	adult	at Mt. Pleasant; 1733 INV, 5th
Harry	1766	JMS	M	adult	hired out to John Cave 1766, 1771; PPT 1782–85, 8th; "tradesman" and English shoe size 6, 1787; choose his own master, 1801
Harry	1787	JMS	M	child	shoe size 4
Henry	1782	AMII	M	child	PPT 1782, 11th
Henry	1783	JMS	M	child	son of Truelove; given to Nelly Hite, 1783; sent to Hites, 1801, valued at £40
Henry	1785	JMS	M	child	son of Margaret; PPT 1785, prob. infant; given to WM, 1787
Isaac	1733	AM	M	adult	at Mt. Pleasant; 1733 INV, 7th

(Continued)

Name	Year First Mentioned	Owner at First Mention	Sex	Age at First Mention	Remarks
Isaac	1780	JMS	M	adult	d. ca.1787; given to AMII; PPT 1782, 1st
Isaac	1794	AMII	M	child	son of Milly; 1794 INV
Isbell	1782	JMS	F	adult	PPT 1782, 18th; shoe size 6
Israel	1801	JMS	M	adult	sent to Hites, valued at £75
Jack	1733	AM	M	child	at Mt. Pleasant; 1733 INV, oldest boy; JMS PPT 1782, 6th; shoe size 10
Jack	1787	JMS	M	adult	"L. Jack" (Little Jack); English shoe size 9
Jacob	1780	JMS	M	adult	given to AMII; PPT 1782, 3d; 1794 INV, valued at £70
James	1768	JMS	M	adult	Jim; hired out to John Cave, 1768, 1774; PPT 1782, 5th
James	1782	AMII	M	child	son of Beck; PPT 1782, 6th; PPT 1783; 1794 INV, 5th and last
Jane	1794	AMII	F	child	1794 INV, valued at £30
Jasper	1787	JMS	M	adult	English shoe size 11
Jemmy	1782	JMS	M	child	given to Nelly Hite, 1783; PPT 1782, 20th; remained with JMS through PPT 1785
Jenny	1787	JMS	F	adult	shoe size 9
Jerry	1782	AMII	M	child	PPT 1782, 9th
Jerry	1783	JMS	M	adult	given to Nelly Hite, 1783; apparently sent to Hites
Jerry	1844	DM	M	adult	b. ca. 1812; deeded to JPT, 1844
Jesse	1782	JMS	M	adult	PPT 1782, 30th; 1787 English shoe size 9

(Continued)

Name	Year First Mentioned	Owner at First Mention	Sex	Age at First Mention	Remarks
Joanna	1782	JMS	F	child	daughter of Eliza; PPT 1782, 29th; given to Nelly Hite, 1793; sent to the Hites
Joe	1733	AM	M	adult	at Mt. Pleasant; 1733 INV, 4th
Joe	1772	JMS	M	adult	hired out to John Cave; PPT 1782, 15th; shoe size 7
Joe	1782	JMS	M	child	PPT 1782, 27th
Joe	1791	AMII	M	adult	bought from estate of Milley Chew (James Coleman administrator)
John	1780	JMS	M	adult	given to AMII; PPT 1782, 2d; 1794 INV, 2d
John	1787	JMJ	M	child	son of Dinar; gift from JMS
John	1804	AMII	M	adult	b. ca.1770; sold ca.1794 to Robert Overall, Stafford Co.; ran away and frequently used Madison as a name (Meaders, *Advertisements*, 41)
John	1844	DM	M	adult	b. ca.1804; deeded to JPT, 1844; freed by JPT with $200 to resettle with, 1852
John	1845	DM	M	adult	b. ca.1827; deed of trust by JPT, aged 18, 1845; described as black smith, 1850 (OCDB 40:26, 42:331)
(Blind) John	1844	DM	M	adult	deeded to JPT, 1844

(Continued)

Name	Year First Mentioned	Owner at First Mention	Sex	Age at First Mention	Remarks
(Black) Jonathan	1782	JMS	M	child	PPT 1782, 36th; shoe size 5; sent to Hites, 1801; valued at £120
Joshua	1782	JMS	M	adult	PPT 1782, 14th
Joshua	1844	DM	M	adult	b. ca. 1822; deeded to JPT, 1844
Juda	1733	AM	F	child	at Mt. Pleasant; JMS PPT 1782, 3d; shoe size 7
Judy	1770	JMS	F	adult	"L. Judy" (Little Judy); hired out 1770, 1772; PPT 1782, 2d
Julia	1782	JMS	F	child	PPT 1782, prob. infant; DM deeds to JPT, 1844; 1852 valued at $150; freed by JPT with $200 to resettle with, 1852
Kate	1733	AM	F	adult	at Mt. Pleasant; 1733 INV, 2d
Katy	1782	JMS	F	child	daughter of Truelove; PPT 1782, 30th; given to Nelly Hite and sent to the Hites, ca. 1784
Letta	1733	AM	F	child	at Mt. Pleasant
Lewey	1772	JMS	M	adult	Old Lewey; 1772 hired out by day, month
Lewey	1772	JMS	M	adult	Little Lewey; 1772 hired out by day, month; shoe size 7

(Continued)

Name	Year First Mentioned	Owner at First Mention	Sex	Age at First Mention	Remarks
Lewis	1765	JMS	M	child	b. 9 Sept. 1765; Ambrose PPT 1782, 5th
Lewis	1782	AMII	M	child	PPT 1782, 10th; 1794 INV, 3d
Lewis	1844	DM	M	adult	deeded to JPT, 1844
Libby	1787	JMS	F	adult	shoe size 6
Livia	1787	JMS	F	adult	shoe size 11
Lucy	1733	AM	F	child	at Mt. Pleasant; 1733 INV, oldest girl
Lucy	1782	JMS	F	adult	PPT 1782, 10th; shoe size 6
Lucy	1794	AMII	F	child	1794 INV, valued at £20
Major Height	1867	Hite?	M	adult	residing/employed at Montpelier
Margaret	1782	JMS	F	adult	PPT 1782, 22d; shoe size 6; given, with son Henry, to WM, 1787
Mary	1769	JMS	F	adult	"in the House"; hired out, 1769, 1772; PPT 1782, 11th; 1787 English shoe size 5
Mary	1794	AMII	F	child	1794 INV, valued at £15
Matthew	1844	DM	M	adult	Matthew Stuart, b. ca.1800; deeded to JPT, 1844; age 45, 1845; married to Winny; at Toddsberth, 1846; 1850 aged "45"; valued at $400, 1852; freed by JPT with $200 to resettle with, 1852

(Continued)

Name	Year First Mentioned	Owner at First Mention	Sex	Age at First Mention	Remarks
Milly	1782	JMS	F	adult	PPT 1782, 26th; given to Nelly Hite, 1783; sent to Hites, 1801, valued at £14
Milly	1782	AMII	F	adult	PPT 1782, 3d; PPT 1783, 3d; with son Isaac, valued at £35, 1794
Milly	1844	DM	F	adult	b. ca. 1804; deeded to JPT, 1844
(Granny) Milly	1782	JMS	F	adult	b. ca. 1721; hired out with her children, 1769, 1772; PPT 1782, 8th; shoe size 8; apparently inherited by JMJ; 1825 living with daughter and granddaughter (aged ca. 70), and owned book by Telemachus, living in Walnut Grove quarter
Minah	1782	AMII	F	adult	PPT 1782, 6th
Molley	1787	JMS	F	adult	shoe size 7
Moses	1782	JMS	M	adult	blacksmith; PPT 1782, 3d; PPT 1783, 1st; PPT 1784, 2d; PPT 1785, 2d; PPT 1786, 1st; 1787 English shoe size 9; 1801 to choose his own master; bought by JMJ for £150, 1802
(Black) Moses	1782	JMS	M	adult	PPT 1782, 4th; PPT 1783, 11th; PPT 1784, 8th; shoe size 10

(Continued)

Name	Year First Mentioned	Owner at First Mention	Sex	Age at First Mention	Remarks
Nancy	1733	AM	F	child	at Mt. Pleasant
Nancy	1782	JMS	F	child	PPT 1782, 41st; 1787 English shoe size 6; DM deeds to JPT, 1844
Nancy	1782	AMII	F	child	PPT 1782, 11th; by 1794 an adult; valued with son Tom at £55
Nancy	1798	JMJ	F	adult	Nancy Barbour, b. May 1798; ca. 1900, 13 children, 4 surviving, a widow, could not read/write, living in house of son-in-law, George Anderson (b. 1840), a farmer, and his wife, Conwayaba (b. 1845), who had been married 21 years with no children (1900 U.S. Census); in 1869 Anderson lived at Montpelier under Frank Carson; in that year Anderson married Ella Barbour (b. 1852), daughter of Phil Barbour and Nancy Rose; in 1902 Nancy Barbour was a very old ex-slave, still living in Orange

(*Continued*)

Name	Year First Mentioned	Owner at First Mention	Sex	Age at First Mention	Remarks
Nanney	1733	AM	F	adult	at Mt. Pleasant; 1733 INV, 1st
Nanny	1782	JMJ	F	adult	PPT 1782, 16th; house slave at Montpelier, 1809
Ned	1782	JMS	M	adult	PPT 1782, "exempted" (superannuated)
Nell	1766	JMS	F	adult	hired out 1766, 1770, January 1774; given, with son, George, to FM
Nelly	1782	AMII	F	adult	PPT 1782, 1st female; PPT 1783, 1st (Nell); 1794 INV, prob. old as valued at only £10
Nelson	1782	JMS	M	child	PPT 1782, 33d
Nicholas	1844	DM	M	adult	b ca.1808; deeded to JPT, 1844
Nicholas Jr.	1844	DM	M	child	b. ca.1831; deeded to JPT, 1844
Patty	1780	JMS	F	child	daughter of Celia; given to AMII
Paul	1799	JMJ	M	child	Paul Jennings, b. ca.1799; mulatto; married to Sukey (pre-1817); at JMJ's deathbed in 1836; stayed with DM until 1845, when purchased by Daniel Webster and manumitted; published memoir, 1865

(*Continued*)

Name	Year First Mentioned	Owner at First Mention	Sex	Age at First Mention	Remarks
Pegg	1765	JMS	F	adult	hired out with her children 1765–66, 1768–69, 1772, 1774; PPT 1782, 4th
Peggy	1783	JMS	F	child	daughter of Truelove; given to Nelly Hite
Pender	1782	JMS	F	child	PPT 1782, 38th
Penny	1787	JMS	F	adult	shoe size 6
Peter	1733	AM	M	adult	at Mt. Pleasant; 1733 INV, 8th
Peter	1782	JMS	M	adult	PPT 1782, 16th; shoe size 10
Peter	1791	AMII	M	adult	bought from estate of Milley Chew (James Coleman administrator)
Phill	1777	JMS	M	adult	hired to T. Bell for 20 5 shillings (£0.25 decimalized) per day, for £5 total
Phoebe	1782	JMS	F	child	PPT 1782, 42d
Phoebe	1783	AMII	F	child	Phebe; PPT 1783, prob. infant; 1794 INV, valued at £30
Pinder	1783	JMS	M	child	son of Eliza; given to Nelly Hite
Polly	1782	JMS	F	child	PPT 1782, 43d
Priscilla	1783	JMS	F	child	daughter of Truelove; given to Nelly Hite
Rachel	1766	JMS	F	adult	hired out 1766, 1770; PPT 1782, 12th
Ralph	1787	JMS	M	adult	shoe size 8; not listed in PPT 1782–86

(Continued)

Name	Year First Mentioned	Owner at First Mention	Sex	Age at First Mention	Remarks
Ralph Jr.	1844	DM	M	adult	Ralph Taylor Jr.; b. ca. 1811; grandson of Old Ralph (Ralph Philip Taylor); deeded to JPT, 1844; freed by JPT with $200 to resettle with, 1852
(Old) Ralph	1846	DM	M	adult	Ralph Philip Taylor, with DM in D.C.; by 1851 was married with Caty; freed by JPT with $200 to resettle with, 1852
Randall	1782	JMS	M	child	PPT 1782, prob. infant; "Old Randall" valued at $150, 1852; freed by JPT with $200 to resettle with, 1852
Reuben	1752	JMS	M	child	b. 3 July 1752, son of Syci (Priscilla?); PPT 1782, 37th
Richmond	1782	JMS	M	child	PPT 1782, 39th; 1801 adult, sent to Hites, valued at £110
Robin	1768	JMS	M	adult	hired out to John Cave 1768, 1770; PPT 1782, 9th; sent to Hites, valued at £100, 1801
Rose	1785	JMS	F	child	PPT 1785, prob. infant
Ruth	1782	JMS	F	child	PPT 1782, 35th
Sally	1782	JMS	F	adult	PPT 1782, 19th; 1783 given to Nelly Hite; sent to Hites
Sally	1794	AMII	F	child	1794 INV, valued at £30
Sam	1733	AM	M	child	at Mt. Pleasant; 1801 superannuated JMS

(Continued)

Name	Year First Mentioned	Owner at First Mention	Sex	Age at First Mention	Remarks
Sam	1782	JMS	M	child	prob. teenager; PPT 1782, 28th
Sam	1782	AMII	M	child	PPT 1782, 8th
Sam	1844	DM	M	adult	deeded to JPT, 1844
Sarah	1733	AM	F	child	at Mt. Pleasant
Sarah	1801	JMS	F	adult	1801 sent to Hites, valued at £66
Sarah	1844	DM	F	adult	b. ca.1794; deeded 1844 to JPT; freed by JPT with $200 to resettle with, 1852
Sarah	1846	DM	F	child	Sarah Taylor, daughter of Ralph and Catharine Taylor; with DM in D.C.
Savina	1780	JMS	F	child	daughter of Celia; given to AMII; PPT 1782, 9th; sold ca.1784–87
Sawney	1769	JMJ	M	adult	(ca. 1737–1830); JMJ's manservant at College of New Jersey (Princeton); suboverseer with own quarter, 1782; PPT 1782, 2d; 1787 English shoe size 6; one of 3 overseers on Montpelier, 1790; overseer, 1794; octogenarian serving Nelly Madison through her death in 1829; her will permits him to choose new master
Shadrack	1782	JMS	M	adult	PPT 1782, 23d; shoe size 12; sent to Hites, 1801, valued at £120

(Continued)

Name	Year First Mentioned	Owner at First Mention	Sex	Age at First Mention	Remarks
Simon	1787	JMS	M	adult	shoe size 12
Sinar	1782	JMS	F	child	PPT 1782, 37th; PPT 1784–86 child
Sophia	1782	JMS	F	child	PPT 1782, 36th; PPT 1783–85 child
Spark	1733	AM	M	adult	at Mt. Pleasant; 1733 INV, 9th
Stephen	1782	AMII	M	adult	PPT 1782, 4th
Stephen	1844	DM	M	adult	deeded to JPT, 1844
Sue	1765	JMS	F	adult	hired out to John Cave 1765, 1769
Sukey	1770	JMS	F	adult	hired out; PPT 1782, 15th; shoe size 6
Sukey	1814	JMJ	F	adult	house slave at White House, fled with DM during War of 1812 burning; married Paul Jennings (pre-1817); deeded to JPT, 1844
Sylvia	1782	JMS	M	adult	PPT 1782, 23d
Sylvia	1844	DM	F	adult	b. ca. 1811; deeded with 4 children to JPT, 1844
Tabby	1782	JMS	F	adult	PPT 1782, 13th
Tabby	1794	AMII	F	child	1794 INV, valued at £15
Tamar	1765	JMS	F	adult	Tam, d. ca. 1765; hired out to John Cave
Tamar	1782	JMS	F	adult	PPT 1782, 24th
Tidal	1782	JMS	M	child	b. ca. 1779; PPT 1782, 38th; DM deeds to JPT, 1844; at Toddsberth, 1846
Tom	1733	AM	M	adult	at Mt. Pleasant; 1733 INV, 1st
Tom	1770	JMS	M	adult	hired out to John Cave, 1770, 1773; PPT 1782, 11th; shoe size 8

(Continued)

Name	Year First Mentioned	Owner at First Mention	Sex	Age at First Mention	Remarks
Tom	1794	AMII	M	child	son of Nancy; 1794 INV
Tom	1844	DM	M	adult	deeded to JPT, 1844
Tony	1782	JMS	M	child	possibly Anthony; PPT 1782, 40th; PPT 1783–86 child
Truelove	1783	JMS	F	adult	given with her 4 children (Peggy, Priscilla, Henry, Katey) to Nelly Hite, 1783; sent to Hites, 1801, valued at £85
Turk	1732	AM	M	adult	at Mt. Pleasant; convicted conspirator in Ambrose's murder, given 29 lashes, remanded to FM; 1733 INV, 2d male
Violet	1733	AM	F	child	at Mt. Pleasant
Violet	1782	JMS	F	adult	PPT 1782, 17th
Violet	1845	DM	F	child	deed of trust by JPT; child, 1850
Webster	1782	JMS	M	child	son of Eliza; PPT 1782, 41st (last male listed, prob. infant); given to Nelly Hite, 1783
William	1844	DM	M	child	William Henry Taylor, son of Ralph and Catharine Taylor; deeded to JPT, 1844; with DM in D.C., 1846
Willoughby	1785	JMS	M	child	(poss. Willoughby Taylor), b. ca. 1785; PPT 1785, prob. infant; PPT 1786, last child named; DM deeds to JPT, 1844; at

(Continued)

Name	Year First Mentioned	Owner at First Mention	Sex	Age at First Mention	Remarks
					Toddsberth, 1846; age 60, 1850; valued at $100, 1852; freed by JPT with $200 to resettle with, 1852; an aged man named Willoughby Taylor "migratory" [homeless] in Orange Co., 1869
Wilson	1794	AMII	M	child	son of Patty; 1794 INV
Winny	1765	JMS	F	adult	hired out 1765, 1771, 1775; PPT 1782, 9th; shoe size 6
Winny	1787	JMS	F	child	daughter of Dinar; given to JMJ, 1787
Winny	1844	DM	F	adult	Winny Stuart, b. ca. 1799; deeded to JPT, 1844; married to Matthew Stuart, 1845; at Toddsberth, 1846; valued at $150, 1852
York	1768	JMS	M	adult	hired out 1768, 1773 to John Cave; PPT 1782, 13th; shoe size 6

Notes:

AM = Ambrose Madison (ca. 1696–1732), patriarch of Montpelier; AMII = Ambrose Madison (1755–93), son of JMS; DM = DM Madison (1768–1849); FM = Francis Madison (1753–1800), son of JMS; JMJ = James Madison Jr. (1751–1836); JMS = James Madison Sr. (1723–1801); JPT = John Payne Todd (1792–1852); PPT = Orange County Personal Property Tax Lists; INV = Probate inventory; OCDB = Orange County Deed Book; OCWB = Orange County Will Book; WM = William Madison (1762–1843), son of JMS.

[a] Ranked or listed in this order in subgroups of males, females, and children.

[b] All shoe sizes from shoe list, Madison Account Books and Miscellaneous Papers.

Statistical Profile

N = 261
M = 139
F = 122   Sex ratio (M:F) 114:100

Year of First Mention	Number	Year of First Mention	Number
1732	2	1785	4
1733	27	1786	2
1752	3	1787	22
1765	6	1791	2
1766	4	1794	17
1767	1	1798	1
1768	4	1799	1
1769	2	1801	4
1770	3	1804	1
1772	3	1814	1
1773	5	1834	1
1777	1	1844	27
1780	8	1845	2
1782	89	1846	3
1783	7	1852	3
1784	3	1867	1
		1868	1

Total Number: 261

1738 Tithables (from Little, *Orange County*, 14, 19) William Bell, constable

		Overseer
George Taylor quarter	3	William Harvey
James Taylor quarter	7	Henry Thornton
John Baylor quarter	15	Robert Boannan
Zachary Taylor	9	
Mr. Beale quarter	5	James Coward
Mrs. Madison quarter	6	Erasmus Taylor
Capt. Todd quarter	9	John Botts
Madame Todd quarters (2)	10	John Lucas
Colonel Willis quarter	9	John Burch
Thomas Edmundson	5	John Mackcoy
James Barbour	6	
Thomas Scott	9	
Colonel Chew	10	
Mrs. Madison	8	Edmund Powell
Benjamin Winslow quarter	6	Tod Daultin

117

232

1739 Tithables (from "Orange County Tithe Lists," 22, 23) Elijah Daniel, constable (includes John Scott quarter [3], James Barbour [8] from James Pickett list; Little, *Orange County*, 17)

Overseer

George Taylor	6	
James Taylor quarter	7	Mark Thornton
Baylor quarter	17	Robert Bohanugh
Zachary Taylor	10	
Beale quarter	6	James Choward
Mrs. Madison quarter	6	Black Level
	[9]	
Madame Todd quarters (2)	19	John Botts (9 tithes); John Lucas (10 tithes)
Colonel Willis quarter	8	
Thomas Edmondson	5	John McCoy
James Barbour	8	
Captain Scott quarter	9	
Colonel Chew	8	
	7	Ambrose Powell
Benjamin Winslow quarter	7	Octonia Grant
Erasmus Taylor	3	
Taliaferro quarter	7	William Clark
John Scott quarter	3	
Anthony Head	3	Octonia Grant (not counted as absentee owned, even though Head was overseer under the general ownership of Robert Beverley)
Richard Winslow	3	Octonia Grant (not counted as absentee owned, even though Winslow was overseer under the general ownership of Robert Beverley)

151

Estimated Slave Population: 300

1755 Tithables (from Little, *Orange County*, 38–39) Thomas White, constable

Joseph Molton	14
John Baylor	32
Richard Beale	11
James Madison	13
Frances Madison	5
Richard Winslow	3
George Taylor	16
Madame Taylor	16
Zachary Taylor	11
Francis Taliaferro	27
Richard Barbour	5
Johnny Scott	5
Thomas Chew	4

162

1756 Tithables Thomas White, constable

Joseph Molton	14
John Baylor	32
Richard Beale	11
James/Frances Madison	13
	[3]
George Taylor	22
Mrs. Taylor	13
Zachary Taylor	12
	[27]
Richard Barbour	3
Johnny Scott	5
Thomas Chew	5
Erasmus Taylor	6

(*Continued*)

Thomas White	4
Edmund Taylor	6
Beverly Winslow	10
James Taylor	8
Richard Todd	7

201

Estimated Slave Population: 364

1766 Tithables (from Little, Orange County, 81, 88) William Leak, constable

Richard Brook	7
Hay Taliaferro	3
James Taylor	17
Rowland Thomas	11
George Taylor	19
James Taylor Jr.	3
Robert Terrill	17
Zachary Taylor	15
James Madison	42
Thomas Bell	10
Benjamin Winslow	5
John Baylor	44
Erasmus Taylor	12
Thomas Chew	4
Dangerfield and Hunter	17
Johnny Scott	11

237

1767 Tithables William Leak, constable

	[7]
	[3]
James Taylor	16
	[11]
George Taylor	17
James Taylor Jr.	4
	[17]
Zachary Taylor Sr.	11
James Madison	30
Thomas Bell	10
Benjamin Winslow	5
John Baylor	43
Erasmus Taylor	13
Thomas Chew	4
William Dangerfield quarter	11
	[11]
Prettyman Merry	6
William Moore	18
Jonathan Taylor	5
Hunter quarter	8
Zachary Taylor Jr.	3
Baylor Walker	5
William Dangerfield quarter	5

263

Estimated Slave Population: 500

1782 Selected Taxable Property (Neighbors)

All Slaves	Land Tax[a]	Acres	Value/Acre[b]	Total Value
Zachariah Burnley	61	2,100	£0.60	£1,260.00
Garland Burnley	12	1,700	£0.60	£1,020.00
Thomas Bell	27	729	£0.69[c]	£499.75
John Baylor	83	7,441	£0.42[d]	£3,146.40
Jonathan Cowherd	13	800	£0.60	£480.00
Martha Chew	9	398	£0.60	£238.80
James Coleman Jr.	25	290	£0.25	£72.50
Catlett Conway	25	2,540	£0.51[e]	£1,284.50
John Daniel	8	536	£0.40	£214.40
Benjamin Johnson	18	1,124	£0.52[f]	£581.10
Prettyman Merry	6	377	£0.65	£245.05
James Madison	84	4,186	£0.62[g]	£2,577.35
James Newman	16	707	£0.65	£459.55
James Taylor Jr.	22	462	£0.50	£231.00
James Taylor Sr.	39	2,260	£0.31[h]	£700.60
Charles Taylor	13	632	£0.53[i]	£334.25
George Taylor	18	730	£0.40	£292.00
Zachary Taylor	15	240	£0.35	£84.00
Chapman Taylor	4	400	£0.15	£60.00
Erasmus Taylor	32	695	£0.90	£625.50
Hay Taliaferro	20	1,000	£0.66[j]	£660.00
Henry Winslow	4	1,188	£0.35[k]	£414.60
John Willis	25	2,116	£0.44	£926.40
Ambrose Madison	27	350	£0.45	£157.50
Benjamin Winslow	9	1,600	£0.70	£1,120.00
Johnny Scott	17	1,000	£0.60	£600.00
Thomas Barbour	30	—	—	—[l]

662

[a] From Sparacio and Sparacio, *Orange County.*

[b] Decimalized; presumably pounds sterling.

[c] In two quarters: 470 acres at £0.65 (=£305.50); 259 acres at £0.75 (=£194.25).

[d]In two quarters: 5,741 acres at £0.40 (=£2,296.40); 1,700 acres at £0.50 (=£850).

[e]In two quarters: 1,645 acres at £0.40 (=£658); 895 acres at £0.70 (=£ 626.50).

[f]In two quarters: 542 acres at £0.75 (=£406.50); 582 acres at £0.52 (=£174.60).

[g]In six quarters: 1809 acres at £0.70 (=£1,266.30); 560 acres at £0.35 (=£196); 663 acres at £0.90 (=£596.70); 773 acres at £0.45 (=£347.85); 281 acres at £0.50 (=£140.50); 100 acres at £0.30 (=£30). Figures suggest two arms substantially more developed than the neighborhood average, two farms noticeably less developed (or more worn out) than average, and two at the neighborhood average worth.

[h]In four quarters: 945 acres at £0.60 (=£567); 390 acres at £0.10 (=£39); 400 at £0.10 (=£40); 525 at £0.10 (=£52.50). Therefore, it would appear that three of the four planting farms were obviously worn out or undeveloped.

[i]In two quarters: 215 acres at £0.10 (=£21.50); 417 acres at £0.75 (=£312.75). Both apparently belonged to Charles Taylor Sr., who died during the year. His son, Charles Jr., ran the presumably worn-out (or undeveloped) 215-acre planting farm.

[j]From 1795 list, where it appears that lands were evaluated at just pence (usually three or four) per acre above the 1782 list.

[k]In two quarters: 400 acres at £0.15 (=£60); 788 acres at £0.45 (=£354.60).

[l]The 1795 list had an entry for "Bell & Barbour" with 915 acres at £0.20 (=£183).

Selected Quarters and Plantations near Montpelier, 1782

Name of Household	Number of Free White Males	Number of Total Slaves
Thomas Barbour	3	30
Benjamin Head	2	11
Benjamin Johnson	1	18
William Taliaferro	1	33
Francis Taliaferro	1	31
Laurence Taliaferro	1	61
John Willis	1	10
Zachariah Burnley	4	61
Catlett Conway quarter	1	12
Catlett Conway	1	25
John Baylor quarter	4	85

(*Continued*)

Name of Household	Number of Free White Males	Number of Total Slaves
Mery Bell quarter	——	28
William Beale	1	19
Thomas Coleman	1	6
Martha Chew quarter	——	9
Zachariah Herndon	2	15
James Madison	2	84
Erasmus Taylor	2	32
Charles Taylor	1	13
George Taylor quarter	1	18
James Taylor	2	39
James Taylor Jr.	1	22
Chapman Taylor	2	4
Hay Taliaferro	1	20
Benjamin Winslow	1	9
James Coleman	1	25
Ambrose Madison	1	27
James Newman	——	16
Johny Scott	2	17
Zachary Taylor	1	15
John Willis	1	25

820

APPENDIX E: Dispersal of Madison Family Slaves, 1770s–1850s

By	To	Year	Number	Remarks
James Madison Sr.	Francis Madison	ca. 1773	6	Gideon Aaron Hannah Nell and her son, George Amey (ca. 16 in 1787)

James Madison Sr.	Ambrose Madison	ca. 1780	9	Jacob
				John
				Celia and
				4 children;
				    Savina (sold ca.
				    Patty, Beck,
				    and Casloe
				Catherine (d. ca.
				1783)

James Madison Sr.	James Madison Jr.	ca. 1782	9	Billy (sold before 1787) Davy Dinar and (*Continued*)

By	To	Year	Number	Remarks
				6 children: Dinah, Alice, Winny, Alexander, John, and Amey
James Madison Sr.	William Madison	ca. 1783	3	Abraham Margaret and her son, Henry
James Madison Sr.	Nelly Hite	ca. 1783	15	Upon marriage of Nelly Madison and Isaac Hite of Belle Grove, Frederick County, Va. Jerry Jemmy Sally Milly Eliza and 5 children; Joanna, Dianna, Demas, Pinder, and Webster Truelove and 4 children: Peggy, Priscilla, Henry, and Katey; Truelove and Henry apparently remained at Montpelier until 1801, when James Madison Sr.'s

(*Continued*)

By	To	Year	Number	Remarks
				estate was divided and all slaves bequeathed to Nelly Hite were sent to Belle Grove
James Madison Sr.	Nelly Hite	1801	10	Upon division of James Madison Sr.'s probate estate (*Hite v. Madison*, Orange County Circuit Court, Clerk's Office) Shadrack Robin Anna Milly Black Jonathan Frank Israel Abraham Sarah Richmond
Nelly Madison	Reuben C. and Conway C. Macon[a]	1818	8	(not given)
James Madison Jr.	William Taylor	1834	16	
James Madison Jr.	not known	Feb. 1835	ca. 12	Martineau, *Retrospect*, 2:5; see also Rutland, *James Madison*, 250

(Continued)

By	To	Year	Number	Remarks
Dolley Madison	John Payne Todd	June 1844[b]	ca. 23	Tydal (age 65) Willoughby (60) John (40) Jerry (32) Matthew (45) Winny (45) Milly (40) Sarah (50) Caty (22) and her young children Charlotte (20) Ralph Jr. (33) Joshua (22) Nicholas (36) Nicholas Jr. (13) Gabriel (50) Charles (30) Sylvia (33) and 4 children
Dolley Madison	John Payne Todd	July 1844[b]	20	Lewis Stephen Ralph Sr. Guy Randall Ellick Blind John "as he is called" Sam Tom Ben Sr. Julia Amy Suckey

(Continued)

By	To	Year	Number	Remarks
				Harriett
				Becca
				Nancy
				Fanny
				Abraham
				William
				Ellen
John Payne Todd	Henry W. Moncure	1845	20	leased at Montpelier[c]
John Payne Todd	manumitted out of Virginia	1852	13[d]	each with $200 to resettle with

Notes:

[a] Grandsons of Nelly Madison; children of Sarah Catlett Madison (1764–1843) and Thomas Macon (1765–1838), who married in 1790. Sale price was one dollar (Orange County Court Deed Book, 32:223). This sale represented about half of Nelly Madison's slaves; she distributed the other half among her four children by her will, with James Jr. keeping four (Orange County Court Will Book, 1829, 134).

[b] D. P. Madison deed for slaves to John P. Todd, [16 June 1844], Madison Family Papers. Dolley had remained resident with the majority of the slave community after selling the core 750 acres and the mansion (and perhaps a few slaves) in November 1842 to Richmond lawyer Henry W. Moncure. She left Virginia for Washington, D.C., with one family of domestic slaves (the Taylors) and Paul Jennings. The number of tithables (aged over twelve) dropped from 53 (out of 105 slaves total) in 1840 to 39 in 1843, and there was a total of only 53 slaves of all ages in 1844 (Orange County Court Deed Book, 38:459, 39:416).

[c] Todd apparently leased half of his slaves to Moncure at Montpelier (Personal Property Tax Lists, Orange County). It is likely that Moncure kept about forty slaves (of whom roughly half were tithables), because his successor absentee owner, Benjamin Thornton of England (who bought the declining plantation in 1849), was assessed for forty in 1850 and for seventeen tithables in 1853. In 1854 there were only five tithable slaves at Montpelier (and 180 head of stock). By 1854, then, the historical Madison/Montpelier slave community was entirely dispersed.

[d] Only ten were listed and valuated in his estate inventory, conducted in September (Orange County Court Will Book, 12:18).

Account of Montpelier Plantation, ca. 1795,
from Deposition of Thomas Melton, 28 January 1835,
Hite v. Madison, Orange County Circuit Court, Clerk's Office

[Melton] lived four years as overseer for Colo James Madison decd at his own house in Orange and two years on his farm in Madison which years were in succession. That he was at the burial of said Madison which was in the month of February and in or about the sixth year from the time this deponent commenced living with him as overseer. Colo Madison had four plantations, but one was a very small and unprofitable one, he keeping on it only a few old negros who did not support themselves. His land generally was much worn but he made as good crops as were generally made in the neighborhood. The two last years this deponent lived with him [ca. 1798–99] there was made in each year on all the plantations about 1200 barrels of Corn or a little upwards. Fine crops of wheat were made each of these years for the land but the exact quantity is not known but he supposes it was at least 1500 bushels. The last year this deponent lived with the sd Madison no Tobo [tobacco] was made but the year before a part of a crop was made and the year before that another part crop was made which was all the Tobo made by said Madison while this deponent was with him.* These parts of crops amounted to about 26 Hhds [hogsheads]

---

* Madison's 1801 estate inventory listed 4,445 pounds of finished tobacco at Rocket's commercial tobacco warehouse in Richmond and a further 28,251 pounds of export-quality tobacco at Royston's in Fredericksburg. The plaintiffs in the chancery suit also alleged that the executor of Madison's estate, his son, William, had at some point prior to 1801 been advanced "about 40,000 lbs of tobacco paid by the testator" (*Hite v. Madison,* Orange County Circuit Court, Clerk's Office).

weighing about 1500 [pounds] each & were carried to Market the year pre-
ceeding the said Madison's death. That the plantation of said Madison generally produced about 100,000 [pounds] Hay which was generally worth about
one Dollar per Hundred [hundredweight] but he never sold any except from
the Madison plantation where most of it was made. At the ears [heirs'] sale
there was sold from the Madison plantation 18 or 19 stacks [of hay] which were
parts of two crops. At the death of said Madison there were on hand a large
stock of cattle, but they were very sorry[;] about 180 Hogs of all descriptions.
There were usually Killed for the use of the plantations about sixty fattened
Hogs & this deponent thinks about this number were killed the fall of the year
before the said Madison died. The Horses on the plantations were numerous
but very in different except two [?] of what sold for 141 or 142 $ at the Sale.
The stock of sheep was likewise considerable but they were indifferent the said
Madison having sold off the choice from his flock a short time before his death.
The said Madison had a Blacksmith shop and kept two fires almost constantly
going during working hours & had of course two sets of tools & a large neybor-
hood custom to his shop & further this deponent saith not.

NOTES

ABBREVIATIONS

ECOB	Essex County Court Order Book
JMMB	James Madison Sr. Memorandum Book (1744–1757)
OCOB	Orange County Court Order Book
OCDB	Orange County Court Deed Book
OCWB	Orange County Court Will Book
PPT	Personal Property Tax Lists, Orange County
SCOB	Spotsylvania County Court Order Book
SCWB	Spotsylvania County Court Will Book
TSTD	David Eltis et al., *Trans-Atlantic Slave Trade*

CHAPTER 1

1. SCOB, 1730–38, 151.

2. Ibid., 163.

3. SCOB, 1730–38, 151, 163; see also the thorough but purposefully antiquarian account in Ann Miller, *Short Life,* as well as her argument for Ambrose's birth in 1696 (9).

4. SCOB, 1730–38, 151. Though Philip J. Schwarz, in his fine book on slave "crimes" in colonial and antebellum Virginia, noted the novelty of Madison's murder, he apparently missed the connection with poison; see Schwarz, *Twice Condemned,* 81, 111.

5. Joseph Hawkins, probably an overseer on a neighboring plantation in the 1720s, had patented a small tract of 670 acres nearby in present-day southeastern Orange County (Ann Miller, *Short Life,* 47 n.51). Thus, Pompey was likely a slave in the neighborhood immediately surrounding the Madison enslaved community.

6. SCOB, 1730–38, 151.

7. For Dido, see Madison Account Book and Miscellaneous Papers; PPT; for use of Ambrose, see Henry, *Genealogies*, 137–48.

8. See OCOB, 4:454–55, 5:247, 8:154; see also Grinnan, "Historical Notes," 308–10; cf. Schwarz, *Twice Condemned*, 92.

9. Chambers, "'He Gwine Sing'"; Walsh, "Chesapeake Slave Trade"; Web-based data at http://www.wm.edu/WMQ/Jan01/WalshTableA1.htm [August 2001].

10. OCOB, 2:281.

11. Such as the girl Luckum (Lucumi?) in Caroline County 1740 (Caroline County Order Book, 1:624).

12. For references to Sapony in 1742, see OCOB, 3:309; for other American Indian individuals, see ECOB 4:51; SCOB, 1751, 129; see also the will of Patrick Belsches (1763), which referred to one of his slaves named Indian Ben (Jerdone Account Books). In Essex County in the 1690s–1700s, there was even an "East India Indian" named Occanough who had been panyarred and taken to Virginia by way of England about 1688 and who successfully sued for his freedom in 1707 (ECOB 3:362, 379).

13. Cf. Mullin, *Africa in America*, 24–25.

14. For the Asante-style drum, see Vlach, *By the Work*, 63, 65; Epstein, *Sinful Tunes*, 48–49; see also Bushnell, "Sloane Collection." The drum, now in the Sloane Collection (exhibit 1368) of the British Museum, may be made of a wood other than American cedar (Philip Morgan, personal communication, February 1996).

15. ECOB 4:277. For the Akan day name system, see Quartey-Papafio, "Use of Names," 179–80; Migeod, "Personal Names," 39–40; cf. the list of day names from Jamaica in Long, *History of Jamaica*, 2:427; Gosse, *Naturalist's Sojourn*, 232–33; see also DeCamp, "African Day-Names."

16. Cumberland County Order Book, 9:105; OCOB, 8:127. Between 1761 and 1775, about 1,000 slaves were imported from Gold Coast areas.

17. For Essex County individuals, see Order Book, 5:59, 466, 6:59. For Caroline County individuals, see Order Book, 3:352. For Solomon and Mamout, respectively, see Curtin, *Africa Remembered*, 17–34; Austin, *African Muslims*, 9–15.

18. For examples of age adjudgments, see Amelia County Order Book, 8A:195, 7:29; Cumberland County Order Book, 9:173; SCOB, 1730–38, 334. Mingo might very well be a contraction of Domingo (in Kikongo rendered as Ndolumingo or Ndorumingo), which appears on eighteenth-century Kongolese baptismal lists (John Thornton, personal communication, March 1996).

For the point that Kongolese sent slaves out using Portuguese or Spanish saints' names, see Thornton, "Central African Names," 729–36. For Jefferson, see Betts, *Thomas Jefferson's Farm Book*, 9. Those slaves came from his wife's father, John Wayles. For the point on bottle-trees, see Thompson, *Flash*, 142–45.

19. Ira Berlin's interesting conception of Atlantic Creoles able to negotiate the Scylla and Charybdis of slavery by claiming a sort of cosmopolitan cultural praxis seems to apply largely to the seventeenth century, when slaves (African as well as Creole) constituted only a tiny minority of the colonial population; by the early decades of the eighteenth century, everything would change. Cf. Berlin, "From Creole to African"; see also Berlin, *Many Thousands Gone*.

20. See Douglas Hall, *In Miserable Slavery;* Matthew Lewis, *Journal;* Handler and Bilby, "On the Early Use."

21. Thomas, *Anthropological Report*, 2:303; with different tones, *ôbia* could also mean "stranger" and "wood used by blacksmith." By the mid–nineteenth century, the term *dibia* (*di-* "expert," lit. "husband," and *ôbia* "knowledge/wisdom") had largely replaced the Nri-Awka term to connote "masters of wisdom," or sorcerers/doctors (Umeh, *After God*, i, 73, 76).

22. "Common Era," which simulates A.D.

23. Cf. Berlin, *Many Thousands Gone*, who privileges the influence of the small percentage of black people in the seventeenth century and who tends to see the changes in the eighteenth century as only an African moment.

24. Cf. the arguments for Kongo warfare in the South Carolina Stono Rebellion (1739) and for later Mende/Temne *poro* societies among the Gullah in Thornton, "African Dimensions"; Creel, *"Peculiar People,"* 38–63, 276–302. For intraethnic marriage among "Angolans" in sixteenth-century Mexico, see Palmer, "From Africa to the Americas." For the Yoruban (Nago) *ogboni* cult in the 1809 slave rebellion in Bahia (Brazil), see Reis, *Slave Rebellion*.

25. See Mulroy, "Ethnogenesis."

26. Stuckey, *Slave Culture*, 3–97.

27. Bennett Green, *Word-Book*, 172; Stacy Moore, "'Established and Well Cultivated,'" 82. For the use of *Guinea* as an adjective for variant kinds of fowl, corn, and melon in 1730s Virginia, see Beatty and Mulloy, *William Byrd's Natural History*, 21, 23, 72.

28. Caroline County Order Book, 2:313, 3:356; Betts, *Thomas Jefferson's Farm Book*, 9. It may be that *Guinea* became the functional equivalent of *Igbo*. For example, see the two separate folk rhymes collected in the Upper South by a professor at Tennessee's Fisk University in the early twentieth century, each of which was noted as being a "Guinea or Ebo Rhyme" (Talley, *Negro Folk Rhymes*, 167, 168).

29. Frey, *Water from the Rock,* 286, 287.

30. See, for example, Thornton, "African Experience."

31. The approximate pronunciation stresses are given for the first use of Igbo words and names.

CHAPTER 2

1. Europeans used a slightly broader term, the Bight (Bay) of Biafra, to include the minor trading sites even further east (by south) which included coastal Cameroon and into modern Gabon (to Cape Lopes); however, the main locations within the Bight of Biafra always were along the coast of Calabar. I recently reestimated that overall, 75 percent of slaves exported from the Bight of Biafra were Igbo and that throughout the eighteenth century, the percentage was 80 percent (Chambers, "Significance of Igbo," 107–13). Other peoples embarked in relatively small numbers would have included so-called Moko (that is, Ibíbio and Éfik, including Andóni and Okríka) and in the nineteenth century Ejágham, Ékoi, and perhaps Bámun.

2. The modern Ímo, Enúgu, and Anámbra states of Nigeria. *Isu* is a derogatory term approximating "peasant," originally applied by Aro peoples to farming peoples on the upper Ímo River (Nwokéji, "Biafran Frontier," 155 n.1).

3. Table A.3.

4. Though the statistics on the slave trade in this volume approximate exactness, these are based on estimates and samples, even if they involve large numbers. For further information, see various explanations of the data and their organization in *TSTD*.

5. Equiano, *Interesting Narrative,* ed. Allison, 39, 45, 50, 54–55; Baikie, *Narrative,* 307.

6. Koelle, *Polyglotta Africana,* 7–8; see also Margaret Green, "Igbo Dialects."

7. The self-reference as Umuchukwu was clearly used to intimidate others, as when the headmen at the important site of Bende in 1896 used it to refer to themselves a "god boys" (Leonard, "Notes," 191). For its deeper meanings, see Nwokeji, "Biafran Frontier," esp. 94.

8. Robin Horton, quoted in Hair, "Ethnolinguistic Inventory," 252n.

9. Alagoa, *History,* 138–40.

10. Henderson, *King.*

11. Northrup, *Trade;* see also Nwokeji, "Biafran Frontier."

12. Founded by a man named Usua from an intermixed Igbo-Ibibio town called Mente-Ifufu. The market town's name was anglicized after Leonard's visit in 1896 (Oriji, *Traditions,* 139).

13. Baikie, *Narrative*, 309–10. For evidence on seventeenth century existence of Bende as a market town, see Nwokeji, "Biafran Frontier," 4, 45–46. Northrup has termed the trade system based on coordinated markets a series of "market rings" (*Trade*, 150).

14. Cookey, "Ethnohistorical Reconstruction," 339–40.

15. Northrup, *Trade*, 142. The historiography is growing on the Aro: for new syntheses, see Díkè and Ékèjiúba, *Aro;* Nwokeji, "Biafran Frontier."

16. Nwokeji, "Biafran Frontier," esp. 89–93. The concept incorporated the ends of accumulating wealth and followers and influence and could perhaps be glossed as aggrandizement.

17. A useful concept developed in ibid., 80.

18. Izuogu Mgbóko Ògunúkpo Akúma Nnáchi was an elite freeborn Aro, the great-grandson of Nnachi (b. ca. 1590), the Igbo cofounder of Aro; Ikelionwu was an Awka-born elite who had received the ennobling *ichi* marks that signified high status in the Nri "cultural zone" and who had been enslaved and then served his Aro master Ùfére Mgbókwu Áka (Dike and Ekejiuba, *Aro*, 176–79; Nwokeji, "Biafran Frontier," 75). Dike and Ekejiuba give his birth date as 1703; Nwokeji dates his birth as 1718. The third-most-important Aro "colony" was Inokun in Ibibioland (Nwokeji, "Biafran Frontier," 17).

19. Dike and Ekejiuba, *Aro*, 176. Other major settlements included Aro Ìkwérre, cofounded by Okóro Àkpa and Ìgburúkwu, and site of the most powerful oracle (Kamánu [Kalu]) in southern Igboland. The name Ikwerre literally means "obedient" (Oriji, *Traditions*, 167).

20. Nwokeji, "Biafran Frontier," 2, 24.

21. Ibid., 27. If anything, Dike and Ekejiuba stress even more directly the role of intimidation in Aro expansion, especially Izuogu (*Aro*, 176–78); see also Oriji, *Traditions*, 100. On the violence associated with the Aro throughout Isuama, see Northrup, *Trade*, 131–37.

22. Nwokeji, "Biafran Frontier," 97.

23. Northrup, *Trade*, 129.

24. Alagoa and Fombo, *Chronicle*, 7–16, 74; Baikie, *Narrative*, 314–15, 438; Oriji, *Traditions*, 157–59.

25. Alagoa, *History*, 153–57; for contemporary descriptions, see Baikie, *Narrative*, 337; Crow, *Memoirs*, 83, 212.

26. Alagoa, *History*, 141.

27. Cookey, "Ethnohistorical Reconstruction," 330–32; Ìsichei, *History of the Igbo People*, 10–14; Oriji, *Traditions*, 4; Northrup, *Trade*, 16–20. The main site, Igbo-Ukwu, is located twenty-five miles southwest of Awka and nine miles

from Agukwu. Some 165,000 beads, some of them of red carnelian and possibly originating in India, suggest contact with northern peoples with access to the early trans-Saharan trade (Shaw, *Igbo-Ukwu*, 237–39; for dating, 260–62). Significantly, no cowrie shells were found at Igbo-Ukwu (Northrup, *Trade*, 158).

28. Ònwùejeógwu, *Igbo Civilization*, 79.

29. Ibid., esp. 14–16; see also Àfîgbo, *Ropes of Sand*, chap. 2; Ìsichei, *History of the Igbo People*, 10–16.

30. Equiano, *Interesting Narrative*, ed. Carretta, 32–33; see also Ònwùejeógwu, *Igbo Civilization*, 14.

31. Onwuejeogwu, *Igbo Civilization*; Mébuge-Òbáa II, "Oral History Research Project." When interviewed in April 2002, Ìsínze Ichie Ànágo Òkóye was ninety years old; he died later that year. Much of the following is based on Ichie Anago Okoye's accounts, as written down and organized by Mébuge-Òbáa II. Chief Okoye's death is a supreme tragedy in the ongoing effort to reconstruct Nri history.

32. Mebuge-Obaa II, "Oral History Research Project."

33. Onwuejeogwu, *Igbo Civilization*, 11; for Nri cosmology and religious beliefs, see chap. 3.

34. Based on a comparison of king lists in Thomas, *Anthropological Report*, 1:49–50; Onwuejeogwu, *Igbo Civilization*, 22–29; and Mebuge-Obaa II, "Oral History Research Project," which is the most complete; and a refigured chronology. Very long interregna often occurred between reigns and are incorporated into the preceding reign. My assumptions are that Òbalíke (r. 1889–1926) and Jimófor II (1935 or 1947–ca. 1980) were normative; that Mébuge Òkpóko (r. 1935–47), after a short interregnum of only seven years) was short; that, in the distant past, an undistinguished reign was twenty-five years (including the following interregnum), an average or usual reign was fifty years, an exalted or distinguished reign was seventy-five years, and a magical or watershed reign was a hundred years, with the added assumption that the more distinguished the reign, the longer the interregnum because of the special requirement that the next person be "spiritually inspired" to claim the title. Two early *Eze Nri* (Àmamílo, fl. 1425, and Ànúo, fl. 1500) were omitted from Onwuejeogwu's list.

35. Or 948–1253 (Onwuejeogwu), dates that are improbably early and precise.

36. 1465–1512 and 1512–83 (Onwuejeogwu), respectively.

37. Because of the extreme magical power of his reign and the fact that it came to a bad end, his minimal lineage never again presented a candidate for the office (Mebuge-Obaa II, "Oral History Research Project").

38. Onwuejeogwu, *Igbo Civilization*, 30 n.10; Chambers, "Tracing Igbo," 62; Mebuge-Obaa II, "Oral History Research Project." Onwuejeogwu inexplicably assigns Agu a very long reign (1583–1677).

39. 1677–1701 (Onwuejeogwu).

40. Onwuejeogwu, *Igbo Civilization*, 26; Mebuge-Obaa II, "Oral History Research Project."

41. 1701–24 (Onwuejeogwu).

42. 1724–95 (Onwuejeogwu).

43. Nwankpo (r. ca. 1775–90) is not included in Onwuejeogwu. Nwankpo was the grandson of the assassinated Ezimilo and son of Ewenetem and apparently asserted the right to succession by birth, an idea that itself was an abomination because it violated the criteria of being "spiritually inspired." Nwankpo was deposed by Enweleana with the support of the Council of Advisers, who stripped Nwankpo of his *ozo* title, fined him, and finally declared that he was an imposter (Mebuge-Obaa II, "Oral History Research Project").

44. See also Dike and Ekejiuba, *Aro*, 179.

45. See also Afigbo, *Ropes of Sand*, 64.

46. The two claimants were Mébuge Òkpóko (r. 1935–47) and Jimófor Tabánsi Ùdéne (Jimófor II) (1936 or 1947–1980s). After Mebuge died in 1947, Jimófor II was recognized as the legitimate *Eze Nri*. Mebuge was not included in Onwuejeogwu's list.

47. The *Adama* are the descendants of the indigenous peoples in the Anambra Valley who served as the palace servants of the *Eze Nri* in his ritual seclusion and in effect have maintained a veto power in the choice of a new king. Diodo and Akampisi are currently campaigning to formally secede from Nri and establish themselves as a legally autonomous community, which would entitle them to their own traditional leader (*Eze*); interviews in Nri, Anambra State, December 2003–January 2004.

48. An interesting development in the 1990s was the launching of a revivalist movement of traditional Nri culture, especially the efforts of Prince N. Mebuge-Obaa II, the youngest son of the *Eze Nri*–designate in 1980 (who unexpectedly died that year) and the founder of Museum Piece International. For example, the last age grade to receive *ichi* markings (*Ìfedióra*) was born in the 1910s and 1920s, and two of Eze Mebuge's sons were marked; Eze Mebuge's

ÀkkaNrí (palace dwarf), Àdaéze (1917–2002), was the last living one in Nri (Mebuge-Obaa II, "Oral History Research Project").

CHAPTER 3

1. Onwuejeogwu, *Igbo Civilization,* 8, 38–40; Afigbo, *Ropes of Sand,* 51–54; Dike and Ekejiuba, *Aro,* 109–13; Meek, *Law and Authority,* 166.

2. Igwe, *Onye Turu Ikoro Waa Ya Eze,* 111; Thomas, *Anthropological Report,* 2:353, 291.

3. Oguagha, "Historical and Traditional Evidence," 198.

4. Oriji, *Traditions,* 2–4. The complete phrase is "Igbo neri ji na ede unu nokwa ebea" (Igbo who eat yams and cocoyams), meaning, "Who domesticated these crops, are you around?"

5. Margaret Green, *Ibo Village Affairs,* 7.

6. Okiy, "Indigenous Nigerian Food Plants."

7. Isichei, *History of Nigeria,* 28. Okra is *Hibiscus esculentus.* The plant was cultivated throughout Atlantic Africa and was called *nkru-ma* in Akan, variations of *gombo* in KiKongo; see also Turner, *Africanisms,* 194. In precolonial southern Igboland, okra was considered an aphrodisiac (Leonard, "Lower Niger," 369). See also Captain Crow (ca. 1790–1810), who noted that around Bonny there "are also some vegetables of the Calilue kind (which are much like spinach), and there is no want of ocra, well known in the West Indies as a good ingredient in making soup" (*Memoirs,* 258).

8. Thomas, *Anthropological Report,* 2:70. *Done* may be supposed to read *gone.* The "oil for eating speech" proverb is a staple of Igbo oral literature, much of which speaks to the singular value Igbo place on oblique speech (i.e., signifying).

9. Jackson, *Journal,* 70; Allen, *Narrative,* 1:388. Cassava was incorporated in village agriculture largely after 1900.

10. Crow, *Memoirs,* 195; see also Noble, "Measuring Vernacular Buildings." The "West and Central Africa" norm of ten by ten is from Vlach, *Back of the Big House,* 165. This supposed ten-by-ten protoform is also cited in Ferguson, *Uncommon Ground,* 73. For examples of twelve-by-twelve dwellings and/or statements about the ubiquity of that dimension, see Deetz, *In Small Things Forgotten,* 149–50; Sobel, *World They Made,* 72, 112, 117, 277 n.38.

11. Crowther, "Journal," 430; Equiano, *Interesting Narrative,* ed. Carretta, 36; see also Cookey, "Ethnohistorical Reconstruction," 336; Meek, *Law and Authority,* 88–164, for more general description of the segmentary nature of Igbo social structure.

12. Isichei, *Igbo Worlds*, 97. Of course, this contrasts with the more widely publicized Igbo saying, "Igbo enwegh eze" (Igbo have no king) (Isichei, *History of the Igbo People*, 19).

13. Crowther, "Journal," 19, 432, 434.

14. Oldfield, "Mr. Oldfield's Journal," 1:391; Allen, *Narrative*, 1:391; Crowther, "Journal," 434; Baikie, *Narrative*, 310.

15. Taylor, "Journal," 254, 264; Leonard, "Notes," 197.

16. See, for example, Talbot, *Peoples*, 3:807–17.

17. Ogbalu, *Ilu Igbo*, 119.

18. Taylor, "Journal," 255; Thomas, *Anthropological Report*, 2:161.

19. Ogbalu, *Ilu Igbo*, 47. In general, dance in northern Igboland was associated with masquerades or "mask dramas" (or what one Igbo art historian has called "performance cults"); see Okeke, "Art Culture," 271–72, 279–80. As Okeke wrote, "Dance is central to Igbo arts culture, and the masqueraders' art is very highly regarded" (279). For two examples of such plays or masquerades, see Crow, *Memoirs*, 35 (New Calabar ca. 1791); Jackson, *Journal*, 89–90 (Bonny ca. 1825).

20. For a discussion of the historical uses of these terms, see Chambers, "Significance of Igbo," 105–7, and notes therein. Taylor noted that *beke* had connotations of "foreigner," "stranger," "coming from over the sea," and "spirits," or *mòá* ("Journal," 247, 251, 261, 281). See also the change in use of terms and the persistence of *beke* in the colonial era in Afigbo, *Ropes of Sand*, 284, 347.

21. Lander and Lander, *Journal*, 2:233; see also 193. The two Landers had traveled overland through Yorubaland and then by canoe downriver from Hausaland into riverine Niger Igboland. Richard Lander was generally familiar with the Muslim Fulani and Hausa of the Sokoto Caliphate.

22. Hutchinson, *Narrative*, 252; Crowther, "Journal," 30, 34; Isichei, *Igbo Worlds*, 158–64, 349; Allen, *Narrative*, 1:190; Baikie, *Narrative*, 49; Taylor, "Journal," 278, 279. Cf. Crow, *Memoirs*, 219–220, 277–78. In the 1920s, Talbot wrote, "One of the first things to strike a visitor to this region is the variety of elaborate coiffures displayed by Ibo women" (*Tribes*, 210; see also 211–15).

23. He also noted that the blue dye was "extracted from a berry, and is brighter and richer than any I have seen in Europe" (Equiano, *Interesting Narrative*, ed. Allison, 36). A hundred years later, a member of Baikie's 1854 expedition noted that at Aboh, "they dye their native manufactured cloths with indigo, and so do not appreciate ours of the same hue" (Hutchinson, *Narrative*, 252); see also Isichei, *History of Nigeria*, 57, 61–62.

24. Crow, *Memoirs*, 232; Allen, *Narrative*, 1:394; Becroft and King, "Details," 275, 268; Crowther, "Journal," 34.

25. See Okeke, "Art Culture," 283–84; Alutu, *Nnewi History,* 397.

26. Both quoted in Isichei, *Igbo Worlds,* 159, 163. In the glossary, Isichei gives a half dozen named locally made cotton cloths that were made in places ranging from southern to northern and western Igboland (335, 337, 341, 342).

27. Northrup distinguished between the subsistence-based "marketing" by women (who exchanged local goods) and the profit-based "trading" by men (which was long distance) ("Growth of Trade," 226); see also Oguagha, "Historical and Traditional Evidence," 200; Leith-Ross, *African Women,* 74–75. In the 1930s, Meek wrote, "Perhaps the most striking feature of Ibo life is the keenness displayed by the women in petty trade. Many women, indeed, seem to do little else but attend markets" (*Law and Authority,* 19).

28. Northrup, "Growth of Trade," 225. This basic trade was one of food-stuffs and of salt for livestock (221–25, 226–30; see also Northrup, *Trade,* 16–29; Ukwu, "Development," 648–55).

29. For definitions, see Thomas, *Anthropological Report,* 2:213; Ukwu, "Development," 648; Isichei, *Igbo Worlds,* 340; Alutu, *Nnewi History,* 405. For nineteenth-century references to the Igbo *izu,* see Baikie, *Narrative,* 316; Taylor, "Journal," 296; see also Leonard, "Lower Niger," 332. For mythic and cosmogenic accounts of the origins of the four-day week and the eight-day big week, see Isichei, *Igbo Worlds,* 23; Oguagha, "Historical and Traditional Evidence," 270.

30. Allen, *Narrative,* 1:398.

31. Equiano, *Interesting Narrative,* ed. Allison, 38.

32. See Isichei, *History of the Igbo People,* 61–63; Cookey, "Ethnohistorical Reconstruction," 339–40; Dike and Ekejiuba, *Aro,* 108–9. The timing of the major fairs may have changed during the nineteenth century, becoming twice as frequent: one account from the 1780s suggested that the biggest fairs in the Igbo interior occurred "at uncertain periods, but generally every six weeks" (Falconbridge, *Account,* 12).

33. For ownership and role of local deities, see Talbot, *Tribes,* 281; Arinze, *Sacrifice,* 6.

34. Cf. Baikie, *Narrative,* 297, 337, 316; Crowther, "Journal," 436.

35. Holman, *Holman's Voyage,* 5. Holman was in Old Calabar in 1828.

36. Green, *Ibo Village Affairs,* 253. Green's fieldwork was in Agbaja in 1934 and 1937; see Margaret Green, *Ibo Village Affairs,* xiii. The Onitsha account is from Taylor, "Journal," 288. The Igbo have had a reputation as entrepreneurs and traders par excellence for much of the colonial and postcolonial eras.

37. Barbot, "Abstract," 461; Talbot, *Tribes,* 252–54.

38. Equiano, *Interesting Narrative*, ed. Carretta, 36–37; Allen, *Narrative*, 1:403–4.

39. The story of the Onitsha market women appears in Taylor, "Journal," 362. Taylor may have meant Nike, which was also the site of a powerful regional or intergroup market affiliated with the Aro; see Taylor, "Journal," 276, 301, 303. Talbot asserted that market rule breakers were not simply killed but were bound to a stake driven into the ground at the site of the Market Juju and left there until dead (*Tribes*, 281).

40. Taylor, "Journal," 364.

41. By plundering the Onitsha women, the Nkwerre not only risked war with Onitsha but perhaps more importantly risked the reputation of their market and of their market's deity. After all, who would go to Nkwerre if the market deity there did not punish such things; even if it did, who would want to be there to catch the misfortunes such retributive justice must bring?

42. For Bonny, see Crow, *Memoirs*, 219, 250, 196; Jackson, *Journal*, 71; for Old Calabar, see Holman, *Holman's Voyage*, 16, 5; Duke, "Diary," 72.

43. Jackson, *Journal*, 71; Simmons, "Ethnographic Sketch," 12; for the interior in the early twentieth century, see also Leith-Ross, *African Women*, 74–75; Margaret Green, *Ibo Village Affairs*, 38–39.

44. Leonard, "Lower Niger," 11. The 1896 expedition is described in Leonard, "Notes," 190–207. Leonard eventually married "a number of" Igbo women and wrote an account of Igbo religion that one modern Nigerian historian has called "a work of tremendous insights whose grasp of the conceptual roots of the traditional religion is yet to be equalled or surpassed" (Obiechina, "Introduction," 6). In some places, the first whites did not arrive until 1912 (Ukwu, "Development," 653).

45. For example, writing in the 1930s, one ethnographer in Okigwi Division in central Igboland noted that "On the whole, diet has been surprisingly little affected by Western contact" (Leith-Ross, *African Women*, 64).

46. For the importance of sacrifice to pre-Christian Igbo "cult" or religious worship and community culture, see Arinze, *Sacrifice*. Early ethnographies stressed the animism of Igbo-speaking peoples: see especially Leonard, "Lower Niger," 1906; Thomas, *Anthropological Report*, vol. 1; Talbot, *Tribes*; Meek, *Law and Authority*. One local village historian writing in the 1950s described Igbo animism as "a system of worship attitudes, practices and beliefs rooted in spiritism. It is a religious concept that sees humanity living in the midst of a host of invisibles (good and bad). These invisibles watch unceasingly our actions and appropriately reward or punish us. . . . All these invisibles are of different temperaments and powers" (Alutu, *Nnewi History*, 199).

47. Equiano, *Interesting Narrative,* ed. Carretta, 40; cf. Leonard's observation that "It is customary, as a mark of esteem, gratitude, and fear to their ancestors, but especially to the protector and daily giver of food, to offer up a short prayer or petition, in addition to a certain amount of food and libations of water or liquor, in accordance with what they may happen to be drinking at the time" ("Lower Niger," 434).

48. For a summary treatise on sacrifice in Igboland, see Arinze, *Sacrifice.*

49. Ibid., 22, 111.

50. Baikie wrote, "'Mo ndjó' means a bad or evil spirit" (*Narrative,* 314).

51. See Nwala, *Igbo Philosophy,* 57, 125–26; Arinze, *Sacrifice,* 34–46.

52. Nwala, *Igbo Philosophy,* 57. The ancestors are so important because they have a vested interest in the welfare of the living, and vice versa. This symbiotic relationship also accounts for the incredible proliferation of deities, as basically anyone and everyone can "adopt" or be adopted by a deity, creating a covenant that is binding across generations. See, for example, Alutu's statement that "One peculiar quality of these jujus is that, because they are anthropomorphic, the have issues [children], and because they are botanical, they have branches" (*Nnewi History,* 224).

53. Dike and Ekejiuba, *Aro,* 132; Arinze, *Sacrifice,* 37. The closest thing to "chance" in Igbo ontology is accidentally bumping into a particular type of spirit, *udo,* that is "wicked" and "like electric wire. . . . They do not consider bona fide transgression [of any kind]" (Arinze, *Sacrifice,* 13–14).

54. For *ichu aja,* see Arinze, *Sacrifice,* 37–38, 57, 83.

55. Jackson, *Journal,* 83, 89.

56. Equiano, *Interesting Narrative,* ed. Carretta, 41; cf. Arinze, *Sacrifice,* 42–44.

57. Jackson, *Journal,* 89. Jackson's description reads, "The Priests dressed most fantastically paraded the Town followed by groups of Negroes, all arrayed in singular & uncouth apparel. Some were besmeared with yellow, others with dark paint; many had their faces and bodies striped with curious devices, & wore upon their heads rush Caps, or Hats, ornamented with feathers & the beards of Goats." By the late nineteenth century, *okonko* societies also were regulating trade by maintaining tollhouses on the major roads between Bonny/Opobo and Bende; see Leonard, "Notes," 197–98. Jackson's description also reads remarkably like an *Ekpe* "play" (as well as the Afro-Cuban derivation, *Abakuá*).

58. Jackson, *Journal,* 89–90.

59. Becroft and King, "Details," 276.

60. Taylor, "Journal," 283–84.

61. There have been many fanciful etymologies offered for the word *juju*, including Yoruba/Igala *egugu,* French *dju-dju* (doll), Hausa *dzu-dzu,* and others. Following Leonard, "Lower Niger," this word as used in the Bight of Biafra seems to have local (and probably Igbo) origins; cf. the Efik/Ibibio, who used the term *doctor* to translate, as in "drinking doctor" or "making doctor" (Duke, "Diary," 33–34) or "doctor off it" (Becroft and King, "Details," 261) for doing *mbiam* (swearing oaths by drinking). The other basic Efik/Ibibio reference was directly to *Egbo* (Snelgrave, *New Account,* x) or "blowing Egbo" (Crow, *Memoirs,* 282–83) to describe sacrifice and/or "making medicine." Various specific terms in the modern (1950s) Efik variant of Ibibio were *ndem* (supernatural powers, or local deities), *mbiam* (a magically potent liquid used in swearing oaths), *ibok* (general class of magicomedicines; see also Leonard, "Lower Niger," 290), *ifot* (sorcery/witchcraft), *esere* (poison bean ordeal) (Simmons, "Ethnographic Sketch," 20–22). Koelle's Igbo informants in Sierra Leone (Group V.:A.) all gave exactly the same word for "medicine" (*ogu;* i.e., *ogwu*) (*Polyglotta Africana,* 28).

62. The most useful gloss for Igbo *juju* therefore is "medicine"; see Leonard, "Lower Niger," 290–91; Talbot, *Tribes,* 32.

63. Leonard, "Lower Niger," 291; Arinze, *Sacrifice,* 21.

64. Northrup noted that the origin of the Long Juju term was "obscure" (*Trade,* 137 n.64). Dike and Ekejiuba note that the term came from the Delta States (New Calabar and Bonny) (*Aro,* 154 n.1). See Leonard, "Notes," 191, for the way an Aro man tried to intimidate Leonard by rearing back and saying, "Me be 'God boy'—me be 'God boy.' You be white man; me be 'God boy.'" For the point that Igbo saw early whites as juju, see Jackson, *Journal,* 77; speeches by King Holiday and King Pepple (ca. 1807) in Crow, *Memoirs,* 137, 141; Taylor, "Journal," 247, 261; Cardi, "Ju-ju Laws," 59, who wrote that "in those days [before 1860] a white man was looked upon as Ju-Ju." The four most powerful oracles in Igboland—*Ibinokpabi* (Aro), *Agbala* (Awka), *Igwe-ka-Ala* (Umunneoha), and *Haba* (Agulu)—were physically blown up by British military forces during several invasions or "expeditions" in 1901–6 (Nwala, *Igbo Philosophy,* 17–19, 61).

65. Barbot, "Abstract," 462. Grazilhier went on to note about Andony that, "They are so superstitiously bigotted, that any person whatever, who offers to touch any of those things with his hand, is sure to be severely punished, and in danger of his life. Besides those idols they worship bulls, and a large sort of lizards, called Gouanes in the French Caribbee islands, as their prime gods; and it is not less than death to kill them." The iguana was sacred at Bonny in the early nineteenth century as well; see Crow, *Memoirs,* 212.

66. Talbot, *Tribes*, 108, 125.

67. Crow, *Memoirs*, 208, 244–45.

68. Allen, *Narrative*, 1:242. For a similar "dish of indescribables," see Hutchinson, *Narrative*, 42. Taylor described such a dish as "a small bowl . . . tinged with blood and fowls' feathers, kola-nuts, and cowries" ("Journal," 253–54). For ethnographic references to such "god basins," see Meek, *Law and Authority*, 22–24, 25; Arinze, *Sacrifice*, 20–22. Arinze wrote that charms or medicine (*ogwu*) often comprised "pots containing water, earth, leaves, roots, sticks, rags, etc., buried before the family gate. . . . [T]he farther the place of origin the greater the power ascribed to them" (*Sacrifice*, 21). For a similar artifact among pre-1850s Efik (which was no longer performed in the twentieth century), see Simmons, "Ethnographic Sketch," 71 n.41.

69. For "juju houses," see Leonard, "Notes," 201; Leonard, "Lower Niger," 355–56, 409. Based on the many structures Leonard saw, he wrote, "Inside the Ju-Ju houses . . . are various and numerous clay images of human beings, beasts of different kinds, snakes, leopards, the moon, stars, and the rainbow. Further, the walls are ornamented with the cheap hardware plates of commerce that are brought to them by New Calabar and Aro middlemen in return for produce" ("Lower Niger," 409). Although his observations were limited to southern Igboland and Bende, these juju houses probably were not the celebrated *mbari*, which were supremely decorated structures full of figurines and so forth built specifically so that they could be neglected and fall apart. On the contrary, these juju houses were very well maintained, as Leonard's descriptions make clear.

70. Allen, *Narrative*, 1:244.

71. Margaret Green, *Ibo Village Affairs*, 78.

72. Leonard, "Lower Niger," 415; see also Onwuejeogwu, *Igbo Civilization*, 41, for the *Nri* ideal of what "a good man" was, which basically was to treat everybody right. As a common saying went, "A good man is a man who is upright in his dealings with men—he does not pervert the truth, justice or the peace of Nri. He breaks no taboos and does nothing of which the ancestors will disapprove." For the later importance of revenge and the *lex talionis* (life for a life), see Arinze, *Sacrifice*, 30; Talbot, *Tribes*, 296–99.

73. Margaret Green, *Ibo Village Affairs*, 251; Talbot, *Tribes*, 201–2. Compare with "drinking doctor" at Old Calabar (Duke, "Diary," 33; Simmons, "Ethnographic Sketch," 20–22). Both Igbo and Efik/Ibibio also had a "poison ordeal" (Igbo *oratshi;* Efik *esere*). The Igbo ordeal involved ingesting "sassawood" (sass wood), whereas the Efik ordeal involved the celebrated Calabar

bean (*Physostigma venenosum*), which often killed its subject; see Taylor, "Journal," 341; Leonard, "Lower Niger," 367, 480.

74. Crow, *Memoirs*, 246; Jackson, *Journal*, 77.

75. Leonard, "Notes," 192–94; Crowther, "Journal," 429.

76. Leonard, "Notes," 195–96. Other more permanent forms of such oaths and the reciprocal relationships they created were known as *igbandu* or *ebwando* (joining life together), which were blood-brotherhood pacts to create fictive kinship, often for trading purposes but also between sons-in-law and fathers-in-law, and which the Aro utilized extensively to gain entrée to new communities; see Thomas, *Anthropological Report*, 1:42; Dike and Ekejiuba, *Aro*, 118–19, 163. Northrup (*Trade*, 156) glossed Leonard's "oathing" as "oaths of friendship," but I believe that "oaths of safe passage" is more accurate.

77. Talbot, *Tribes*, 100–101; Meek, *Law and Authority*, 61–65, 105; Margaret Green, *Ibo Village Affairs*, 12, 58–60; see also Njaka, *Igbo Political Culture*, 46–49, which drew on the symbolism of the *ofo* to describe a constituent element of Igbo political culture as "ofoism."

78. Taylor, "Journal," 338, 288; see also Nwala, *Igbo Philosophy*, 63–65, which likens the use of the *ofo* in oathing to the formal Christian use of the Bible when swearing the truth.

79. Crowther, "Journal," 430.

80. The root word is clearly *obia*, as *dibia* is a compound word, *di-* (expert or specialist, lit. "husband") and *-obia* (knowledge/wisdom) (Umeh, *After God*, i, 53, 73–74).

81. Crow, *Memoirs*, 226; Crowther, "Journal," 435; Meek, *Law and Authority*, 82.

82. Talbot, *Tribes*, 131; see also Margaret Green, *Ibo Village Affairs*, 54, for how *dibia* in central Igboland were consulted for any misfortune, theft, or illness as well as for every birth and death.

83. Crowther, "Journal," 435; Crow, *Memoirs*, 211, 225.

84. Crow, *Memoirs*, 227.

85. Equiano, *Interesting Narrative*, ed. Carretta, 42. A couple of sentences are omitted describing how these specialists were called "Ah-affoe-way-cah, which signifies calculators or yearly men, our year being called Ah-affoe." This information is problematical but may be related to the annual new yam festival (*ji-njokku*), as the root of *afo* is the Igbo word for "year." The term *dibia* apparently was universal in and around Igboland; see Koelle, *Polyglotta Africana*, 28; Thomas, *Anthropological Report*, 2:27, 303.

86. Igwe, *Onye Turu Ikoro Waa Ya Eze*, 67; Arinze, *Sacrifice*, 117, 119–20. For more on the *chi* concept, see Taylor, "Journal," 348; Nwala, *Igbo Philosophy*,

46–47; Meek, *Law and Authority*, 55–57. The *chi* concept was also bound up with the central concept of reincarnation, which is why *dibia* were called in at births and to help name babies (Thomas, *Anthropological Report*, 1:30; Meek, *Law and Authority*, 53–54; Margaret Green, *Ibo Village Affairs*, 50).

87. Taylor, "Journal," 341; see also Margaret Green, *Ibo Village Affairs*, 64–65; Dike and Ekejiuba, *Aro*, 170.

88. Arinze, *Sacrifice*, 81.

89. Compare, for example, the description of how the king at New Calabar sacrificed a chicken ca. 1699 and how the king of Old Calabar sacrificed an infant ca. 1713 (see also 1704); Barbot, "Abstract," 462; Snelgrave, *New Account*, vii, x, xiii.

90. For the importance of vultures, see proverbs in Thomas, *Anthropological Report*, 2:157, 382; Arinze, *Sacrifice*, 44.

91. Equiano, *Interesting Narrative*, ed. Carretta, 42.

92. Ibid., 46.

Chapter 4

1. Schwarz, *Twice Condemned*, 45, 103.

2. Ibid., 95–97, 110–11; Morgan, "Slave Life," 438–44; Morgan, *Slave Counterpoint*, 617; see also Berlin, *Many Thousands Gone*, 122–23, even though the slaves clearly were not "confined" to the plantations, whether in the Tidewater or the Piedmont.

3. Based on a systematic search of county order books that found twelve trials involving sixteen slaves: five trials in Caroline, three in Spotsylvania, and four in Orange.

4. For example, see the case of one slave in the Shenandoah Valley who was convicted for "exhibiting or administering to them the seed of a certain Noxious and Poisonous Herb, called James Town Weed" (Norris, *History*, 165).

5. Castiglione, *Viaggio*, 426.

6. Thomas Mann Randolph to Thomas Jefferson, [25 April 1800], ALS, Jefferson Papers.

7. Bennett Green, *Word-Book*, 95.

8. For recent *historical* treatments of obeah, see Chambers, "'My Own Nation,'" 88–90; Handler, "Slave Medicine"; Handler and Bilby, "On the Early Use"; Brown, "Spiritual Terror," 35–45; for contemporary descriptions of practices called "obeah" (sometimes by slaves, and other times by whites) in Jamaica, see Douglas Hall, *In Miserable Slavery*, 56, 61, 279; Matthew Lewis, *Journal*, 62, 84–87, 216, 220–24, 242–43; for elsewhere in the Anglophone

Caribbean, see Abrahams and Szwed, *After Africa*. A full historical understanding of this "sacred science" system as it operated (and as it changed over time) throughout the British West Indies still awaits writing, in part due to the reluctance to begin with the beginning (Igbo *obia/dibia* and to a lesser extent, Ibibio/Efik "doctoring," known variously as *ábíà íbɔk, ákù ídìòŋ, átâ ifìòk, àkɔk íbɔk,* and *ifót*); see Kaufman, *Ibibio Dictionary*, 4, 23, 46, 179, 185. The multiplicity of terms for "sacred science [men]" among Ibibio and other Cross River peoples, who made up an estimated 20 percent of slaves embarked from the Bight of Biafra, in conjunction with the pan-Igbo core concept of *obia*, may account for why this general term was selected, over time and in the British Americas only, for these related practices. Cf. the evidently spurious etymology usually given for *obeah*,—that is, Akan *o-bàyifó* (witchcraft) (most recently in Morgan, *Slave Counterpoint*, 620).

9. Cf. Morgan, *Slave Counterpoint*, 612, 614–15; cf. Sobel, *Trabelin' On*, 43.

10. A thorough analytical, ethnographic, or historical treatment of Igbo *ôbia* and *dibia* also is yet to be written, though many observers and scholars have noted the importance of this practice in "traditional" Igbo culture. The earliest specific reference I have found is Crow, *Memoirs*, writing from his experiences as a slave trader on the Calabar coast ca. 1791–1808, where he noted the prominence of "Oboe doctors, or Dibbeah" who "cure diseases by charms" and whose work included sacrifices, incantations, and herbal concoctions (226–27). See also Taylor, in the vicinity of Onitsha, who defined *dibia* as "doctors" ("Journal," 309, 341). Significantly, by the early nineteenth century, the terms for *doctor* and *medicine* were basically the same across Igboland; see Koelle, *Polyglotta Africana*, 28.

11. Umeh, *After God*, 44–45.

12. Sobel, *Trabelin' On*; Frey, *Water from the Rock*; Frey and Wood, *Come Shouting*; for local studies of plantations in Virginia and South Carolina that suggest only a minority of Christians at the advent of the antebellum era, see Willis, "From the Dictates of Pride"; Cody, "There Was No 'Absalom,' " 588.

13. See, for example, Hyatt, *Hoodoo*, who conducted his research in the 1930s and 1940s.

14. Geier and Reeves, "Digging for Madison," 54, 56–57; for a discussion of blue glass beads in African American archaeology, see Stine, Cabak, and Groover, "Blue Beads"; for African influences in the making of clay tobacco pipes in eighteenth-century Virginia, see Emerson, "Decorated Clay Tobacco Pipes." For more general discussions of the archaeology of African American folk religious practices and artifacts, see Orser, "Archaeology"; Wilkie, "Magic

and Empowerment"; Wilkie, "Secret and Sacred"; Young, "Archaeological Evidence."

15. Samuel Smith, *Essay*, 26–27.

CHAPTER 5

1. *TSTD* no. 16207. Hooke flourished 1710s–30s. He was elected sheriff of Bristol in 1706 and master of the Society of Merchant Venturers in 1712 and was one of the port's leading merchants before 1729 (Minchinton, King, and Waite, *Virginia Slave-Trade Statistics*, 86; Richardson, "Introduction," xxi).

2. Baylor Family Papers, Ledgers, vol. 1. Though the date in the ledger was given as 1721, the sale was listed in vol. 1 (1718–20).

3. Richard Morton, *Colonial Virginia*, 2:444–53, 536–82.

4. Chambers, "Transatlantic Slave Trade," 13; Walsh, "Chesapeake Slave Trade," 150–51.

5. Minchinton, King, and Waite, *Virginia Slave-Trade Statistics*, 100 note d. This commission remained standard through the 1770s; see Boyd, *Papers*, 15:654–55.

6. For example, in the 1730s Baylor's son, John Baylor II (1705–72), owned 143 slaves distributed on eight quarters; Carter, reputedly the richest man in the colony at his death in 1732, owned more than 700 slaves on forty-seven plantations in eighteen counties (Baylor Family Papers, Ledgers, vol. 3, "A List of All the Negroes Belonging to Baylor"; Chambers, "Transatlantic Slave Trade," 12).

7. Minchinton, "Virginia Letters," 281; see also Rawley, *Trans-Atlantic Slave Trade*, 190, which recognized the concentration of Bristol ships to the York River (1715–40).

8. *TSTD*; Query, "Where slaves disembarked = Virginia, and Port of departure = ( )" [Bristol, Liverpool, London, which together comprised 96 percent of Africans landed], and "Where slaves disembarked = Virginia."

9. Though in the third quarter of the century, that capital investment dropped to an annual average of about £93,500. Their investment would decrease dramatically after 1776 to relatively low levels (annual averages of £44,000) not seen since the first quarter of the century. Throughout the eighteenth century, metropolitan merchants could expect a clear profit of 8–10 percent on their initial investment in slaving voyages (Rawley, *Trans-Atlantic Slave Trade*, 261–65).

10. Richardson, "Introduction," xvii. If each voyage represented a capital investment of £3,000, perhaps rising to £4,000 by ca. 1760, then over the course of the Bristol trade to Virginia (1699–1769), metropolitan merchants invested more than £400,000 sterling in supplying Africans to Virginia and thus could

have expected some £1.2 million sterling (or £1.5 million in Virginia money-of-account) in revenues from the sales. See Price, "Buchanan & Simson," 30; Minchinton, "Slave Trade," 42; Donnan, *Documents,* 4:102–17, 120 n.2.

11. Based on various Queries of the *TSTD,* including "25-year period, Where voyage begins = Britain, and port of departure = Bristol." The invested capital figures are estimated based on an initial cost of £3,000 per voyage before 1750 and of £4,000 after 1751, per Richardson, "Introduction," viii; Price, "Buchanan & Simson," 30. These estimates suggest that Bristol merchants invested some £3.6 million in 1701–50 in their overall slaving business, averaging £71,820 annually; the figure for 1701–75 is £5.94 million, an average of £79,200 annually. The number of shipments to Virginia suggests estimates for 1701–50 of a total of £468,000, an average of £9,360 annually; for 1701–75 the estimated figures are 188 ships (32 after 1751), a total of £596,000, and an average of £7,947 annually.

12. Walsh, "Summing," 60, 65, 92–93; Minchinton, "Virginia Letters," 285–86; Price, "Buchanan & Simson," 10.

13. Some 96 percent of the slaves were shipped on Bristol-owned vessels, and 77 percent originated in the Bight of Biafra. See the following eight ships in the *TSTD: Parnel Gally* (no. 16191); *Prince Eugene* (no. 16224); *Anna & Sarah* (no. 16207); *Berkley Gally* (no. 16209); *Greyhound* (no. 16218); *Callabar Merchant* (no. 16240); *Tiverton* (no. 16255); *Hunter* (no. 16266). The ninth ship, the 1719 *Little John* (Captain George Selburn, Virginia registry, from Calabar with fifty-three slaves) is not included in the *TSTD*. See also Minchinton, King, and Waite, *Virginia Slave-Trade Statistics;* Baylor Family Papers, Ledgers, vol. 1.

14. Braxton (1677–1748), of King William County and Newington in the Mantapike neighborhood of King and Queen, also was a slave trade consignment agent for Bristol merchants on the York River and in 1718 was a major tobacco broker with his own tobacco warehouse. He served as burgess for King and Queen 1718–28 and 1742–48, when he was succeeded by his son, George Braxton II (d. 1761), who had married King Carter's youngest daughter, Mary (d. 1736) in 1732. George II's son, Carter Braxton (b. 1736), was a signer of the Declaration of Independence. See King and Queen County Committee, "True Relation," 14, 16; Minchinton, King, and Waite, *Virginia Slave-Trade Statistics,* 88, 96, 102; Glover and Standard, *Colonial Virginia Register,* 54, 56, 60, 67, 79, 83; *State Historical Markers,* 67; Dowdey, *Virginia Dynasties,* 361, 367; Stanard, "Virginia Council Journals," 32:134 n.8.

15. Baylor died shortly before 27 September 1720, the date of Robert Carter's letter to Micajah Perry, which contains the reference to Baylor as "the

great negro seller." At his death, Baylor's estate was valued at £6,500 (presumably sterling), or about £8,650 in Virginia current money (assuming the usual 25 percent discount for colonial money-of-account). Baylor died heavily in debt to the Bristol merchant firm of Isaac Hobhouse and Company, whose partners included Lyonel Lyde and William Challoner (Minchinton, "Virginia Letters," 283 n.50). Before 1729, Challoner financed seven slaving voyages to Virginia, with a specialty in Calabar slaves; between 1722 and 1742, Hobhouse and Company financed at least eleven slaving voyages to Virginia, bringing some 2,100 Africans, apparently all from the Bight of Biafra (Richardson, *Bristol*, vols. 1, 2). Values based on the assumption of an average price of £25 (sterling) per slave, or ca. £33 in Virginia current money.

16. The slaves arrived on the *Tiverton* and the *Callabar* (Baylor Family Papers, Ledgers, vol. 1). The *Callabar Merchant*, owned by Francis Stevens and Company, left Bristol in September 1719, purchased 181 slaves at Calabar, and arrived on the York River in April 1720 with 156 slaves; the *Tiverton*, owned by Abraham Hooke, departed Bristol in December 1719, purchased an estimated 260 slaves at Calabar, and arrived on the York River in July 1720 with 210 slaves (*TSTD*, nos. 16240, 16255). As early as 1707, Larkin Chew owned 5,200 acres in upper King and Queen (now Spotsylvania) county, and by 1724 the young Thomas Chew was church warden of Mattaponi (Brick) Church, St. George's Parish, in eastern Spotsylvania County. By 1734, he was sheriff of the newly formed Orange County (Chew and Chew, "Antient Burial Ground"; SCOB, 1724–30, 31; Scott, *History*, 33).

17. Clark, "Madison Family Bible Records," 81; Bruce, "Public Officers," 6–7; Harrison, "Robert Beverley," 339–41; Alexander, *Journal*, 14.

18. Grymes, *Octonia Grant*, 9–20; Nugent, *Cavaliers and Pioneers*, vol. 3. In addition, in 1728 a patent for an additional 10,000 acres was awarded to Henry Willis, part of "a great survey made by Mr. John Baylor, dec'd, James Taylor, Major Todd, & others" (Nugent, *Cavaliers and Pioneers*, 3:342).

19. See plat of land patents in Klein, *Montpelier Periphery*, 26; Ann Miller, "Counterpoints," 2.

20. For a transcript of the original patent, see Ann Miller, *Short Life*, 51–52.

21. Stanard, "Virginia Council Journals," 33:297; SCOB, 1724–30, 113.

22. Stanard, "Virginia Council Journals," 33:392.

23. Glover and Standard, *Colonial Virginia Register*, 7; Dowdey, *Virginia Dynasties*, 294; Stanard, "Virginia Council Journals," 34:205–6; "Will of Ambrose Madison," 484; OCDB, 2:10; Alexander, *Journal*, 13.

24. Grymes, *Octonia Grant*, 5–6.

25. Assuming an average price of £25 sterling (ca. £33.33 current money) per slave, Madison would have spent over half of his required amount for seating the patent in purchasing these Africans. During the trip, he stayed at three different ordinaries (Magrath, Deniak, Storey) and spent a total of 19 shillings, 2 pence (£0.95), including 5 shillings (or 7 pence each) to feed the slaves (Account Book of Ambrose Madison, 1725–26," Shane Collection).

26. Ann Miller, *Short Life,* 41 n.27, 42–43 n.33.

27. Hugh Jones, *Present State,* 101.

28. Durand de Dauphine (1687), quoted in Upton, "Vernacular Domestic Architecture," 96.

29. These valuations presumably were made in Virginia current money; conversion to pounds sterling would give the following amounts (decimalized); Chew's two quarters at £183.75 (£131.25 and £52.50), and Madison's two at £285 (Mt. Pleasant £255 and the other £30), assuming a 25 percent discount between Virginia money and pounds sterling. Hence, without their direct investment of £400 (£300 sterling), presumably in slaves, Madison and Chew would not have qualified their patent for title.

30. Ann Miller's argument for Madison and Chew both moving to the patent lands in the spring of 1732 is convincing (*Short Life,* 18, 42–43 nn. 30, 33). The year 1729 has been the conventional date of Madison's move to Mt. Pleasant/Montpelier (Brant, *James Madison,* 26; Ketcham, *James Madison,* 4). The name Mt. Pleasant was used in the 1720s, though apparently not afterward; the first recorded use of the name Montpelier appeared in a 1781 letter to James Madison Jr. from his cousin, Edmund Pendleton (*Montpelier Fact Sheet 5*).

31. Daniel Lamport to Ambrose Madison, [12 November 1731], ALS, Shane Collection.

32. Lynne Lewis and Parker, *From Aborigines to Aristocrats,* 22–23, 80, 97, 102; *Montpelier Fact Sheet 3;* Geier and Reeves, "Digging for Madison," 50–51. The Walnut Grove site is marked on a ca. 1865 map (Lynne Lewis and Parker, *From Aborigines to Aristocrats,* 110); the possible northernmost slave quarter is designated as site #UVA-MP19 in Klein, *Montpelier Periphery,* 56, 121.

33. Samford, "Archaeology," 95; see also Fountain, "Historians and Historical Archaeology," 74; Samford, "Power Runs"; for the signal importance of these root-pit cellars for African American archaeology, see Kelso, *Kingsmill Plantations;* Neiman, *"Manner House";* Kelso, "Archaeology"; Kelso, *Archaeology;* Wheaton, "Colonial African American Plantation Villages"; Franklin, "Early Black Spirituality."

34. For the abroad-spouse custom in Piedmont Virginia, see Madison to Morse, [28 March 1823]; for the Negro grapevine in Virginia, see Bennett Green, *Word-Book*, 252 ("Negro-news"); Washington, *Up from Slavery*, 19 ("grape-vine telegraph"); for the historical reality of "Negro daytime" in Virginia, see Davis, *Travels*, 385; Anonymous, "Manner of Living"; Janson, *Stranger*, 404 (for Orange County, ca. 1790s). As George Tucker noted, "The day was their masters; but the night is their own" (*Letters*, 79).

35. The process of creating communities out of these settler groups, therefore, could well have been quite different historically than the model of anthropological creolization would suggest; cf. Mintz and Price, *Birth;* Morgan, *Slave Counterpoint.* However, for new evidence and arguments along the lines of historical creolization, see Gwendolyn Hall, *Africans;* Chambers, "'He Is an African'"; Walsh, *From Calabar to Carter's Grove;* Thornton, *Africa and Africans;* Gomez, *Exchanging;* and, in part, Berlin, *Many Thousands Gone.*

36. The Beverley tract (the Octonia Grant) was for 24,000 acres, though about 10,000 were in the Mt. Pleasant/Montpelier neighborhood, with Winslow inheriting the easternmost 3,000 acres (Grymes, *Octonia Grant,* 8). In 1728, Willis divided his grant (which was located between present-day Gordonsville and Madison Run), and sold 3,333 acres to Thomas Beale of Richmond County, who made it his new seat (Ann Miller, *Antebellum Orange,* 36). In that same year, Willis sold another 3,333 acres, this time to Ambrose Madison, who called this settlement the Black Level quarter (Ann Miller, *Short Life,* 24, 45 n.43).

37. McGroarty, "Family Register," 145–46, 150.

38. Though Todd sold significant parcels early on, including 1,000 acres to his brother-in-law, John Scott of Caroline County, in 1730 (which passed immediately to his son Johny Scott) and several thousand acres to James Barbour; both of these families seated themselves on these lands to the south of Montpelier, even as the Todd family fortunes steadily declined (Ann Miller, *Antebellum Orange,* 31, 59). For reconstructed plats of the major patents in the vicinity, see Ann Miller, *Short Life,* 76–79. The Baylor lands (and presumably the slaves) in Orange County were divided and sold off after 1808 (Ann Miller, *Antebellum Orange,* 66, 110).

39. Walsh, *From Calabar to Carter's Grove,* 92–93.

40. Adapted from 1782 Census; all of these quarters were within an hour or two by foot from Montpelier. The planters were John Bell, Elijah Craig, John T. Hamilton, Joseph Smith, Johnny Scott, Edward Dearing, John Willis, Zachary Taylor, William Webb, Thomas Barbour, John Brookes, John Carter Jr., Benjamin Johnson, William Lucas, Robert Sanford, John Baylor, Mary Bell, James Madison, Ambrose Madison, Martha Chew, Hay Taliaferro, James Taylor,

James Taylor Jr., Erasmus Taylor, George Taylor, Robert Terrell, William Beale, Zachary Herndon, James Newman, John Stockdell, Charles Taylor, Chapman Taylor, Zachariah Burnley, and Catlett Conway.

41. The ship, owned by John Duckinfield, departed Bristol in December 1718, purchased an estimated 229 slaves in Calabar, and arrived on the York River in July 1719 (Baylor Family Papers, Ledgers, vol. 1; *TSTD* no. 16209). Earlier in 1718, the same ship and captain had purchased an estimated 177 slaves at New Calabar (Elem Kalabari) on the Calabar coast and had delivered 141 Africans to the York River (*TSTD* no. 16179).

42. Chambers, "Making of Montpelier," 51, 84–86, 88–89.

CHAPTER 6

1. Cutts, *Memoirs,* 154–55; Levasseur, *Lafayette,* 1:220–25; Virginia Moore, *The Madisons,* 392; see also Ketcham, *James Madison,* 664–65; McCoy, *Last of the Fathers,* 309; for the importance of French style to the Madisons, see Hunt-Jones, *Dolley,* chap. 2. Beazée and his wife came to Virginia in the 1790s and in around 1802 designed the formal garden to the rear of the mansion. They reputedly taught French to a number of slaves (Cutts, *Memoirs,* 157; Hunt-Jones, *Dolley,* 74). In the early nineteenth century, Beazée was paid an annual salary of seven hundred dollars, and he trained a number of slaves as gardener's assistants and lived at Montpelier for "many years" (*Montpelier Fact Sheet* 2).

2. For a stimulating explication of the concept that objects, including books, may constitute "sites of memory" in contradistinction to "history," see Nora, "Between Memory and History."

3. Ibid., 295–96.

4. Ibid., 298.

5. For the 1773–1801 estimate, see "Hite's Acct. for His Distribution [of] Slaves," 12 November 1803, *Hite v. Madison,* Orange County Circuit Court, Clerk's Office. James Madison Sr.'s heirs apparently agreed that he had owned 150 slaves, including 42 whom he had "advanced" to his children before his death in 1801; the total value of those slaves in 1800 Virginia money was about £10,000; see also appendixes A and C; *Hite v. Madison.* For a description of Madison's farm operation ca. 1795, see appendix F. In 1784–85, Madison apparently owned a further 28 slaves across the Rapidan River in Culpeper (now Madison) County (Fothergill and Naugle, *Virginia Tax Payers,* 79). In that year his son, Francis, owned 21 slaves on his 1,000-acre farm next door; in 1783, another son, Ambrose, owned 28 slaves adjacent to Montpelier; and in 1787, James Jr., owned between fifteen and twenty slaves (PPT).

6. Over this period, the number of slaves ranged from a low of 69 in 1800 to a high of 80 in 1801 (PPT).

7. Cf. this schema with that of Ira Berlin for pre-1800 North America, in which he distinguishes charter, plantation, and revolutionary generations.

8. John Maddison died sometime between July 1724 and March 1725 (Nugent, *Cavaliers and Pioneers*, 3:267, 299; see also Ann Miller, *Short Life*, 6–8).

9. N = 354; Caroline County, 1732–45 (196), Spotsylvania County, 1733–43 (110), Orange County, 1735–46 (48) (Caroline County Order Book; SCOB; OCOB).

10. See Cohen, "Slave Names," 106; Long, *History of Jamaica*, 2:427; see also Puckett, "Names"; Turner, *Africanisms*, 101. Of ten examples in Virginia court records, however, only one (Jubo, Essex County, 1725), was female; see ECOB 6:308.

11. Puckett, *Black Names*, 18, 33.

12. Ònyejiúba (Who holds wealth) and Ònwujúba (Death holds wealth) (Njoku, *Dictionary*, 46). The historian is Felicia Ékèjiúba, whose surname can be translated as signifying one of the days of the customary Igbo four-day week, *Ékè* (who/which holds wealth).

13. Phonetically cognate words, such as *úgbo/úbwo* (farm) and *úbê/úbeh* (cowry) (for gambling/gaming), touch on the same structural semantic field (Thomas, *Anthropological Report*, 2:32, 22, 375, 376). The word *úbä* for "canoe" is identified in the early to mid–nineteenth century for the two dialects of Abadsha (Agbaja) and Isoama, or the Nri-Awka/Isuama heartland of north-central Igboland (Koelle, *Polyglotta Africana*, 94; for regional identifications, see Oriji, *Traditions*, 26–41, 82–91).

14. Caroline County Order Books; SCOB; OCOB; Amelia County Order Books; Louisa County Order Books; Jerdone Family Slave Record Book. The Jerdone slaveholding, owned by Francis Jerdone Sr. (1720–71) and then his son, Francis Jr. (1756–1841), included quarters in Louisa, Albemarle, and Spotsylvania Counties and was a heavily Igbo-influenced population; names of slaves included Juba (2), Breechy (2), Calabar (3), Coomba (2), Doctor, Eboe Sarah, and Malebo (b. 1814). In 1810, Eboe Sarah's son, Barnet (b. 1769), was convicted of attempted poisoning and transported out of Virginia; two slaves (a man named Minny and a woman named Violette) were hanged in 1816 for "being concerned in a Conspiracy and insurrection."

15. Bennett Green, *Word-Book*, 206; Ingraham, *Sunny South*, 146; Puckett, "Names," 483; Epstein, *Sinful Tunes*, 141–44; on North Carolina Jonkonnu, see Warren, *Doctor's Experiences*, 202.

16. The name is not known in records for west-central Africa in the six-teenth through nineteenth centuries (John Thornton, personal communica-tion, March 1996), nor does it appear in an extensive (and sometimes fanciful) list of "Bantu" vocabulary of American English (Holloway and Vass, *African Heritage*). And though it was known as a female name in the 1930s, by the 1970s–80s it was no longer used among South Carolina and Georgia Sea Islanders (Gullah) (Baird and Twining, "Names and Naming," 43–52).

17. Lawrence Taliaferro owned a slave named Anica in 1782 as well as a Willoby and a Queen (Little, *Orange County*, 117). James Madison Jr.'s first cousin, Captain Catlett Conway (1751–1827), of Hawfield in central Orange County, also owned a large quarter to the west of Montpelier by 1782. In the nineteenth century, his son, John Fitzhugh Conway (1783–1859), owned a slave named Anica (b. 1785) and two slaves named Madison (b. 1831, 1852, respectively), on his plantation, Firnew, in what is now Madison County (Conway Family Papers). For a Conway family genealogy, see Hayden, *Virginia Genealogies*, 223–64; see also Dove, *Madison County Homes*, 106–7. In the 1782 land enumeration, both of Conway's quarters were in the "room" of Ambrose Madison, who was one of the enumerating constables (Sparacio and Sparacio, *Orange County*, 3). President Madison's niece (the daughter of his sister, Sarah Catlett Macon) later married another of Catlett Conway's sons, Reuben (1788–1838) (Slaughter, *History*, 147). The deep and tangled connections between the Madison and Conway families went back to 1749, when James Sr. married Nelly Conway; James Jr. was born among his maternal relatives at Port Conway on the upper Rappahannock River in 1751.

18. May Burton Sr. owned seven slaves on his 770-acre farm. His son, May Burton Jr., also owned seven slaves that year on a 360-acre farm. The Burton family holdings comprised some twenty slaves on five farms totaling 2,000 acres in the area south of Montpelier (room of Thomas Barbour). See Little, *Orange County*, 111; Sparacio and Sparacio, *Orange County*, 1.

19. For the derivation of the name, see Njoku, *Dictionary*, 38, 54. The female name Anika was uncommon but can be documented in nineteenth-century southern records as well; see Puckett, "Names," 478; Puckett, *Black Names*, 25, 54. In some parts of the South such as Mississippi, the name continues in use even today. For Annika Cumba, see "Each a Mighty Voice"; for Jesse Scott, see Stanton, *Free Some Day*, 150–51. Scott married the daughter of Mary Hemmings.

20. The root is *nná* (father) and the name could mean something like "father watching me"; see Wieschoff, "Social Significance," 219. There were at least two slave women named Annaca in 1782 in Orange County (Little, *Orange*

County, 123, 139). Jefferson's Anakey was born in 1775, likely the daughter of Ned and Phoebe (whom Jefferson had inherited from his slave trader father-in-law, John Wayles, in 1774), and was sold to Reuben Smith in 1791 (Betts, *Thomas Jefferson's Farm Book*, 8, 26, 30; "Jefferson Slaves Database," no. 228).

21. Little, *Orange County*, 130. Bell lived in the same enumeration room and in the same militia precinct as Montpelier. At one point, Ibibio were known to Europeans as Kwa Ibo, as that is what Igboized people in the coastal slave trade entrepôt of Bonny called Ibibio (Forde and Jones, *Ibo and Ibibio-Speaking Peoples*, 9, 68). For the wide phonemic use of *kwa* in precolonial Igbo dialects, see Thomas, *Anthropological Report*, 2:228–30, 232–33. In Moko dialects (Ibibio and Efĩk), the phoneme is extremely widespread, though it is a softer labio-velar and usually represented by -*kp*- (Kaufman, *Ibibio Dictionary;* Goldie, *Dictionary*).

22. Equiano, *Interesting Narrative*, ed. Allison, 39. For tobacco in West Africa at this time, see Walsh, *From Calabar to Carter's Grove*, 61–65, 73. Although recently a scholar who is not a historian but a professor of literature has questioned the veracity of Equiano's claim to have been born in Africa, I do not find the evidence questioning his nativity convincing. In fact, much internal evidence within *Interesting Narrative* suggests that Equiano was indeed Igbo and grew up in north-central Igboland, and the ambiguities and "mistakes" would be consistent with the account of a man who was remembering events that had occurred three decades earlier, when he was a boy; cf. Vincent Carretta, "Olaudah Equiano."

23. SCWB, A:183, et seq.

24. "Orange County Tithe Lists," 22. Erasmus's land was three miles northeast of Orange on the road to Fredericksburg; he married Jane Moore of King George County, the half-sister of Nelly Conway Madison, in about 1750 (Dandridge, "Family Notes," 6, 8, 47). Anne S. Dandridge was the stepdaughter of Elizabeth (Taylor) Bliss (1824–1909), the daughter of President Zachary Taylor (1784–1850). Anne married Philip Pendleton Dandridge (d. 1881) in 1858 (Dandridge, "Family Notes," ii, 111–12; Dandridge, "Addenda," 11, 13). In 1782, Erasmus Taylor had thirty-two slaves on his 695-acre farm; the land was valued at 18 shillings per acre, which was far above the average valuation in the county (Little, *Orange County*, 132; Sparacio and Sparacio, *Orange County*, 13).

25. Both Mt. Pleasant and Todds Folly were on the north side of the mountain that roughly bisected the patent (Ann Miller, *Short Life*, 54).

26. Forde and Jones, *Ibo and Ibibio-Speaking Peoples*, 16; see also Margaret Green, *Ibo Village Affairs*, 12; Meek, *Law and Authority*, 127–28; Talbot, *Peoples*, 3:541–42; Leonard, "Lower Niger," 69, for the importance of philosophical "dualism."

27. Meek, *Law and Authority,* 127–28.

28. Data derived from Little, *Orange County.*

29. It is plausible that the regional numbers of slaves and patterns of slave-holding in 1782 were comparable to the 1760s and early 1770s, as appears to have been the case at Montpelier, though the figures for 1782 would have reflected at least some of the disruption and loss (or gain) relating to the Revolutionary War.

30. As a whole, there were 3,195 enumerated slaves in Orange in 1782 and 393 slave owners out of 704 households. The region of densest slave population was perforce the region of the larger plantations; in the Little Mountains–Blue Run district, there were 6 slaves for every 1 free white male. In figuring precinct- and district-level numbers, it is important to watch for the many addition errors in Little's compilation; these numbers are corrected.

31. Madison to Morse, [28 March 1823].

32. Meek, *Law and Authority,* 19, writing of Onitsha and Owerri provinces of north-central Igboland in the late 1920s and early 1930s; for suggestions of extensive road or trade path networks from at least the early eighteenth century, see Díkè and Ékèjiúba, *Aro,* 122–23.

33. See also Lynne Lewis and Parker, *From Aborigines to Aristocrats.*

34. OCOB, 1:459.

35. Cf. Forde and Jones, *Ibo and Ibibio-Speaking Peoples,* 17, summarizing the early colonial Igbo ethnography: "The land and homesteads along a given path (*ama*) are usually those of the men of one patrilineage."

36. This was the case for places as diverse as Philadelphia, the Chesapeake, the Carolina low country, Jamaica, Barbados, and the Leeward Islands. For the derivation, see Turner, *Africanisms,* 191; Kaufman, *Ibibio Dictionary,* 223.

37. Turner, *Africanisms,* 191; Oxford English Dictionary (compact ed.), 288; Barclay, *Voyages and Travels,* 26; cf. Becroft and King, "Details," 261. Interior Igbo did not have a common term for white folks until at least the 1850s. It is noteworthy that Mande *toubab,* Akan *abroni,* or Western Bantu *mundele* did not resonate with slaves in the British Americas; this is especially so for *mundele,* since Kongo and Angolan peoples were widely distributed. By comparison, the Igboesque *buckra* was commonly adopted, even where, as in South Carolina, there were comparatively few Igbo.

38. See Schuler, "Afro-American Slave Culture," 124, 131, 132.

39. "The Life, History, and Unparalleled Sufferings of John Jea, the African Preacher [1815]," in Hodges, *Black Itinerants,* 90.

40. Taylor, "Journal," 264. The locals routinely called Taylor *eze.*

CHAPTER 7

1. For an excellent account of a similarly predominant Eboe community of slaves in eighteenth-century Tidewater Virginia, see Walsh, *From Calabar to Carter's Grove.*

2. See various County Order Books. Madison was brought onto the county court in Orange in 1749.

3. SCWB, A:172.

4. For an interesting discussion of entail and slave property in colonial Virginia, see Walsh, *From Calabar to Carter's Grove.*

5. In 1745, James Sr. and his mother, Frances, together were levied for eighteen adult slaves; Elizabeth (Madison) Willis was widowed in 1750 and remarried the following year to Richard Beale (1723–ca. 1771), whose plantation was just to the south of Montpelier. Her one-third widow's dower when the Willis estate was divided in 1753 was eight adults (PPT; Clark, "Madison Family Bible Records," 81; Willis to Smith, 3 February 1986; OCWB, 2:180).

6. John was the son of Colonel Henry Willis (1692–1740) of Willis Hall near Fredericksburg, but he had a plantation near the Madisons. John apparently seated part of the large 10,000-acre tract patented by his father in 1728; the original description of the land was along "Bleuing Run; on the County Line; to the poison fields, on line of Todd & Company; to the SE side of the Ragged Mts." (Nugent, *Cavaliers and Pioneers,* 3:342).

7. OCOB, 2:23. Erasmus Taylor had been the young overseer of the newly established Black Level quarter in 1738.

8. Madison was appointed guardian in November 1752 and posted his bond (giving surety) to secure her estate in February 1753 (OCOB, 5:392, 411). For the division of the Willis estate, see OCWB, 2:146, 179–80. A trustee in effect acquired the usufruct of the beneficiary's estate and guaranteed to preserve the property until the child either came of legal age or married.

9. Crop Memoranda 1745–48, JMMB; 1745–49 accounts, JMMB. In 1745, James paid quitrents on 750 acres; in 1747, his mother paid the quitrents on the 1,900 acres of Montpelier proper.

10. JMMB, including Crop Memoranda. The overseer at the Home House quarter was Thomas Dauhany.

11. Johann Schoepf, *Travels in the Confederation, 1783–1784* (1911), quoted in Brant, *James Madison,* 42.

12. Orange County 1785 Census.

13. Cf. Carson et al., "Impermanent Architecture."

14. Chambers, "Making of Montpelier," 107–8 nn.36–41.

15. Based on estimates of land-use from crop figures in Crop Memoranda, JMMB; see also Brant, *James Madison*, 41.

16. Crop Memoranda, [16], JMMB. In August 1755, Rev. James Maury wrote, "Our spring crops of wheat, barley, oats, and rye, have been ruined by an early drought. Our Indian corn, the main support of man and beast in this part of the world, has been so much hurt by a later drought, that I fear scarce enough will be made for the sustenance of the people, exclusive of our stocks, the great numbers of which must in all probability perish this winter" (Richard Morton, *Colonial Virginia*, 2:681).

17. Walsh, "Plantation Management," 395; cf. Williams, "Small Farmer," 417, who gave a rough estimate of 1,500–2,000 pounds per hand.

18. Crop Memoranda, JMMB. Figures for 1755 are excluded; in 1757, Montpelier farms produced 38,650 pounds of tobacco.

19. It appears that 1745–57, Madison generally paid the overseers with one-sixth of the crop.

20. Madison averaged £176.34 (decimalized) between 1750 and 1754; the greatest jump in tobacco production came after his marriage, when his income surged from £44.94 in 1749 to £188.29 in 1750. Prices in these years varied from an estimated 1.17 pence per pound (or £0.49 per hundredweight) to 3.1 pence per pound (£1.29 per hundredweight). The most common prices were 18 shillings (£0.90) per hundredweight (1750, 1752, 1754); 25 shillings (£1.25) in 1755; 20 shillings (£1.00) in 1756; and 26 shillings (£1.30) in 1757.

21. Based on changes in tobacco marks on hogsheads listed 1745–57, in Crop Memoranda, JMMB.

22. Madison's executorship of John Willis's estate between 1750 and 1752 produced at least £200 in cash income (tobacco sales, slave hirings, pork sales). The estimated total cost of starting the Mill Quarter, including the buildings, provisions, rebuilding the millworks, and miller's pay, was around £75–100 (Chambers, "Making of Montpelier," 115 n.81).

23. Material on Willis slaves drawn from "Book of Accompts Belonging to Mary Willis (1755 to 1763)," which was misaccessioned as Madison's own accounts (see archivist's postscript), Shane Collection.

24. About half the Willis slaves were at the Spotsylvania plantation under Robert Dudley; a quarter were at her father's old Mountain Quarter; another quarter were at the Mine Run farm under Connor; one or two working hands were on a 100-acre plot leased for Mary's direct financial benefit; and at least three, including two carpenters, were leased out in Spotsylvania.

25. She married Captain William Daingerfield of Coventry, Spotsylvania County. During this year, the trustee accounts for the slaves in Spotsylvania and Mine Run end ("Book of Accompts Belonging to Mary Willis," Shane Collection).

26. See note from Daingerfield acknowledging receipt of his new wife's slaves (Madison-Pendleton Correspondence).

27. For architectural history, see Hunt-Jones, *Dolley*, 59–61; Ann Miller, *Antebellum Orange*, 100; for the symbolic importance of the "gentleman's seat" in the reproduction of social structure and hierarchy in eighteenth-century Virginia, see Isaac, *Transformation*, 34–42; Upton, "White and Black Landscapes."

28. Scott, *History*, 44, 208, 260–61. Cf. the slower rise of James Madison Sr.'s cousin, George Taylor, who served as captain, burgess, clerk of the court, and lieutenant colonel before being appointed county lieutenant in 1757. Taylor was not commissioned a full colonel until 1760 (Scott, *History*, 258–59, 279; OCOB, 6:334, 552).

29. OCOB, 7:449, 8:55.

30. In this world where hierarchy was closely guarded, respected, and enforced, at least among the gentry, lists were generally composed in rank order.

31. OCOB, 8:27–28.

CHAPTER 8

1. Barbour, *Eulogium*, 28.

2. Cf. Berlin, *Many Thousands Gone*.

3. Madison Account Books and Miscellaneous Papers; PPT 1782. In 1777, James Madison Sr. purchased fifteen skillets and eighteen "small ovens." Around 1787, at least six families numbering 27 slaves can be identified (OCWB, 4:1 et seq.; *Hite v. Madison*, Orange County Circuit Court, Clerk's Office). In 1782, Colonel Madison, James Jr., and Ambrose (next door at Woodley) together owned 124 slaves.

4. In 1785, Woodley contained one dwelling and seven other buildings; the absentee-owned Baylor plantation had nineteen buildings.

5. There is no evidence that Walnut Grove was organized as a single street.

6. Madison to Clay and Midgley, 24 August 1760, 19 June 1770, ALS, Shane Collection.

7. James Madison Sr.'s 1801 probate inventory included a third bellows (of "little value") and the following tools: three anvils, three vises, six branding irons, ten pairs of tongs, three shovels, fourteen hammers, two pair of pincers, two butteries, thirteen files, one drill, and three steelyards (OCWB, 4:54).

8. Quoted in Schlotterbeck, "Plantation and Farm," 64. In 1801 Colonel Madison owned one set of cooper's tools and the following carpenter's tools: one bung borer, three augurs, one chisel, one gouge, one set of joiner's tools (including a plow plane and a jack plane), one adze, two handsaws, and three grindstones; he also owned three brandy stills and pewter coils (worms) (OCWB 4:54; see also Scott, *History,* 73).

9. "Ciphering by J. M. Sr. on the Production Corn, Wheat, & Tobacco 1774–1779—Presumably Dated [1779] [*sic*]," AMs, Shane Collection.

10. Cf. 1801 probate inventory, when Madison had 32,700 pounds at warehouses, and the later assertion by some of his heirs that he had advanced 40,000 pounds to his son, William, before 1801 (*Hite v. Madison,* Orange County Circuit Court, Clerk's Office).

11. In 1774 Madison produced only forty-nine bushels of wheat. Between 1774 and 1777, corn production increased from 1,102 barrels to 1,487 (in 1776) to 2,575 barrels (1777) ("Ciphering by J. M. Sr. on the Production Corn, Wheat, & Tobacco 1774–1779—presumably dated [1779] [*sic*]," AMs, Shane Collection). Colonel Madison apparently invested in wheat production only after the revolution and perhaps did so in part by cutting back on the effort on corn. Prices for corn in the 1760s and 1770s generally were high—perhaps 25 percent higher than they had been (on average) in the 1750s (Bureau of the Census, *Historical Statistics,* 1197).

12. Based on his ownership in 1801 of eighteen hilling hoes, fourteen plows and colters, twelve scythes, and nine "cradles." He also had nine ox yokes, ten pair of hames, and six swingletrees, all used to harness plows and carts. He also owned one harrow, used to smooth the plowed field just before planting.

13. Based on Madison's ownership of seventeen narrow axes; the probate inventory also included two broadaxes, one crosscut saw, and seven pair wedges (for splitting larger logs).

14. Hunt, *Writings,* 2:15.

15. Bear, *Thomas Jefferson's Account Books,* 3:538, 580.

16. For shoe list, see Madison Account Books and Miscellaneous Papers; for Colonel Madison's directive concerning Moses and Harry, see his will (written 1787); for Sawney, see chap. 10. Madison paid £150 to the estate for Moses in 1802, "according to will of testator" (OCWB, 5:242 et seq.).

17. *Richmond Virginia Gazette or American Advertiser,* 8 November 1786, in Windley, *Runaway Slave Advertisements,* 1:388–89. Anthony's rather colorful dress also contrasts interestingly with the generally austere clothing of James Madison Jr. (Cutts, *Memoirs*).

18. For the long unresolved chancery court case, see *Hite v. Madison,* Orange County Circuit Court, Clerk's Office.

19. At least sixty-eight whites purchased items during these sales.

20. Hackett et al., *Papers,* 154, 155 n.3.

21. *Hite v. Madison,* Orange County Circuit Court, Clerk's Office. Each one-fifth share of the children was valued at some £1,650 [£1,646.50]; the total value therefore is estimated at £12,375 (or $41,250).

22. "Hite's Acct. for His Distribution [of] Slaves," 12 November 1803, *Hite v. Madison,* Orange County Circuit Court, Clerk's Office. For the Hites and their seat of Belle Grove, see Terry Morton, *Belle Grove.*

23. James also bought fifteen grubbing hoes, twelve hilling hoes, and twelve narrow axes ("Account of Sales of Estate of James Madison, 1801," *Hite v. Madison,* Orange County Circuit Court, Clerk's Office).

24. *Hite v. Madison,* Orange County Circuit Court, Clerk's Office. The colonel had even left about two hundred pounds in gold coin locked in his "cabinet" (safe), which James turned over to his mother (Brugger et al., *Papers,* 123–24; *Hite v. Madison,* Orange County Circuit Court, Clerk's Office). On the verso of an undated receipt (ca. 1801–18), the conversion rate of pounds to dollars was figured at 6 shillings per dollar, or .3 pounds per dollar; therefore, two hundred pounds, fourteen shillings, nine pence (£200.74 decimalized) in gold coin was worth $669.13.

25. *Madison v. Madison;* see also Hackett et al., *Papers,* 126. The local chancery suit was not resolved until 1838. The court ordered that all the residuary slaves at Colonel Madison's death in 1801 were to be "divided among the wife and children who survived him, equalie, the bequest as to those who died before him being lapsed." It is interesting that James Jr. sought this order since he had received a legal opinion in June 1801 in which his lawyer, Richmond's Edmund Randolph, determined that "The bequest of negroes and other personal estate to the testator's children does not exclude the representatives of those, who died between the date of the will and his death" (Brugger et al., *Papers,* 359).

26. The sources for this discussion are Hackett et al., *Papers,* 125–26 n.1; Hunt, *Writings,* 6:214–15; *Hite v. Madison,* Orange County Circuit Court, Clerk's Office; Fothergill and Naugle, *Virginia Tax Payers,* 79.

27. Colonel Madison's farm may have been the tract that he bought from Benjamin Grymes in 1784. The commercial mill was situated on a 16.5 acre lot.

28. An example of the complicated figuring that occasionally came with partible inheritance of personal property is how this sum was divided among the heirs in 1811. The executor was William Madison, but James Jr. apparently

did the rather complicated math needed to arrive at the amounts dispersed: James got a one quarter share ($461.25) plus a quarter of his father's share ($115.31) plus two-fifths of half of his father's share ($92.24) plus half of the remaining fifth of his father's share ($23.07), for a total of $692.41. William got the same amount, and the rest ($460.18) was split up among the various nephews and nieces with an interest in the property. But William actually received $958.15, since several of James's shares were paid to William between 1808 and 1811 (*Hite v. Madison*, Orange County Circuit Court, Clerk's Office). It is instructive that Colonel Madison's slaves were worth about twelve times the market value of a commercial flour mill in 1800–1810.

29. Because Francis died in 1800, it is unlikely that he or his heirs inherited many slaves from this group. In effect, these slaves offset the departure of the Hite slaves, at least in numbers. It is also possible that these slaves were among the people divided out to Sarah Madison Macon, Frances Madison Rose, or William Madison, though they apparently did not go to Nelly Madison Hite.

30. See Virginia Moore, *The Madisons*, 371–87, 406; Ketcham, *James Madison*, 623; McCoy, *Last of the Fathers*, 257. Madison's salary as president had been $25,000 per year, but between 1813 and 1836 he paid out about $20,000 to discharge Todd's bad debts and may have paid out as much as $40,000 total (Ketcham, *James Madison*, 616, 623). By the summer of 1832, Madison had mortgaged half of his landholdings (Virginia Moore, *The Madisons*, 448).

31. Virginia Moore, *The Madisons*, 419.

32. Ketcham, *James Madison*, 625–29; McCoy, *Last of the Fathers*, 281–84.

33. Scott, *History*, 178.

34. Rutland, *James Madison*, 250. For the difficulties that faced slaves who accepted transportation in exchange for manumission (in this case, from 1833), see the letters to Madison's close friend, John Hartwell Cocke of Bremo, in Randall M. Miller, *"Dear Master."*

35. In 1835, Madison believed that about a third of his slaves were under the age of five (Rutland, *James Madison*, 250). In 1840, the U.S. Census recorded Madison owning 105 slaves, 33 of them age ten or younger. Of the slaves owned by Dolley Madison in that year, 33 were employed directly in agriculture, 3 in manufactures, and 9 in "mining."

36. Between 1845 and 1849, the number of slaves on which Todd paid county levies declined sharply from twenty to four; in 1851, he paid taxes on five slaves over age sixteen. In 1850, his eleven slaves were all aged over fifty, but his 1851 will mentioned fifteen slaves by name, all of whom were to be manumitted. Thornton bought the reduced plantation in October 1849 and

was not assessed for a single slave in that year and in 1850; however, the 1850 U.S. Census listed forty slaves for Thornton. For the various 1844 deeds of personal property from Dolley to her son, see Madison Family Papers. These possessions included James Madison's personal library, which contained 4,000 published volumes and thousands of broadsheet pamphlets that Todd purportedly sold off in the late 1840s ("Papers Concerning the Madison Papers by William Cabell Rives [1857–66]," Ms., Madison Family Papers).

37. OCWB, 12:18.

38. 1850 and 1860 U.S. Census, Agriculture Schedule. Much of the land itself may have been left fallow during this decade, as the estimated property cash value more than doubled to $46,600 in 1860.

39. Ann Miller, *Antebellum Orange*, 30.

40. McCoy, *Last of the Fathers*, 255–56, 259–60, 318. Taylor refused to accept a girl named Betty because of a "condition . . . annulling her sale," and he refused to pay the final installment of $1,800.

41. Martineau, *Retrospect*, 2:5, mentions this sale, which likely was not a reference to the earlier sale to Taylor. If Madison, even as a reluctant seller, followed the general conventions in the domestic slave trade to Louisiana at this time, most of those sold would have been "prime-aged slaves" between ten and thirty see Pritchett and Freudenberger, "Peculiar Sample," 110–11, 121.

42. See deeds dated 16 June, 17 July 1844, 28 September 1846, in Madison Family Papers. It is unclear whether these slaves were included among those Todd manumitted by his will in 1852.

43. PPT 1867.

44. The sources for the following discussion are Orange County Marriage Book, 2:3; 1900 U.S. Census, Population Schedule; Hunt, *Life*, 380–81; Tyler, "Chart Pedigree," 39; Clark, "Madison Family Bible Records," 80–84; PPT 1869.

45. Elmer Vivian Johnson, Burr Hill, Va., 10 March 1936, in Works Progress Administration, "Virginia Historical Inventory"; for other references to conjuring among ex-slaves in the 1930s in Virginia, see Perdue, Barden, and Phillips, *Weevils*, 221, 244, 246, 263, 267, 278, 310, 324.

46. Souders and Souders, *Rock*, 49. This fine little book is an exemplar of local "amateur" scholarship in the sense that the work is a labor of love.

CHAPTER 9

1. See, for example, McCall, "Rethinking," 259–60, 264.

2. Gutman, *Black Family*, 198–204; Inscoe, "Carolina Slave Names," 527; Cody, "There Was No 'Absalom,' " 573, 595–96.

3. Cody, "There Was No 'Absalom,' " 572–73.

4. Based on a biographical data set of 261 separate slaves owned by Madison and descendant masters (Frances Taylor, Colonel James Madison, Nelly Madison, Ambrose Madison II, Francis Madison, William Madison, Nelly Madison Hite, President James and Dolley Madison, John Payne Todd) and including one man, Edward Taylor, who was resident on Montpelier in 1868.

5. SCWB, A:183.

6. Though I have counted her as the same person in my biographical database. As a classical or whimsical name, of course, Dido was not uncommon among enslaved women; the classical reference is Virgil's *Aeneid*, in which she is the mythical founder and queen of Carthage who killed herself when her lover, Aeneas, deserted her.

7. Chambers, "Madison Slaves Biographical Database," nos. 79, 80.

8. Further research or the inclusion of slaves of allied families such as the Beales, Conways, Macons, Taliaferros, Taylors, Willises, and Hites in Frederick County, some of whom may have been descended from Madison's ca. 1733 population, may increase this proportion.

9. See Cutts, *Memoirs*, 154–55; McCoy, *Last of the Fathers*, 309.

10. PPT 1785, 1869; Little, *Orange County*, 117, 118, 130, 134.

11. Battaile's father, Nicholas, married Hannah Taylor (b. 1718),the sister of Frances Taylor Madison, Ambrose Madison's wife (Dandridge, "Family Notes," 7). Nicholas Battaile also was a close associate of Francis Conway (d. 1733), the father of Nelly Conway Madison (see "Extracts," 203). Lawrence owned two quarters (total 1,800 acres) in 1782 in the room of Ambrose Madison II (Sparacio and Sparacio, *Orange County*, 2). In 1780, Major John Willis married Anne Willis (d. 1799), the daughter of Colonel Madison's sister, Elizabeth Madison Beale, by her first marriage (Willis to Smith, 3 February 1986, citing Byrd C. Willis, *A Sketch of the Willis Family, Fredericksburg Branch* [1909], and B. C. Willis and R. W. Willis, *A Sketch of the Willis Family of Virginia* [1906]). In 1782 Major Willis owned two quarters (total of 2,116 acres) in Madison's room of the county (Sparacio and Sparacio, *Orange County*, 13). Catlett Conway (1751–1827) of Hawfield was the son and namesake of Nelly Conway Madison's brother, Catlett (1719–ca. 1750), and in 1782 the younger Catlett owned two quarters (2,540 acres) in Madison's room (Hayden, *Virginia Genealogies*, 244, 257; Dove, *Madison County Homes*, 106–7; Sparacio and Sparacio, *Orange County*, 3). For Taliaferros, see Hayden, *Virginia Genealogies*, 254; "Extracts," 203.

12. OCDB, 40:26.

13. D. P. Madison deed for slaves to John P. Todd, [16 June 1844], Madison Family Papers; OCDB, 40:26, 129, 210. Toddsberth was a 9.5 acre residence on Madison's Run, southeast of Woodley, probably part of a 50-acre mill site Dolley deeded to her son in 1838; by the 1860s, it was in complete ruin (OCDB, 37:177; Ann Miller, *Short Life*, 30).

14. D. P. Madison deed for slaves to John P. Todd, [16 June 1844], Madison Family Papers; OCWB, 11:476.

15. 1850 U.S. Census, Slave Schedule; OCWB, 11:476, 12:18. Virginia's Manumission Act of 1806 required that all slaves manumitted had to leave the commonwealth within twelve months of achieving their freedom, although freed slaves increasingly petitioned for permission to remain or simply evaded prosecution (Berlin, *Slaves without Masters*, 146–48).

16. Elizabeth Lee was the daughter of the powerful Hancock (d. 1709) and Sarah Allerton Lee, of Ditcheley, Northumberland County.

17. All relations and dates are from Dandridge, "Family Notes."

18. The following men worked or resided on Montpelier in the aftermath of Emancipation and may have included former Madison slaves: (1867) John Allen, Jack Brook, Walker Brook, Wilson Banister, John Albert, George Gilmore, Major Height [Hite], Benjamin Jones, James K. Polk; (1868) James Horde, Edward Taylor, Dangerfield Walker; (1869) George Anderson, Jack Brock, George Gilmer, James K. Jackson, Thomas Jackson (PPT 1867–69).

19. Advertisement by Robert Overall, who lived twelve miles above Dumfries in Stafford County (Meaders, *Advertisements*, 41).

20. In 1910 in Orange County, there were at least seven black heads of households named Taylor (including Conway G. Taylor, a clothes cleaner, and gardener named Jefferson Taylor); there also was one Madison Hoord, a farm laborer and perhaps the son of the James Horde who lived at Montpelier in 1868 (1910 U.S. Census).

21. For Madison's basic antipathy to slavery and his political positions for generalized antislavery, see Ketcham, *James Madison*, 625–30; McCoy, *Last of the Fathers*, 108–18, 230–32, 298.

22. Jennings, *Colored Man's Reminiscences*, 19–20.

23. Very old works such as Cutts, *Memoirs*, and Hunt, *Life*, are at least understandable as reflecting their own times. But Virginia Moore, *The Madisons*, is too recent to be explained this way. Even the standard modern works usually strike a nostalgic pose; see Brant, *James Madison*, 29–71; Ketcham, *James Madison*, 1–16, 370–90, 613–29.

24. McCoy, *Last of the Fathers*, 253–322.

25. Hunt-Jones, *Dolley;* Robert Rutland and Conover Hunt-Jones, "James Madison: Intellectual Planter," in Hunt-Jones, *Dolley,* 97–108.

26. For very preliminary attempts at the larger story, see Chambers, "Making of Montpelier"; Scott Parker et al., "Crafty Businessmen."

27. Even McCoy's sensitive account mentions only three slaves by name.

28. Virginia Moore, *The Madisons,* 308, 315; Jennings, *Colored Man's Reminiscences,* 10.

29. In a draft of Dolley's will written in 1841, she intended to free Jennings upon her death; however, if he had not secured his freedom through Webster, Jennings would have been inherited by John Todd; see "Papers Concerning the Madison Papers by William Cabell Rives" [1857–66], Ms., Madison Family Papers.

30. Hunt, *Life,* 381; McCoy, *Last of the Fathers,* 7; Ketcham, *James Madison,* 619; Virginia Moore, *The Madisons,* 308, 313, 343, 374, 443, 477.

31. Further research on the Conway family and in papers relating to them is necessary to confirm Sawney's origins, but the circumstances of the Conways in the 1730s suggest that this was the case.

32. His age is inferred from the fact that he was an octogenarian in 1817 and that he was probably one of the four or five adults that Nelly Madison kept in her own name until her death in 1829 (Ketcham, *James Madison,* 374, 614; PPT 1820–28).

33. She had inherited the slaves from her father, Francis (1696–1732), who ran a tobacco warehouse on the upper Rappahannock River, although in the 1740s her slaves apparently were kept at her brother's farm, also in Caroline County ("Extracts," 203; Francis Conway Account, JMMB). Nelly married James Madison Sr. on 15 September 1749 (Clark, "Madison Family Bible Records," 81).

34. Orange County Minute Book, 5:392.

35. Based on the tobacco marks used by Madison (1749–57) when marketing his finished tobacco (Crop Memoranda, JMMB). For the building spree, see Chambers, "Making of Montpelier," 127.

36. Shortly before his death in 1732, Francis Conway I had copatented 5,000 acres in what became Orange County; in 1737 the tithables were listed as those of "Mrs. Conoway" (Conway Family Papers; Little, *Orange County,* 5; Hayden, *Virginia Genealogies,* 244; see also Dove, *Madison County Homes,* 106).

37. Little, *Orange County.*

38. Brant, *James Madison,* 71, 83.

39. In 1787 Moses was mentioned in Colonel Madison's will (probated 1801) as a blacksmith; Moses was specifically allowed to choose his own master

on the colonel's death (OCWB, 4:1). In 1802, James Madison Jr. purchased Moses in the estate division for £150, "according to the will of testator," so Moses must have chosen James (Executor's Account, OCWB, 5:242 [recorded 1818]).

40. Madison Account Books and Miscellaneous Papers. The tobacco mark was J&N,S M (James and Nelly Madison/Sawney), meaning it was produced by Nelly's slaves, whom James controlled, and overseen by Sawney at "his" quarter.

41. The owners were Thomas Barbour, William Taliaferro, Lawrence Taliaferro, James Madison Sr., James Taylor Jr. (Little, *Orange County*, 111, 117, 131, 133, 136, 139).

42. 1787 Shoe List, Madison Account Books and Miscellaneous Papers. Of the fifty slaves issued shoes that year, only ten received "English" shoes.

43. The three white overseers were Thomas Gilbert, James Coleman, and Conrad Ash.

44. In 1790, he was listed as one of the three overseers at Montpelier, per James Madison's "Instructions for the Montpelier Overseers and Laborers" [8 November 1790], Hobson and Rutland, *Papers*, 302–4. Sawney was also referenced in a late November 1790 letter from James Madison Jr., in Philadelphia, to his father: "I hope you have not forgotten to pay Majr. Lee, and that Robin & the [torn] will have given Sawney the aids necessary for the jobb I left unfinished" (Hunt, *Writings*, 22). A 1794 letter from James Madison Jr. noted, "I hope M.C. and Sawney will make ready for harvest without waiting for my presence, as I cannot be sure of being there in time" (Madison, *Letters*, 2:16). For a description of some of Sawney's responsibilities as overseer in these years, see Ketcham, *James Madison*, 374.

45. In an 1838 deed of gift of 400 acres from Dolley Madison to her son John Todd, which was bounded "On the West by Reuben Newman, on the South and East by James Newman & John H. Lee and on the North by the Mont Pelier tract," as devised in President Madison's will, she noted that the farm was "Called Edmondson's and more recently Sawney's" (OCDB, 37:178).

46. OCWB, 1829, 134.

47. Virginia Moore, *The Madisons*, 392.

48. For statement that Sawney served Nelly Conway Madison until her death, see Ketcham, *James Madison*, 374.

49. McCoy, *Last of the Fathers*, 295–309; Ketcham, *James Madison*, 629.

50. Ann Miller, *Short Life*. Brant (see *James Madison*, 26–27, or more generally 24–28, 49) clearly went through the relevant court order books; see also Ketcham, *James Madison*, 5.

51. Even after seventeen years of archaeological investigations and the recent identification of several descendants of some of the nineteenth-century enslaved people, there are no known National Trust publications, self-guided tour materials, or pamphlets dedicated to explaining or interpreting the African American community at Montpelier, including black employees and residents in the twentieth century under the Du Ponts. Cf. the programmatic efforts at Monticello, including their "Getting Word" oral history and Jefferson Slave Database projects in the 1990s and the several publications sponsored by the Thomas Jefferson Foundation, including most recently Stanton, *Free Some Day*.

52. See, for example, Ann Miller, *Short Life*, 10.

CHAPTER 10

1. For a theoretical discussion of ancestral and common traditions in the context of small-scale societies in equatorial Africa, see Vansina, *Paths*, 71–100, 249–63. For bricolage, see Lévi-Strauss, *Savage Mind*, 16–22.

2. The following discussion is based on Jerdone Family Slave Record Book; Jerdone Account Books, Accounts and Receipts 1773–1818, folder 4, and Jerdone Accounts, folder 6; Jerdone Family Business Records.

3. Variations of Breechy are found in age adjudgments in Goochland in 1734 and in Amelia in 1753 and 1760. In eighteenth-century Igboland, *mbreechi* was the title for those who bore *ichi* scars, which Equiano called the "mark of grandeur" (*Embrenché*) (Equiano, *Interesting Narrative*, ed. Allison, 34). G. I. Jones transliterated the Igbo term as *mbreechi* ("Olaudah Equiano," 70); Acholonu translates the term the same way but clarifies that in the Nri-Awka area it was more precisely *mgburichi* (*Igbo Roots*, 12; see also chap. 2).

4. The only Mingo was a boy born in 1766. He died, was sold, or changed his name. This 1796 Anakey in New Kent County may be the same person listed as an aged Anaky "valued at nothing on account of infirmities" at a Jerdone-owned plantation on the Chickahominy River in Charles City County, whom Francis Jerdone Jr. (1756–1841) allotted to his son, William, in 1836 ("Inventory of the Landed Estate, Slaves, Money, etc. of the late Francis Jerdone [1841]," Jerdone Family Business Records).

5. Littlefield, *Rice and Slaves*, table 9, 138–39. As discussed earlier, in Igbo, both *obea* and *dibia* meant "doctor."

6. Puckett, *Black Names*, 27, 30, 32. Of course, Beck could have been a contraction of Rebecca/Becky, but the Jerdones' Breechy (d. 1779) was married to a Beck. There are so many words formed from the *mgb-* and *ka-* (and *kwa-*) phonemes in Igbo that even this morpheme may represent an Igboism.

7. All of these names appear in the Jerdone Family Slave Record Book. It is not clear when Jerdone wrote these entries in his ledger.

8. As for example in Thompson, *Flash*, 103–59; Thompson, "Kongo Influences"; Douglas Hall, *In Miserable Slavery;* and more generally the papers in Heywood, *Central Africans*. Thompson suggests that a covert Kongo influence is to be seen in some mid–twentieth century blues lyrics from the Mississippi Delta, largely from the geographical proximity to New Orleans. However, I believe that at least some of these core terms are references to Igboized creolisms derived from the descendants of people whose ancestors in many cases were taken from the Chesapeake region. Much of the Delta area was not settled until after the Civil War and was often settled by freedpeople who were born (or whose parents were born) in Virginia—for example, the founders of Mound Bayou, the famous black town, who were taken from Loudoun County, Virginia, to Mississippi as slaves (see the state historical marker at Mound Bayou). Thompson quotes a stanza from the blues standard "Hoochie Coochie Blues" (*Flash*, 131):

> I got a black cat bone
> I got a mojo tooth
> I got John the Conqueroo
> I'm gonna mess with you.

9. Of course, no single "trait" (or cultural artifact) in and of itself is meaningful; rather, sets of such artifacts have importance. There is a reference to H. esculentus as "Gumbs" in an 1825 Virginia cookbook, but the recipe was subtitled "a West India Dish," and that is the only such reference I have found for the Upper South. Furthermore, the recipe text uses the term *ocra* (Stacy Moore, "'Established and Well Cultivated,'" 80).

10. DeCamp, "African Day-Names," 142–47; Cohen, "Slave Names." Cf. Reynolds, *Stand the Storm*, 113: "In the Gullah Islands and Virginia, traditions from the Gold Coast predominated."

11. For an excellent account of Juba in antebellum American minstrelsy, see Abrahams, *Singing the Master*, 146–53.

12. That historical Igbo paid attention to the sun's movements is indicated by Equiano, who wrote, "We compute the year from the day on which the sun crosses the line, and on its setting that evening, there is a general shout throughout the land" (*Interesting Narrative*, ed. Allison, 41).

13. A historical geographer, however, noted that "Eastern Nigeria is not, and probably never was, a land completely covered with vast impenetrable rain-forests or 'jungles'" (Floyd, *Eastern Nigeria*, 53, 153).

14. Òkpóko, "Archaeology and Ethnoarchaeology," 7.

15. Perdue, Barden, and Phillips, *Weevils*, 278. Ironically, however, yam agriculture in Igboland would have encouraged the anopheles mosquito, and thus malaria, as the insect vector does not thrive under dense rainforest canopies but does thrive in cleared fields and lowland marshes (Vansina, *Paths*, 43; see also Robert Hall, "Savoring Africa," 171). It is likely that in Tidewater Virginia, the draining and reclaiming of swamps or of swampy areas around quarters for planting could have decreased the ideal conditions for breeding mosquitoes.

16. Jackson, *Journal*, 70; Oldfield, "Mr. Oldfield's Journal," 1:393.

17. "Frog in a Mill" and "Tree Frogs" (Talley, *Negro Folk Rhymes*, 167, 168, 247 (commentary); see also Puckett, *Folk Beliefs*, 16–17).

18. See, for example, Igbozurike, "Vegetation."

19. Castiglioni, *Viaggio*, 401–2.

20. Beatty and Mulloy, *William Byrd's Natural History*, 26.

21. See Floyd, *Eastern Nigeria*, 241–44. Oldfield, "Mr. Oldfield's Journal," 1:377, recorded seeing "hawks." Tilapia is a bony white fish, as is herring, which is what George Washington gave his home plantation slaves as part of their monthly rations; see White, "'To Indulge Themselves,' " 9.

22. Herskovits, *Myth*, 113.

23. Equiano, *Interesting Narrative*, ed. Allison, 37, 39; Oldfield, "Mr. Oldfield's Journal," 1:394; see also Equiano's description of clay-bowl tobacco pipes in his Eboan community (*Interesting Narrative*, ed. Allison, 36). There are several species of cotton (*Gossypium*) that are indigenous to West Africa, and in Igboland the cotton plant is called *olulu* (Oyenuga, *Agriculture*, 106–12).

24. See Castiglioni, *Viaggio*, 114–15, 197, 376–78; see also Janson, *Stranger*, 405, for apple brandy as the common drink of the central Piedmont. Rev. Peter Randolph, b. ca. 1828 in Prince George County, Virginia, remembered that in his youth, slaves made persimmon beer, which they put into gourds and carried with them to work in the fields (*Sketches*, 31).

25. See, for example, Crow's description of the common foods of Bonny around 1800 (*Memoirs*, 252).

26. For examples, see, Humphreys, *Historical Account*, 234; Farish, *Journal and Letters*, 129; Betts, *Thomas Jefferson's Farm Book*, 143, 185, 187; Krzyzanowski, *Julia Ursyn Niemcewicz*, 28; Janson, *Stranger*, 381; St. Mery, *American Journey*, 1947, 306; Madison to Morse, [28 March 1823]; Finch, *Travels*, 235.

27. Equiano, *Interesting Narrative*, ed. Allison, 38.

28. See Perdue, Barden, and Phillips, *Weevils*, 81, 268–69; Randolph, *Sketches*, 49; James Smith, *Autobiography*, 8–9.

29. Puckett, *Folk Beliefs*, 20 (*tingany* was also used for flour; his source was an 1895 *Southern Workman* article); Thomas, *Anthropological Report*, 5:54. Northern Igbo farmers in the mid–twentieth century grew their own short-growing early maturing variety of corn/maize, which was quite different than the modern taller and late-maturing variety. In the wake of the Biafran War (1967–70), when the federal government gave out free corn seed to these farmers, many of them complained about the modern variety, partly because it grew too tall and overshadowed the yams with which the corn was inter-cropped and partly because "the taste is not good and the grains tend to harden soon after boiling" (Uzozie, "Agricultural Land Use," 170–71). Cf. Taylor, who in June 1858 noted that around Onitsha the people were all "busy in reaping their *nhansi*, a kind of corn resembling *kooskoos*, or guinea-corn" (millet or sorghum) ("Journal," 367–68). See also Allen, *Narrative*, 1:388, on how Niger Igbo made a flour out of local millet and cooked "little cakes . . . made of the flour of Dauer, or of Indian-corn, mixed with honey and abundance of pepper, rolled up in balls, or in long pieces, and half-boiled." This may have resembled the Upper South's ash-cake, johnnycake, or hoecake.

30. See Randolph, *Sketches*, 29; James Smith, *Autobiography*, 8.

31. Hugh Jones, *Present State*, 40. For general statements on slave reliance on highly seasoned (peppered) one-pot stews in Virginia, see Stacy Moore, "'Established and Well Cultivated,'" 78–80.

32. Crews, *Plantation Recollections*, 21, (reminiscences of antebellum Halifax County, Virginia).

33. James Smith, *Autobiography*, 8. This resembles what Booker T. Washington described in *Up from Slavery*, 9.

34. See Stacy Moore, "'Established and Well Cultivated,'" 70–83; Robert Hall, "Savoring Africa," 161–69.

35. See Wagner, "Introduction."

36. See Equiano, *Interesting Narrative*, ed. Allison, 36–37; Oyenuga, *Agriculture*, 134–39; Floyd, *Eastern Nigeria*, 174–77; Uzozie, "Agricultural Land Use," 155, 170–71. For historical sources, see Barbot, "Abstract," 379; Adams, *Sketches*, 53; Crow, *Memoirs*, 146, 252–53, 258; Lander and Lander, *Journal*, 2:174, 201, 246; Oldfield, "Mr. Oldfield's Journal," 1:374, 386–87; Allen, *Narrative*, 1:251; Taylor, "Journal," 367–68.

37. See Farish, *Journal and Letters*.

38. Perdue, Barden, and Phillips, *Weevils*, 306.

39. Adams, *Sketches*, 53; see also Robert Hall, "Savoring Africa," 167–68.

40. As for okra, it is highly improbable that, as Stacy Moore suggests, Thomas Jefferson, who started growing it in his garden only in 1809, was "most likely among the first in Virginia to grow this foreign plant" ("'Established and Well Cultivated,'" 79–80). In fact, in the 1790s and 1800s, Jefferson became suddenly interested in the African plants about which the slaves but not he knew. Also, he did not have sweet potatoes planted in his garden; see Betts, *Thomas Jefferson's Garden Book*.

41. Ferguson, *Uncommon Ground*, 44–55, 82–93, 102–7; see also the excellent discussion of colonoware and North American slavery in Kathleen Parker and Hernigle, *Portici*, 220–29.

42. See Singleton and Bograd, *Archaeology*, 25–27; Singleton, "Archaeology," 158–62, although here she points out that the question is still very much open to debate; see Ferguson, "Looking for the 'Afro.'" The Pamunkey Indian tribe absorbed a significant proportion of runaway African and/or Afro-Virginian slaves, so similarities between Pamunkey and Afro-Virginian colonowares should be expected.

43. Kathleen Parker and Hernigle, *Portici*, 85–96, 100, 224–29.

44. Ibid., 89.

45. Ferguson, *Uncommon Ground*, 52; Kathleen Parker and Hernigle, *Portici*, 225.

46. Kathleen Parker and Hernigle, *Portici*, 225.

47. See Òkpóko's extensive comments about "traditional" potting largely in terms of the Anambra Valley based on his archaeological surveys there ("Archaeology and Ethnoarchaeology," 40–60); see also Okeke, "Art Culture," 272–73, about the Nsukka region in northern Igboland.

48. Thomas, *Anthropological Report*, 1:131–32.

49. Equiano, *Interesting Narrative*, ed. Allison, 36–37; Allen, *Narrative*, 1:388.

50. Allen, *Narrative*, 1:388.

51. Perdue, Barden, and Phillips, *Weevils*, 164, 16; cf. Equiano, *Interesting Narrative*, ed. Allison, 37.

52. See, for example, the description of the making of a dugout canoe in Perdue, Barden, and Phillips, *Weevils*, 110.

53. Gosse, *Naturalist's Sojourn*, 193, 205–6.

54. Farish, *Journal and Letters*, 74; see also Knight, *Letters*, 59.

55. Equiano, *Interesting Narrative*, ed. Allison, 36. Cf. the suggestion by one archaeologist that the magical or affective quality of blue suggested by the glass beads came from Islam (Singleton, "Archaeology," 164). For more on blue beads in the context of religiomagical artifacts, see Singleton, "Archaeology,"

162–64; Ferguson, *Uncommon Ground*, 116–20; Klingelhofer, "Aspects," 115–16; Orser, "Archaeology"; Samford, "Archaeology"; Stine, Cabak, and Groover, "Blue Beads"; Young, "Archaeological Evidence"; Wilkie, "Secret and Sacred."

56. See Talbot, *Peoples*, 3:932; see also Cardinall, "Aggrey Beads."

57. Vlach, *By the Work*, 26.

58. Herskovits, *Myth*, 136–37; see, for example, Vlach, *By the Work*, 19–71.

59. This concept sounds much like an old southern black saying, "Every brother ain't a brother."

60. Chambers, "Making of Montpelier," 86–89.

61. Cf. Kulikoff, *Tobacco and Slaves*, 340–42.

62. Madison to Morse, [28 March 1823]; Finch, *Travels*, 237; Perdue, Barden, and Phillips, *Weevils*, 89.

63. This practice was ubiquitous throughout the nineteenth-century South; see Gutman, *Black Family*, 197–224.

64. Perdue, Barden, and Phillips, *Weevils*, 150, 128; Hurmence, *My Folks*, 2; Smedes, *Southern Planter*, 86.

65. Burnaby, *Travels*, 65.

66. See, for example, Oldfield, "Mr. Oldfield's Journal," 374.

67. See Woolman, *Journal*, 59; Anbury, *Travels*, 2:333; Brissot de Warville, *New Travels*, 232; Janson, *Stranger*, 382; Sutcliff, *Travels*, 69–70, 112; see also Barclay, *Voyages and Travels*, 25; Dennett, *South as It Is*, 132.

68. Hurmence, *My Folks*, 36. Presumably, she meant that she wore nothing but a sack dress: she was "naked" under her dress.

69. See Sobel, *World They Made*, 34–35.

70. Perdue, Barden, and Phillips, *Weevils*, 32.

71. Steward, *Twenty-two Years*, 31. He was born in 1799 in Prince William County. This custom may have changed dramatically after Nat Turner's War in 1831.

72. Carr and Menard, "Land, Labor, and Economies of Scale," 414–16: "Slaves were made to work longer days, were denied the Saturday half-day that English custom granted servants (even Sundays were often encroached on by grasping masters), and were allowed fewer holidays than English indentured laborers" (415).

73. Humphreys, *Historical Account*, 24; Anbury, *Travels*, 2:332; Farish, *Journal and Letters*, 137.

74. Perdue, Barden, and Phillips, *Weevils*, 106; see also Smedes, *Southern Planter*, 68; Armstrong, *Old Massa's People*, 137–38.

75. Davies, *Duty*, 45; Anonymous, "Manner of Living," 214; Davis, *Travels*, 366.

76. Humphreys, *Historical Account*, 235.

77. Mullin, *Africa in America*, 67. Basden described the Igbo *ubaw* (thumb piano) as "an instrument which cannot be compared with any foreign one with which I am acquainted" (*Among the Ibos*, 189). For more, see Epstein, *Sinful Tunes*, 30–38; for many Caribbean references to *gambeys*, see 51–62, 85–90; see also Vlach, *By the Work*, 23–25, 63–67. For Igbo instruments ca. 1920, see Talbot, *Peoples*, 3:812–15.

78. Anonymous, "Manner of Living," 215; Equiano, *Interesting Narrative*, ed. Allison, 36; Basden, *Among the Ibos*, 189.

79. Jacobs, *Incidents*, 118; Matthew Lewis, *Journal*, 53.

80. Quoted in Cassidy and LePage, *Dictionary*, 202. They give the word a probable Western Bantu provenance.

81. Bennett Green, *Word-Book*, 206. See Epstein, *Sinful Tunes*, 141–44, for sources and a general discussion. She notes that the word does not appear to have been known in Jamaica.

82. For a long description of juba, see Hungerford, *Old Plantation*, 196–98.

83. Vass, *Bantu Speaking Heritage*, 110; Holloway and Vass, *African Heritage*, 100. Many of Vass's etymologies, however, are suspect; cf. Jacobs, *Incidents*, 118–19, where the phrase "so dey say" seems to take the place of "juba!"

84. For discussions and accounts of Jonkonnu in North America and the Anglo-Caribbean islands, see Cameron, "Christmas," 5; MacMillan, "John Kuners"; Reid, "John Canoe Festival"; Cassidy, "'Hipsaw' and 'John Canoe'"; Walser, "His Worship"; Bettelheim, "Afro-Jamaica Jonkonnu Festival"; Bettelheim, "Jonkonnu Festival"; Fenn, "'Perfect Equality'"; see also Mullin, *Africa in America*, 70, 326 n.35; Patterson, *Sociology of Slavery*, 238–39, 243–44; Stuckey, *Slave Culture*, 68–73; Levine, *Black Culture*, 13, 449 n.22; Epstein, *Sinful Tunes*, 131; Norfleet, *Suffolk*, 43, 124 n.130; Abrahams and Szwed, *After Africa*.

85. See Cassidy and LePage, *Dictionary*, 249–50; see also Abrahams and Szwed, *After Africa*, 29–30, and the extracts of primary accounts on 226–79.

86. The Gold Coast provenance is originally from Long, *History of Jamaica*, vol. 2; see reprint in Abrahams and Szwed, *After Africa*, 229.

87. Norfleet, *Suffolk*, 43; Jacobs, *Incidents*, 118–19; Warren, *Doctor's Experiences*, 200–202; *Blue Ridge Guide* (Rappahannock County), September 9, 1920, based on Professor Charles Perdue, personal communication, 1987.

88. Long, *History of Jamaica*, attributed the custom to a Fante caboceer named John Conny in the 1720s, but the wide distribution of Jonkonnu, especially after 1750, suggests that such a limited origin was unlikely at best and fanciful at worst; see Craton, "Decoding Pitchy-Patchy." Stuckey suggests a Yoruban or Fon influence, from the Egun masquerade, overlooking the fact that neither

ethnic group was numerically important to the British trade (*Slave Culture,* 68–73). Others such as Cassidy argue for possibly a Bambara or an Ewe derivation; see Craton, "Decoding Pitchy-Patchy," 38–39.

89. Bettelheim, "Afro-Jamaica Jonkonnu Festival," 12–13, 20. She also writes, "This Kalabari peaked hat is so close in style to those worn in Jamaica that one is tempted to make certain assumptions. Yet, the region of Kalabari demonstrates as varied a culture history as does Jamaica and any firm conclusions are impossible" (45–46).

90. See Oguagha, "Historical and Traditional Evidence," 268–69; Okeke, "Art Culture," 271–72.

91. See Patterson, *Sociology of Slavery,* 245, which recognizes that the Igbo *mmo,* Yoruba *egugun,* and Ga *homowo* were most like the Jamaican Jonkonnu, but again, the proportion of Yoruba and Ga (who if enslaved would have been sent from the Bight of Benin) in the eighteenth-century British trade was negligible. For a description of *homowo,* see Quartey-Papafio, "Ga Homowo Festival."

92. For an historical description of such a masquerade in Bonny in the 1820s, see Jackson, *Journal,* 89–90.

93. Kathleen Parker and Hernigle, *Portici,* 195; Kelso, "Archaeology," 7.

94. Kelso, *Kingsmill Plantations.*

95. For Igbo ca. 1911, see Talbot, *Peoples,* 3:817.

96. Oldfield, "Mr. Oldfield's Journal," 1:394.

97. Hogendorn and Johnson, *Shell Money,* 101–24, esp. 106–12.

98. Equiano, *Interesting Narrative,* ed. Allison, 51–52.

99. Pearce, "Cowrie Shell"; cf. Singleton, "Archaeology," 157–58, 188 n.9.

100. One has been recovered in North Carolina and one in Louisiana. There have been a number of large-scale excavations in the Carolina low country, including such major rice plantations as Middleton Place, Drayton Hall, and Yaughan Plantation, which are comparable to the efforts at both Williamsburg and Yorktown in Virginia; see the bibliographical entries in Singleton and Bograd, *Archaeology,* 35–81. Ferguson does not include an entry for cowrie in the index to his account of archaeology and early African American life, *Uncommon Ground.*

101. Pearce, "Cowrie Shell," 64–65.

102. Ibid., 56–67, esp. 60, 62–63.

103. Singleton, "Archaeology," 157–58. The Afro-Barbadian charm necklace sounds quite like Ingraham's Juba in antebellum Mississippi. Carnelian (reddish) beads have been found archaeologically in Nri-Awka (Igbo Ukwu sites), dating from about the ninth century C.E. (Hartle, "Archaeology,"

199–200; Ìsichei, *History of the Igbo People*, 10–15). Some 165,000 "carnelian" (including some likely Venetian) beads have been found at Igbo-Ukwu sites.

104. Pearce, "Cowrie Shell," esp. 25, 72–74. Most of her ethnographic examples are contemporary Yoruba, even though she noted that Nri-Awka and northern Ika Igbo used cowries as currency in the nineteenth century.

105. Talbot, *Peoples*, 3:955. In the Chesapeake, Orion/Pleiades sets out of the night sky in the late spring/summer, leaving as the most prominent constellation (at least to modern eyes) the Big Dipper (which antebellum African Americans learned to call the Drinking Gourd).

106. Schwarz, *Twice Condemned*, 111.

107. For a standard account, see ibid., 92.

108. Ibid.; for Eve's trial and the order for her execution, see OCOB, 4:454–55. Eve was owned by Peter Mountague (Montague). In 1750, Mountague came into court and acknowledged a deed of gift to his children (the eldest of whom was also named Peter), and in 1771 "Peter Mountague Senr, an Antient poor man" was exempted from paying the county tithable or capitation tax (OCOB, 5:247, 8:154).

109. Stacy Moore, "'Established and Well Cultivated,'" 77.

110. Kretchner, "Lactose and Lactase," 136–37. Although the association of lactose intolerance with tsetse fly would suggest that a broad swath of West and West Central Africa, from Liberia through Angola, would be areas of lactose intolerance, this appears not to have been the case; see Vansina, *Paths*, 60, 89–92. Lactose intolerance is not obvious in Upper Guinea or in Kongo/Angola, although that does not mean it does not exist.

CONCLUSION

1. SCWB, A:183; Baylor Family Papers, Ledgers, vol. 1.

2. Gutman, *Black Family*, 196. Unfortunately, Gutman did not cite the source for these quotations, and they are not included in David Lewis, *W. E. B. DuBois*.

3. *Three Negro Classics*, 48. In another edition, apparently a reprint of the first book edition, though differing from the serial version in *Outlook* (3 November 1900–23 February 1901), this sentence is rendered "but I have no knowledge as to where most of them are" (Washington, *Up from Slavery*, liii, 36). In the year that Washington published his autobiography, 1901, the core of Montpelier (some 1,240 acres) was purchased by William Du Pont of Bellevue, Delaware (OCDB, 59:180). The property remained in the Du Pont family until 1984.

4. Quoted in Gutman, *Black Family,* 196.

5. Most notably in *The Myth of the Negro Past* (1941) and in the pioneering work of his many students, especially William Bascom, now largely overlooked, as well as others—particularly George E. Simpson and Harold Courlander—whom Herskovits deeply influenced; see Simpson, *Melville J. Herskovits;* Baron, "Africa in the Americas."

MANUSCRIPT SOURCES

Baylor Family Papers. Acc. #2257, Special Collections, Alderman Library, University of Virginia, Charlottesville.

Conway Family, Papers of, 1732–1904. Acc. #2485, Special Collections, Alderman Library, University of Virginia, Charlottesville.

Jefferson Papers, 1732–1828. Microfilm, Roll 4, M119, Special Collections, Alderman Library, University of Virginia, Charlottesville.

Jerdone, Francis, Account Books, 1762–1773, Jerdone Family Papers. Acc. #21607 (manuscript), Virginia State Library, Richmond.

Jerdone Family, Louisa County, Slave Record Book, 1761–1865. Acc. #20415 (manuscript), Virginia State Library, Richmond.

Jerdone Family Business Records. Acc. #21655 (manuscript), Virginia State Library, Richmond.

Madison, James, to Jedidiah Morse, [28 March 1823]. ALS, Acc. #8347, Special Collections, Alderman Library, University of Virginia, Charlottesville.

[Madison, James, Sr.]. Memorandum Book, 1744–1757. AMs. Accessioned as "Small octavo day book supposedly belonging to a James Madison Sr." C. Russell Caldwell Papers, 1901–1922. Acc. #10558, Special Collections, Alderman Library, University of Virginia, Charlottesville.

Madison, James, Sr., Montpelier, Orange County, Account Books and Miscellaneous Papers, 1752–1817. Acc. #28529 (microfilm), Misc. Reel 8, Virginia State Library, Richmond.

Madison Family, Papers of, 1768–1866 (manuscript). Acc. #2988, Special Collections, Alderman Library, University of Virginia, Charlottesville.

Madison v. Madison, High Court of Chancery for the Richmond District. Cause ended 3 March 1803 (copy). TMs., Madison Papers Manuscript File, Special Collections, Alderman Library, University of Virginia, Charlottesville.

Madison-Pendleton Correspondence, Gilder Lehman Collection. Pierpont Morgan Library, New York. Ms. #17.

Randolph, Thomas Mann, to Thomas Jefferson, [25 April 1800]. ALS, Jefferson Papers 1732–1828 (microfilm), Roll 4, M119, Special Collections, Alderman Library, University of Virginia, Charlottesville.

Shane Collection, Madison Family Papers (microfilm), Sh18 M265. Presbyterian Historical Society, Philadelphia.

Willis, Mrs. Jere M. H., Jr. [Barbara], to George Smith, 3 February 1986, Montpelier Station, Va., ALS.

U.S. Census.
  1850 Slave Schedule (microfilm)
  1900 Population Schedule (microfilm)
  1910 Population Schedule (microfilm)

COURTHOUSE MANUSCRIPT RECORDS

Amelia County Circuit Court, Clerk's Office, Amelia Court House, Va.
  Court Order Books
Caroline County Circuit Court, Clerk's Office, Bowling Green, Va.
  Court Order Books
Essex County Circuit Court, Clerk's Office, Tappahannock, Va.
  Court Order Books
Louisa County Circuit Court, Clerk's Office, Louisa, Va.
  Court Order Books
Orange County Circuit Court, Clerk's Office, Orange, Va.
  County Census 1785 (microfilm)
  Court Deed Books
  Court Order Books
  Court Marriage Books
  Court Minute Books
  Court Will Books
  Hite v. Madison, Papers, Chancery Cause ended 1838, File no. 2, Loose Papers.
Spotsylvania County Circuit Court, Clerk's Office, Spotsylvania, Va.
  Court Order Books
  Court Will Books

PUBLISHED SOURCES

Abrahams, Roger D. 1992. *Singing the Master: The Emergence of African-American Culture in the Plantation South.* New York: Penguin Books.

Abrahams, Roger D., and John F. Szwed, eds. 1983. *After Africa: Extracts from British Travel Accounts and Journals of the Seventeenth, Eighteenth, and Nineteenth Centuries Concerning the Slaves, Their Manners, and Customs in the British West Indies.* New Haven: Yale University Press.

Acholonu, Catherine O. 1989. *The Igbo Roots of Olaudah Equiano—An Anthropological Research.* Owerri, Nigeria: Afa.

Adams, John. 1823. *Sketches Taken during Ten Voyages to Africa, between the Years 1786 and 1800; Including Observations on the Country between Cape Palmas and the River Congo.* London: Hurst, Robinson; New York: Johnson, 1970.

Afigbo, A. E. 1981. *Ropes of Sand: Studies in Igbo History and Culture.* Ibadan, Nigeria: University Press.

Alagoa, E. J. 1972. *A History of the Niger Delta, and Historical Interpretation of Ijo Oral Tradition.* Nigeria: Ibadan University Press.

Alagoa, E. J., and Adadonye Fombo. 1972. *A Chronicle of Grand Bonny.* Nigeria: Ibadan University Press.

Alexander, Edward Porter, ed. 1972. *The Journal of John Fontaine, an Irish Huguenot Son in Spain and Virginia, 1710–1719.* Charlottesville: University Press of Virginia.

Allen, William. 1848. *A Narrative of the Expedition Sent by Her Majesty's Government to the River Niger in 1841.* 2 vols. London: Richard Bentley.

Alutu, John O. Alutu. 1985 [1963]. *Nnewi History.* 2d ed. Enugu, Nigeria: Fourth Dimension.

Anbury, Thomas. 1789. *Travels through the Interior Parts of America.* 2 vols. London: William Lane; repr., New York: Arno, 1969.

Anonymous [Thomas Jefferson?]. 1787. "Manner of Living of the Inhabitants of Virginia." *American Museum* 1, no. 3: 214–16.

Arinze, Francis A. 1970. *Sacrifice in Ibo Religion.* Ibadan, Nigeria: Ibadan University Press.

Armstrong, Orland K. 1931. *Old Massa's People: The Old Slaves Tell Their Story.* Indianapolis: Bobbs-Merrill.

Austin, Allan D. 1984. *African Muslims in Antebellum America: A Sourcebook.* New York: Garland.

Baikie, William B. 1856. *Narrative of an Exploring Voyage up the Rivers Kwora and Binue, Commonly Known as the Niger and Tsadda, in 1854.* London: John Murray; repr., London: Frank Cass, 1966.

Baird, Keith A., and Mary A. Twining. 1991. "Names and Naming in the Sea Islands." In *Sea Island Roots: African Presence in the Carolinas and Georgia,* ed. Mary A. Twining and Keith A. Baird. Trenton, N.J.: Africa World.

Barbot, James. 1732. "An Abstract of a Voyage to New Calabar River, or Rio Real, in the Year 1699." In *A Collection of Voyages and Travels,* ed. Awnshawn Churchill and John Churchill. London: John Walthoe.

Barbour, James. 1836. *Eulogium upon the Life and Character of James Madison.* Washington, D.C.: Gales and Seaton.

Barclay, James. 1777. *The Voyages and Travels of James Barclay, Containing Many Surprising Adventures and Interesting Narratives.* N.p.

Basden, G. T. 1921. *Among the Ibos of Nigeria.* London: Seeley.

Beatty, Richmond Croom, and William J. Mulloy, eds. 1940. *William Byrd's Natural History of Virginia; or, The Newly Discovered Eden.* Richmond: Dietz.

Becroft, Captain, and J. B. King. 1844. "Details of Explorations of the Old Calabar River, in 1841 and 1842, by Captain Becroft, of the Merchant Steamer 'Ethiope,' and Mr. J. B. King, Surgeon of that Vessel." *Journal of the Royal Geographical Society* 14: 260–62.

Berlin, Ira. 1974. *Slaves without Masters: The Free Negro in the Antebellum South.* Oxford: Oxford University Press.

———. 1996. "From Creole to African: Atlantic Creoles and the Origins of African-American Society in Mainland North America." *William and Mary Quarterly,* 3d ser., 53: 251–88.

———. 1998. *Many Thousands Gone: The First Two Centuries of Slavery in North America.* Cambridge: Belknap Press of Harvard University Press.

Bettelheim, Judith. 1985. "The Jonkonnu Festival in Jamaica." *Journal of Ethnic Studies* 13, no. 1: 85–105.

Betts, Edwin M., ed. 1944. *Thomas Jefferson's Garden Book, 1766–1824.* Philadelphia: American Philosophical Society.

———, ed. 1953. *Thomas Jefferson's Farm Book, with Commentary and Relevant Extracts from Other Writings.* Memoirs of the American Philosophical Society, vol. 35; repr., Charlottesville: University Press of Virginia, 1976.

Bosah, S. I. [1975?]. *Groundwork of the History and Culture of Onitsha.* N.p.

Bosman, William. 1705. *A New and Accurate Description of the Coast of Guinea.* English ed. London: Knapton and others; London: Frank Cass, 1967.

Boyd, Julian P., ed. 1958. *The Papers of Thomas Jefferson.* Vol. 15, *27 March 1789 to 30 November 1789.* Princeton: Princeton University Press.

Brant, Irving. 1941. *James Madison.* Vol. 1, *The Virginia Revolutionist.* Indianapolis: Bobbs-Merrill.

Brissot de Warville, J. P. 1792. *New Travels in the United States.* New York: n.p.

Brown, Vincent. 2003. "Spiritual Terror and Sacred Authority in Jamaican Slave Society." *Slavery and Abolition* 24, no. 1: 24–53.

Bruce, Philip A., ed. 1894. "Public Officers in Virginia, 1714." *Virginia Magazine of History and Biography* 2, no. 1: 6–7.

Brugger, Robert J., et al., eds. 1986. *The Papers of James Madison, Secretary of State Series.* Vol. 1, *4 March–31 July 1801.* Charlottesville: University Press of Virginia.

Bureau of the Census. 1975. *Historical Statistics of the United States: Colonial Times to 1970.* Bicentennial ed. Pt. 2. Washington, D.C.: U.S. Department of Commerce.

Burnaby, Andrew. 1798 [1775]. *Travels through The Middle Settlements in North America in the Years 1759 and 1760.* 3d ed. London: T. Payne.

Bushnell, David J. 1906. "The Sloane Collection in the British Museum." *American Anthropologist,* n.s., 8: 676–77.

Cameron, Rebecca. 1891. "Christmas on an Old Plantation." *Ladies' Home Journal* 9, no. 1: 5.

Cardi, Count C. N. de. 1899. "Ju-ju Laws and Customs in the Niger Delta." *Journal of the Royal Anthropological Institute* 29:51–64.

Cardinall, A. W. 1925. "Aggrey Beads of the Gold Coast." *Journal of the African Society* 24, no. 96: 287–98.

Carr, Lois G., and Russell R. Menard. 1989. "Land, Labor, and Economies of Scale in Early Maryland: Some Limits to Growth in the Chesapeake System of Husbandry." *Journal of Economic History* 49, no. 2: 407–18.

Carretta, Vincent. 1999. "Olaudah Equiano or Gustavus Vass? New Light on an Eighteenth-Century Question of Identity." *Slavery and Abolition* 20, no. 3: 96–105.

Carson, Cary, Norman F. Barka, William M. Kelso, Gary W. Stone, and Dell Upton. 1981. "Impermanent Architecture in the Southern American Colonies." *Winterthur Portfolio* 16: 135–96.

Carton, Michael. 1995. "Decoding Pitchy-Patchy: The Roots, Branches and Essence of Junkanoo." *Slavery and Abolition* 16, no. 1: 15–31.

Cassidy, Frederic G. 1966. "'Hipsaw' and 'John Canoe.'" *American Speech* 41, no. 1: 45–51.

Cassidy, Frederic G., and R. B. Le Page, eds. 1980. *Dictionary of Jamaican English.* 2d ed. Cambridge: Cambridge University Press.

Castiglione, Luigi. 1983. *Viaggio: Travels in the United States of North America, 1785–1787.* Trans. and ed. Antonio Pace. Syracuse, N.Y.: Syracuse University Press.

Chambers, Douglas B. 1996. "'He Is An African but Speaks Plain': Historical Creolization in Eighteenth-Century Virginia." In Joseph E. Harris et al., *The African Diaspora: Walter Prescott Webb Memorial Lectures, no. 30*, ed. Alusine Jalloh and Stephen E. Maizlish, 100–133. College Station: Texas A & M University Press.

———. 1997. "'My Own Nation': Igbo Exiles in the Diaspora." *Slavery and Abolition* 18, no. 1: 72–97.

———. 1999. "The Transatlantic Slave Trade to Virginia in Comparative Historical Perspective, 1698–1778." In *Afro-Virginian History and Culture*, ed. John Saillant, 3–28. New York: Garland.

———. 2000. "Tracing Igbo into the African Diaspora." In *Identifying Enslaved Africans: The "Nigerian" Hinterland and the African Diaspora*, ed. Paul Lovejoy, 55–71. London: Continuum.

———. 2002. "The Significance of Igbo in the Bight of Biafra Slave-Trade: A Rejoinder to Northrup's 'Myth Igbo.'" *Slavery and Abolition* 23, no. 1: 101–20.

Clark, Patricia P., ed. 1958. "Madison Family Bible Records." *Virginia Magazine of History and Biography* 66, no. 1: 80–84.

Cody, Cheryll Ann. 1987. "There Was No 'Absalom' on the Ball Plantations: Slave-Naming Practices in the South Carolina Low Country, 1720–1865." *American Historical Review* 92: 563–96.

Cohen, Hennig. 1952. "Slave Names in Colonial South Carolina." *American Speech* 28, no. 1: 102–7.

Cookey, S. J. S. 1980. "An Ethnohistorical Reconstruction of Traditional Igbo Society." In *West African Cultural Dynamics: Archaeological and Historical Perspectives*, ed. B. K. Swartz and Raymond E. Dumett, 327–47. London: Longman, Hurst.

Creel, Margaret W. 1988. *"A Peculiar People": Slave Religion and Community-Culture among the Gullahs*. New York: New York University Press.

Crews, Jennie Wilson. 1945. *Plantation Recollections*. Richmond, Va.: Dietz.

Crow, Hugh. 1830. *Memoirs of the Late Captain Hugh Crow, of Liverpool: Comprising a Narrative of His Life; Together with Descriptive Sketches of the Western Coast of Africa, Particularly of Bonny; the Manners and Customs of the Inhabitants, the Productions of the Soil, and the Trade of the Country*. Repr., London: Frank Cass, 1970.

Crowther, Samuel A. "Journal of the Rev. S. Crowther." 1859. In Samuel Crowther and John C. Taylor, *The Gospel on the Banks of the Niger—Journals and Notices of the Native Missionaries Accompanying the Niger Expedition of 1857–1859*. Repr., London: Dawsons of Pall Mall, 1968.

Crowther, Samuel A., and John C. Taylor. 1859. *The Gospel on the Banks of the Niger—Journals and Notices of the Native Missionaries Accompanying the Niger Expedition of 1857–1859*. Repr., London: Dawsons of Pall Mall, 1968.

Curtin, Philip D., ed. 1967. *Africa Remembered: Narratives of West Africans from the Era of the Slave Trade.* Madison: University of Wisconsin Press.

Cutts, Lucia B. 1886. *Memoirs and Letters of Dolley Madison.* Boston: Houghton, Mifflin.

Davies, Samuel. 1758. *The Duty of Christians to Propagate Their Religion among Heathens, Earnestly Recommended to the Masters of Negroe Slaves in Virginia.* London: J. Oliver; repr., *Hazard Pamphlets,* no. 105.

Davis, John. 1803. *Travels of Four Years and a Half in the United States of America: During 1798, 1799, 1800, 1801, and 1802.* London: R. Edwards.

DeCamp, David. 1967. "African Day-Names In Jamaica." *Language* 43, no. 1: 139–44.

Deetz, James. 1977. *In Small Things Forgotten: Archaeology of Early American Life.* Garden City, N.Y.: Anchor.

Dennett, Robert. 1965. *The South as It Is, 1865–1866.* Ed. Henry M. Christman. New York: Viking.

Dike, Kenneth O., and Felicia Ekejiuba. 1990. *The Aro of South-Eastern Nigeria, 1650–1980: A Study of Socio-Economic Formation and Transformation in Nigeria.* Ibadan, Nigeria: University Press.

Donnan, Elizabeth, ed. 1935. *Documents Illustrative of the History of the Slave Trade to America.* 4 vols. Repr., New York: Octagon, 1969.

Dove, Vee. 1975. *Madison County Homes: A Collection of Pre–Civil War Homes and Family Heritages.* Madison, Va.: the author.

Dowdey, Clifford. 1969. *The Virginia Dynasties: The Emergence of "King" Carter and the Golden Age.* New York: Bonanza.

Duke, Antera. 1956. "The Diary (1785–8) of Antera Duke." Ed. A. W. Wilkie. In *Efik Traders of Old Calabar,* ed. Daryll Forde, 27–78. London: Dawsons of Pall Mall.

Eltis, David, Stephen D. Behrendt, David Richardson, and Herbert S. Klein, eds. 1999. *The Trans-Atlantic Slave Trade: A Database on CD-ROM.* Cambridge: Cambridge University Press.

Emerson, Matthew C. 1994. "Decorated Clay Tobacco Pipes from the Chesapeake: An African Connection." In *Historical Archaeology of the Chesapeake,* ed. Paul A. Shackel and Barbara J. Little, 35–49. Washington, D.C.: Smithsonian Institution Press.

Epstein, Dena J. 1977. *Sinful Tunes and Spirituals: Black Folk Music to the Civil War.* Urbana: University of Illinois Press.

Equiano, Olaudah. 1789. *The Interesting Narrative of the Life of Olaudah Equiano, Written by Himself.* Ed. and intro. Robert J. Allison. Boston: Bedford Books of St. Martin's Press, 1995.

————. 1789. *The Interesting Narrative and Other Writings*. Ed., intro., and notes Vincent Carretta. New York: Penguin, 1997.

"Extracts from the Records of Caroline County." 1912. *Virginia Magazine of History and Biography* 20, no. 2: 203.

Falconbridge, Alexander. 1788. *An Account of the Slave Trade on the Coast of Africa*. Repr., New York: AMS, 1973.

Farish, Hunter Dickinson, ed. 1968. *Journal and Letters of Philip Vickers Fithian, 1773–1774: A Plantation Tutor of the Old Dominion*. Charlottesville: University Press of Virginia.

Fenn, Elizabeth A. 1988. "'A Perfect Equality Seemed to Reign': Slave Society and Jonkonnu." *North Carolina Historical Review* 65, no. 2: 127–53.

Ferguson, Leland. 1980. "Looking for the 'Afro' in Colono-Indian Pottery." In *Archaeological Perspectives on Ethnicity in America: Afro-American and Asian-American Culture History*, ed. Robert L. Schuyler, 14–28. New York: Baywood.

————. 1992. *Uncommon Ground: Archaeology and Early African America, 1650–1800*. Washington, D.C.: Smithsonian Institution Press.

Finch, John. 1833. *Travels in the United States of America and Canada*. London: Longman.

Floyd, Barry. 1969. *Eastern Nigeria: A Geographical Review*. New York: Praeger.

Forde, Daryll, and G. I. Jones. 1950. *The Ibo and Ibibio-Speaking Peoples of South-Eastern Nigeria*. Ethnographic Survey of Africa, Western Africa, pt. 3. London: International African Institute.

Fothergill, Augusta, and John Mark Naugle, eds. 1940. *Virginia Tax Payers 1782–87, Other Than Those Published by the United States Census Bureau*. Baltimore: Genealogical Publishing, 1978.

Fountain, Daniel L. 1995. "Historians and Historical Archaeology: Slave Sites." *Journal of Interdisciplinary History* 26, no. 1: 67–77.

Franklin, Maria. 1998. "Early Black Spirituality and the Cultural Strategy of Protective Symbolism: Evidence from Art and Archaeology." In *African Impact on the Material Culture of the Americas: Conference Proceedings*, 1–25. Winston-Salem, N.C.: The Museum of Early Southern Decorative Arts.

Frey, Sylvia. 1991. *Water from the Rock: Black Resistance in a Revolutionary Age*. Princeton: Princeton University Press.

Frey, Sylvia, and Betty Wood. 1998. *Come Shouting to Zion: African American Protestantism in the American South and British Caribbean to 1830*. Chapel Hill: University of North Carolina Press.

Geier, Clarence R., and Matthew Reeves. 2001. "Digging for Madison." *Montpelier: James Madison University Magazine* 24, no. 2: 48–57.

Glover, William, and Newton Standard, eds. 1902. *The Colonial Virginia Register.* Albany, N.Y.: Munsell's Sons. Available at http://www.ls.net/~newriver/va/vareg1.htm.

Goldie, Hugh. 1862. *Dictionary of the Efik Language, in Two Parts.* Repr., Ridgewood, N.J.: Gregg, 1964.

Gomez, Michael A. 1998. *Exchanging Our Country Marks: The Transformation of African Identities in the Colonial and Antebellum South.* Chapel Hill: University of North Carolina Press.

Gosse, Philip Henry. 1851. *A Naturalist's Sojourn in Jamaica.* London: Longman.

Green, Bennett W. 1899. *Word-Book of Virginia Folk-Speech.* Richmond, Va.: William Ellis Jones.

Green, Margaret M. 1947. *Ibo Village Affairs.* Repr., New York: Praeger, 1964.

———. 1967. "Igbo Dialects in the Polyglotta Africana." *African Language Review* 6: 111–19.

Grinnan, A. G. 1896. "Historical Notes and Queries: The Burning of Eve in Virginia." *Virginia Magazine of History and Biography* 3, no. 3: 308–10.

Grymes, J. Randolph. 1977. *The Octonia Grant in Orange and Greene Counties.* Ruckersville, Va.: Seminole.

Gutman, Herbert G. 1976. *The Black Family in Slavery and Freedom, 1750–1925.* New York: Random House.

Hackett, Mary A., et al., eds. 1993. *The Papers of James Madison, Secretary of State Series.* Vol. 2, *1 August 1801–28 February 1802.* Charlottesville: University Press of Virginia.

Hair, P. E. H. 1969. "An Ethnolinguistic Inventory of the Lower Guinea Coast before 1700: Part II." *African Language Review* 8: 225–56.

Hall, Douglas. 1989. *In Miserable Slavery: Thomas Thistlewood in Jamaica, 1750–86.* Repr., Kingston, Jamaica: University of the West Indies Press, 1999.

Hall, Gwendolyn Midlo. 1992. *Africans in Colonial Louisiana: The Development of Afro-Creole Culture in the Eighteenth Century.* Baton Rouge: Louisiana State University Press.

Hall, Robert L. 1991. "Savoring Africa in the New World." In *Seeds of Change: A Quincentennial Commemoration,* ed. Herman J. Viola and Carolyn Margolis, 161–71. Washington, D.C.: Smithsonian Institution Press.

Handler, Jerome S. 2000. "Slave Medicine and Obeah in Barbados, circa 1650 to 1834." *New West Indian Guide* 74, nos. 1–2: 57–90.

Handler, Jerome S., and Kenneth M. Bilby. 2001. "On the Early Use and Origin of the Term 'Obeah' in Barbados and the Anglophone Caribbean." *Slavery and Abolition* 22, no. 2: 87–100.

Harrison, F. H. [Fairfax]. 1928. "Robert Beverley, the Historian of Virginia." *Virginia Magazine of History and Biography* 36, no. 4: 333–44.

Hartle, Donald D. 1980. "Archaeology East of the Niger: A Review of Cultural-Historical Developments." In *West African Cultural Dynamics: Archaeological and Historical Perspectives,* ed. B. K. Swartz and Raymond E. Dumett, 195–203. The Hague, Holland: Mouton.

Hayden, Horace E. 1891. *Virginia Genealogies.* Repr., Washington, D.C.: Rare Book Shop, 1931.

Henderson, Richard N. 1972. *The King in Every Man: Evolutionary Trends in Onitsha Ibo Society and Culture.* New Haven: Yale University Press.

Henry, Reginald Buchanan, ed. 1935. *Genealogies of the Families of the Presidents.* Rutland, Vt.: Tuttle.

Herskovits, Melville J. 1941. *The Myth of the Negro Past.* Repr., Boston: Beacon, 1958.

Heywood, Linda M., ed. 2002. *Central Africans and Cultural Transformations in the American Diaspora.* Cambridge: Cambridge University Press.

Hobson, Charles F., and Robert A. Rutland, eds. *The Papers of James Madison.* Vol. 13, *20 January 1790–31 March 1791.* Charlottesville: University Press of Virginia.

Hodges, Graham R., ed. 1993. *Black Itinerants of the Gospel.* Madison: University of Wisconsin Press.

Hogendorn, Jan, and Marion Johnson. 1986. *The Shell Money of the Slave Trade.* Cambridge: Cambridge University Press.

Holloway, Joseph E., and Winifred K. Vass, eds. 1993. *The African Heritage of American English.* Bloomington: Indiana University Press.

Holman, James. 1959. *Holman's Voyage to Old Calabar.* Ed. Donald C. Simmons. Calabar, Nigeria: American Association for African Research. Originally published as *A Voyage round the World.* 4 vols. London: Smith, Elder, 1834.

Humphreys, David. 1730. *An Historical Account of the Incorporated Society for the Propagation of the Gospel in Foreign Parts.* London: Joseph Downing.

Hungerford, James. 1859. *The Old Plantation, and What I Gathered There in an Autumn Month.* New York: Harper.

Hunt, Gaillard. 1902. *The Life of James Madison.* New York: Doubleday, Page.

———, ed. 1906. *The Writings of James Madison.* 9 vols. New York: Putnam's.

Hunt-Jones, Conover. 1977. *Dolley and the "Great Little Madison."* Washington, D.C.: American Institute of Architects Foundation.

Hurmence, Belinda, ed. 1984. *My Folks Don't Want Me To Talk about Slavery: Twenty-one Oral Histories of Former North Carolina Slaves*. Winston-Salem, N.C.: John F. Blair.

Hutchinson, T. J. 1855. *Narrative of the Niger, Tshadda, and Binue Exploration*. Repr., London: Frank Cass, 1966.

Hyatt, Harry M. 1970–74. *Hoodoo-Conjuration-Witchcraft-Rootwork: Beliefs Accepted by Many Negroes and White Persons, These Being Orally Recorded among Blacks and Whites*. Memoirs of the Alma Egan Hyatt Foundation. 4 vols. Hannibal, Mo.; New York; and Cambridge, Mass.: Western Publishing.

Igbozurike, U. M. 1978. "The Vegetation of Nsukka Area." In *The Nsukka Environment*, ed. G. E. K. Ofomata, 98–105. Enugu, Nigeria: Fourth Dimension.

Igwe, G. E. 1986. *Onye Turu Ikoro Waa Ya Eze*. Ibadan, Nigeria: University Press.

Ingraham, Joseph H. 1860. *The Sunny South; or, The Southerner at Home*. Philadelphia: G. G. Evans.

Inscoe, John C. 1983. "Carolina Slave Names: An Index to Acculturation." *Journal of Southern History* 49, no. 4: 527–54.

Isaac, Rhys. 1982. *The Transformation of Virginia, 1740–1790*. Chapel Hill: University of North Carolina Press.

Isichei, Elizabeth. 1976. *A History of the Igbo People*. London: Macmillan.

———, ed. 1978. *Igbo Worlds: An Anthology of Oral Histories and Historical Descriptions*. Philadelphia: Institute for the Study of Human Issues.

———. 1983. *A History of Nigeria*. London: Longmans.

Jackson, Richard M. 1934. *Journal of a Voyage to Bonny River on the West Coast of Africa, and in the Ship Kingston, from Liverpool*. [1825–26]. Ed. Roland Jackson. Letchworth, U.K.: Garden City Press.

Jacobs, Harriet A. 1861. *Incidents in the Life of a Slave Girl, Written by Herself*. Ed. Jean Fagan Yellin. Cambridge: Harvard University Press, 1987.

Janson, Charles W. 1807. *The Stranger in America, 1793–1806*. Repr., New York: Press of the Pioneers, 1935.

Jennings, Paul. 1865. *A Colored Man's Reminiscences of James Madison*. Brooklyn, N.Y.: Beadle.

Jones, Hugh. 1956. *The Present State of Virginia, from Whence Is Inferred a Short View of Maryland and North Carolina*. [1724]. Ed. Richard L. Morton. Chapel Hill: University of North Carolina Press.

Jones, G. I. 1967. "Olaudah Equiano of the Niger Ibo." In *Africa Remembered: Narratives by West Africans from the Era of the Slave Trade*, ed. Philip D. Curtin, 60–98. Madison: University of Wisconsin Press.

Jones, Randall B. 2001. "Invisible History." *Montpelier: James Madison University Magazine* 24, no. 2: 58–65.

Kaufman, Elaine M. 1985. *Ibibio Dictionary*. Leiden, the Netherlands: African Studies Centre.

Kelso, William M. 1984. *Kingsmill Plantations, 1619–1800: Archaeology of Country Life in Colonial Virginia*. New York: Academic Press.

———. 1986. "The Archaeology of Slave Life at Thomas Jefferson's Monticello: 'A Wolf by the Ears.'" *Journal of New World Archaeology* 6, no. 4: 5–20.

———. 1997. *Archaeology at Monticello: Artifacts of Everyday Life in the Plantation Community*. Monticello Monograph Series. Charlottesville, Va.: Thomas Jefferson Memorial Foundation.

Ketcham, Ralph, ed. 1959. "An Unpublished Sketch of James Madison by James K. Paulding." *Virginia Magazine of History and Biography* 67, no. 4: 435.

———. 1971. *James Madison: A Biography*. Repr., Charlottesville: University Press of Virginia, 1990.

Klingelhofer, Eric. "Aspects of Early Afro-American Material Culture: Artifacts from the Slave Quarters at Garrison Plantation, Maryland." *Historical Archaeology* 21, no. 2: 112–19.

Knight, Henry C. [pseud. Arthur Singleton]. 1824. *Letters from the South and West; by Arthur Singleton*. Boston: Richardson and Lord.

Koelle, Sigismund W. 1854. *Polyglotta Africana; or, A Comparative Vocabulary of Nearly Three Hundred Words and Phrases, in More Than One Hundred Distinct African Languages*. Repr., Graz, Austria: Akademische Druk-U. Verlagsanstalt, 1963.

Kretchner, Norman. 1978. "Lactose and Lactase." In *Human Nutrition*, ed. Norman Kretchner and William van B. Robertson, 131–38. San Francisco: Freeman.

Krzyzanowski, Ludwik, ed. 1797. *Julia Ursyn Niemcewicz and America*. New York: Polish Institute of Arts and Sciences in America, 1961.

Kulikoff, Allan. 1986. *Tobacco and Slaves: The Development of Southern Cultures in the Chesapeake, 1680–1800*. Chapel Hill: University of North Carolina Press.

Lander, Richard, and John Lander. 1832. *Journal of an Expedition to Explore the Course and Termination of the Niger*. 2 vols. New York: Harper.

Leith-Ross, Sylvia. 1939. *African Women: A Study of the Ibo of Nigeria*. Repr., London: Routledge and Kegan Paul, 1965.

Leonard, Arthur G. 1898. "Notes of a Journey to Bende." *Journal of the Manchester Geographical Society* 14: 190–207.

———. 1906. *The Lower Niger and Its Tribes*. London: Macmillan.

Levasseur, A. 1829. *Lafayette in America, in 1824 and 1825; or, Journal of Travels, in the United States*. 2 vols. New York: White, Gallagher, and White.

Levine, Lawrence. 1977. *Black Culture and Black Consciousness: Afro-American Folk Thought from Slavery to Freedom*. Oxford: Oxford University Press.

Lévi-Strauss, Claude. 1966. *The Savage Mind.* Chicago: Chicago University Press.

Lewis, David Levering, ed. 1995. *W. E. B. DuBois: A Reader.* New York: Holt.

Lewis, Matthew. 1834. *Journal of a West India Proprietor.* Ed. Judith Terry. Oxford: Oxford University Press, 1999.

Little, Barbara V., ed. 1988. *Orange County, Virginia, Tithables, 1734–1782.* Orange, Va.: the author.

Littlefield, Daniel C. 1981. *Rice and Slaves: Ethnicity and the Slave Trade in Colonial South Carolina.* Baton Rouge: Louisiana State University Press.

Long, Edward. 1774. *The History of Jamaica; or, General Survey of the Antient and Modern State of that Island.* 3 vols. Repr., London: Cass, 1970.

MacMillan, Dougald. 1926. "John Kuners." *Journal of American Folk-Lore* 39, no. 151: 53–57.

Madison, James. *Letters and Other Writings of James Madison.* Vol. 2, *1794–1815.* New York: R. Worthington, 1884.

Martineau, Harriet. 1838. *Retrospect of Western Travels.* 3 vols. London: Saunders and Orley.

McCall, John C. 1995. "Rethinking Ancestors in Africa." *Africa* 65, no. 2: 256–70.

McCoy, Drew. 1989. *The Last of the Fathers: James Madison and the Republican Legacy.* Cambridge: Cambridge University Press.

McGroarty, William Buckner. 1921. "The Family Register of Nicholas Taliaferro, with Notes." *William and Mary Quarterly,* 2d ser., 1, no. 3: 145–66.

Meaders, Daniel, ed. 1997. *Advertisements for Runaway Slaves in Virginia, 1801–1820.* New York: Garland.

Meek, C. K. 1937. *Law and Authority in a Nigerian Tribe: A Study in Indirect Rule.* Repr., New York: Barnes and Noble, 1970.

Migeod, F. W. H. 1917. "Personal Names among Some West African Tribes." *Journal of the African Society* 17, no. 65: 39–40.

Miller, Ann L. 1988. *Antebellum Orange: The Pre–Civil War Homes, Public Buildings, and Historic Sites of Orange County, Virginia.* Orange, Va.: Orange County Historical Society.

———. 2001. *The Short Life and Strange Death of Ambrose Madison.* Orange, Va.: Orange County Historical Society.

Miller, Randall M., ed. 1978. *"Dear Master": Letters of a Slave Family.* Ithaca: Cornell University Press.

Minchinton, Walter E., ed. 1958. "The Virginia Letters of Isaac Hobhouse, Merchant of Bristol." *Virginia Magazine of History and Biography* 66, no. 3: 278–301.

———. 1976. "The Slave Trade of Bristol with the British Mainland Colonies in North America, 1699–1770." In *Liverpool, the African Slave Trade, and*

Abolition: Essays to illustrate Current Knowledge and Research, ed. Roger Anstey and P. E. H. Hair, 39–59. Liverpool, U.K.: Historic Society of Lancashire and Cheshire.

Minchinton, Walter, Celia King, and Peter Waite, eds. 1984. *Virginia Slave-Trade Statistics, 1698–1775.* Richmond: Virginia State Library.

Mintz, Sidney W., and Richard Price. 1992. *The Birth of African-American Culture: An Anthropological Approach.* Boston: Beacon Press. Originally published as *An Anthropological Approach to the Afro-American Past.* Philadelphia: Institute for the Study of Human Issues, 1976.

Moore, Stacy G. 1989. "'Established and Well Cultivated': Afro-American Foodways in Early Virginia." *Virginia Cavalcade* 39, no. 2: 70–83.

Moore, Virginia. 1979. *The Madisons: A Biography.* New York: McGraw-Hill.

Morgan, Philip D. 1988. "Slave Life in Piedmont, Virginia, 1720–1800." In *Colonial Chesapeake Society,* ed. Lois Green Carr, Philip D. Morgan, and Jean B. Russo, 433–84. Chapel Hill: University of North Carolina Press.

———. 1998. *Slave Counterpoint: Black Culture in the Eighteenth-Century Chesapeake and Lowcountry.* Chapel Hill: University of North Carolina Press.

Morton, Richard L. 1960 *Colonial Virginia.* 2 vols. Chapel Hill: University of North Carolina Press.

Morton, Terry B., ed. 1969. *Belle Grove.* Washington, D.C.: National Trust for Historic Preservation.

Mullin, Michael. 1992. *Africa in America: Slave Acculturation and Resistance in the American South and the British Caribbean, 1736–1831.* Urbana: University of Illinois Press.

Mulroy, Kevin. 1993. "Ethnogenesis and Ethnohistory of the Seminole Maroons." *Journal of World History* 4, no. 2: 287–305.

Neiman, Frazer D. 1980. *The "Manner House" before Stratford (Discovering the Clifts Plantation).* Ed. Alonzo T. Dill. Stratford, Va.: n.p.

Njaka, Mazi E. N. 1974. *Igbo Political Culture.* Evanston, Ill.: Northwestern University Press.

Njoku, John E. E. 1978. *A Dictionary of Igbo Names, Culture, and Proverbs.* Washington, D.C.: University Press of America.

Noble, Allen G. 1991. "Measuring Vernacular Buildings: A Field Course Unit." *Material Culture* 23, no. 1: 1–14.

Nora, Pierre. 1994. "Between Memory and History: *Les Lieux de Mémoire.*" In *History and Memory in African-American Culture,* ed. Geneviève Fabre and Robert O'Meally, 284–300. New York: Oxford University Press.

Norfleet, Fillmore. 1974. *Suffolk in Virginia c. 1795–1840: A Record of Lots, Lives, and Likenesses.* Richmond: Whittet and Shepperson.

Norris, J. E., ed. 1890. *History of the Lower Shenandoah Valley Counties of Frederick, Berkeley, Jefferson, and Clarke.* Repr., Berryville, Va.: Virginia Book, 1972.

Northrup, David. 1972. "The Growth of Trade among the Igbo before 1800." *Journal of African History* 13, no. 2: 217–36.

———. 1978. *Trade without Rulers: Pre-Colonial Economic Development in South-Eastern Nigeria.* Oxford: Clarendon.

Nugent, Nell Marion, ed. 1934. *Cavaliers and Pioneers: Abstracts of Virginia Land Patents and Grants.* 4 vols. Repr., Baltimore, Md.: Genealogical Publishing, 1979.

Nwala, T. Uzodinma. 1985. *Igbo Philosophy.* Lagos, Nigeria: Lantern.

Obiechina, E. N. 1971. "Introduction." *The Conch* 3, no. 2: 1–15.

Ogbalu, F. C. 1965. *Ilu Igbo (The Book of Igbo Proverbs).* 2d ed. Onitsha, Nigeria: University Publishing.

Oguagha, Philip A. 1984. "Historical and Traditional Evidence." In Philip A. Oguagha and A. I. Okpoko, *History and Ethnoarchaeology in Eastern Nigeria: A Study of Igbo-Igala Relations with Special Reference to the Anambra Valley,* 185–295. Cambridge Monographs in African Archaeology 7, B.A.R. International Series 195. Oxford: B.A.R.

Okeke, Uche. 1978. "The Art Culture of the Nsukka Igbo." In *The Nsukka Environment,* ed. G. E. K. Ofomata. Enugu, Nigeria: Fourth Dimension; repr., with an index, 1985.

Okiy, G. E. O. 1960. "Indigenous Nigerian Food Plants." *Journal of the West African Science Association* 6, no. 2: 117–21.

Okpoko, A. I. 1984. "Archaeology and Ethnoarchaeology in the Anambra Valley." In Philip A. Oguagha and A. I. Òkpóko, *History and Ethnoarchaeology in Eastern Nigeria: A Study of Igbo-Igala Relations with Special Reference to the Anambra Valley,* 1–184. Cambridge Monographs in African Archaeology 7, B.A.R. International Series 195. Oxford: B.A.R.

Oldfield, R. A. K. 1837. "Mr. Oldfield's Journal." In Macgregor Laird and R. A. K. Oldfield, *Narrative of an Expedition into the Interior of Africa, by the River Niger, in the Steam-Vessels Quorra and Alburkah, in 1832, 1833, and 1834.* 2 vols. London: Bentley.

Onwuejeogwu, M. Angulu. 1981. *An Igbo Civilization: Nri Kingdom and Hegemony.* London: Ethnographica.

"Orange County Tithe Lists." 1918. *William and Mary Quarterly* 1st ser., 27, no. 1: 19–27.

Oriji, John N. 1987. "The Slave Trade, Warfare, and Aro Expansion in the Igbo Hinterland." *Transafrican Journal of History* 16: 151–66.

————. 1990. *Traditions of Igbo Origin: A Study of Pre-Colonial Population Movements in Africa.* American University Studies, Series XI, Anthropology and Sociology vol. 48. New York: Lang.

Orser, Charles E., Jr. 1994. "The Archaeology of African-American Slave Religion in the Antebellum South." *Cambridge Archaeological Journal* 4, no. 1: 33–45.

Oyenuga, V. A. 1967. *Agriculture in Nigeria: An Introduction.* Rome: Food and Agricultural Organization of the United Nations.

Palmer, Colin A. 1995. "From Africa to the Americas: Ethnicity in the Early Black Communities of the Americas." *Journal of World History* 6, no. 2: 223–36.

Patterson, Orlando. 1969. *The Sociology of Slavery: An Analysis of the Origins, Development, and Structure of Negro Slave Society in Jamaica.* Rutherford, N.J.: Fairleigh Dickinson University Press.

Perdue, Charles L., Jr., Thomas E. Barden, and Robert K. Phillips, eds. 1976. *Weevils in the Wheat: Interviews with Virginia Ex-Slaves.* Repr., Bloomington: Indiana University Press, 1980.

Price, Jacob M. 1983. "Buchanan & Simson, 1759–1763: A Different Kind of Glasgow Firm Trading to the Chesapeake." *William and Mary Quarterly,* 3d ser., 40, no. 1: 3–41.

Pritchett, Jonathan, and Herman Freudenberger. 1992. "A Peculiar Sample: The Selection of Slaves for the New Orleans Market." *Journal of Economic History* 52, no. 1: 109–27.

Puckett, Newbell Niles. 1926. *Folk Beliefs of the Southern Negro.* Chapel Hill: University of North Carolina Press.

————. 1937. "Names of American Negro Slaves." In *Studies in the Science of Society, Presented to Albert Galloway Keller,* ed. George P. Murdock, 471–94. New Haven: Yale University Press.

————. 1975. *Black Names in America: Origins and Usage.* Ed. Murray Heller. Boston: Hall for the Cleveland Public Library.

Quartey-Papafio, A. B. 1914. "The Use of Names among the Gas or Accra People of the Gold Coast." *Journal of the African Society* 13, no. 50: 179–80.

————. 1920. "The Ga Homowo Festival." *Journal of the African Society* 19, no. 74: 126–34; 19, no. 75: 227–32.

Randolph, Peter. 1855. *Sketches of Slave Life; or, Illustrations of the "Peculiar Institution."* 2d ed. Boston: n.p.

Rawley, James A. 1981. *The Trans-Atlantic Slave Trade: A History.* New York: Norton.

Reid, Ira DeA. 1942. "The John Canoe Festival: A New World Africanism."
    Phylon 3, no. 4: 349–70.
Reis, João José. 1993. *Slave Rebellion in Brazil: The Muslim Uprising of 1835 in*
    Bahia. Trans. Arthur Brakel. Baltimore: Johns Hopkins University Press.
Reynolds, Edward. 1985. *Stand the Storm: A History of the Atlantic Slave Trade.*
    London: Allison and Busby.
Richardson, David. 1986. "Introduction." In *Bristol, Africa, and the Eighteenth-*
    Century Slave Trade to America, vol. 1, *The Years of Expansion, 1698–1729,* ed.
    David Richardson, vii–xxviii. Gloucester, U.K.: Bristol Record Society.
————, ed. 1986–96. *Bristol, Africa, and the Eighteenth-Century Slave Trade to*
    America. 4 vols. Gloucester, U.K.: Bristol Record Society.
Rutland, Robert A. 1987. *James Madison: The Founding Father.* New York:
    Macmillan.
Samford, Patricia. 1996. "The Archaeology of African-American Slavery and
    Material Culture." *William and Mary Quarterly,* 3d ser., 53, no. 1: 87–114.
Schuler, Monica. 1979. "Afro-American Slave Culture." *Historical Reflections* 6,
    no. 1: 121–55.
Schwarz, Philip J. 1988. *Twice Condemned: Slaves and the Criminal Laws of Virginia,*
    1705–1865. Baton Rouge: Louisiana State University Press.
Scott, W. W. 1907. *A History of Orange County, Virginia, from Its Formation in 1734*
    (O.S.) to the End of Reconstruction in 1870; Compiled Mainly from Original
    Records, with a Brief Sketch of the Beginnings of Virginia, a Summary of Local
    Events to 1907, and a Map. Richmond, Va.: Waddy.
Shaw, Thurstan. 1970. *Igbo-Ukwu: An Account of Archaeological Discoveries in*
    Eastern Nigeria. 2 vols. Evanston, Ill.: Northwestern University Press.
Simmons, Donald C. 1956. "An Ethnographic Sketch of the Efik People."
    In *Efik Traders of Old Calabar,* ed. Daryll Forde, 1–26. London: Dawsons of
    Pall Mall.
Simpson, George Eaton. 1973. *Melville J. Herskovits.* New York: Columbia
    University Press.
Singleton, Theresa A. 1991. "The Archaeology of Slave Life." In *Before Freedom*
    Came: African-American Life in the Antebellum South, ed. Edward D. C.
    Campbell Jr. and Kym S. Rice, 155–75. Charlottesville: University Press of
    Virginia.
Singleton, Theresa A., and Mark D. Bograd, eds. *The Archaeology of the African*
    Diaspora in the Americas. Guides to the Archaeological Literature of the
    Immigrant Experience in America 2. Ann Arbor, Mich.: Braun-Brumfield
    for the Society for Historical Archaeology.

Slaughter, Philip. 1877. *A History of St. Mark's Parish, Culpeper County, Virginia, with Notes of Old Church Families and Old Families, and Illustrations of the Manners and Customs of the Olden Time.* Baltimore: Innes.

Smedes, Susan D. 1887. *A Southern Planter: Social Life in the Old South.* Repr., New York: Pott, 1900.

Smith, James L. 1881. *Autobiography of James L. Smith.* Norwich, Conn.: Press of the Bulletin.

Smith, Samuel Stanhope. 1787. *An Essay on the Causes of the Variety of Complexion and Figure in the Human Species.* In *The Negro versus Equality, 1762–1826,* ed. Winthrop D. Jordan, 23–28. Chicago: Rand McNally, 1969.

Snelgrave, William. 1734. *New Account of Some Parts of Guinea, and the Slave-Trade.* London: Knapton.

Sobel, Mechal. 1979. *Trabelin' On: The Slave Journey to an Afro-Baptist Faith.* Princeton: Princeton University Press.

———. 1987. *The World They Made Together: Black and White Values in Eighteenth-Century Virginia.* Princeton: Princeton University Press.

Souders, Bronwen C., and John M. Souders. 2003. *A Rock in a Weary Land, a Shelter in a Time of Storm: The African-American Experience in Waterford, Virginia.* Waterford, Va.: Waterford Foundation.

Sparacio, Ruth, and Sam Sparacio, eds. 1996. *Orange County, Virginia, Land Tax Books, 1782–1790.* McLean, Va.: Antient Press.

Stanard, William G., ed. 1924–26. "Virginia Council Journals." *Virginia Magazine of History and Biography* 32, no. 2: 134; 33, no. 3: 297; 33, no. 4: 392; 34, no. 3: 205–6.

Stanton, Lucia. 2000. *Free Some Day: The African-American Families of Monticello.* Monticello Monograph Series. Charlottesville, Va.: Thomas Jefferson Foundation.

State Historical Markers of Virginia. 1948. 6th ed. Richmond: Virginia Department of Conservation and Development.

Steward, Austin. 1861. *Twenty-two Years a Slave, and Forty Years a Freeman.* 3d ed. Rochester, N.Y.: Allings and Cory.

Stine, Linda France, Melanie A. Cabak, and Mark D. Groover. 1996. "Blue Beads as African-American Cultural Symbols." *Historical Archaeology* 30, no. 3: 49–75.

St. Mery, Moreau de. 1947. *American Journey* [1793–98]. Trans. and ed. Kenneth Roberts and Anna M. Roberts. Garden City, N.Y.: Doubleday.

Stuckey, Sterling. 1987. *Slave Culture: Nationalist Theory and the Foundations of Black America.* Oxford: Oxford University Press.

Sutcliff, Robert. 1815. *Travels in Some Parts of North America, in the Years 1804, 1805, and 1806.* London: Longman, Hurst.

Talbot, P. Amaury. 1926. *The Peoples of Southern Nigeria: A Sketch of Their History, Ethnology, and Languages with an Abstract of the 1921 Census.* 4 vols. Repr., London: Cass, 1969.

———. 1932. *Tribes of the Niger Delta: Their Religions and Customs.* London: Sheldon.

Talley, Thomas W. 1922. *Negro Folk Rhymes: Wise and Otherwise.* New York: Macmillan.

Taylor, John C. 1859. "Journal of the Rev. J. C. Taylor at Onitsha." In Samuel Crowther and John C. Taylor, *The Gospel on the Banks of the Niger—Journals and Notices of the Native Missionaries Accompanying the Niger Expedition of 1857–1859.* Repr., London: Dawsons of Pall Mall, 1968.

Thomas, Northcote W. 1913. *Anthropological Report on the Ibo-Speaking Peoples of Nigeria.* 6 vols. Repr., New York: Negro Universities Press, 1969.

Thompson, Robert Ferris. 1983. *Flash of the Spirit: African and Afro-American Art and Philosophy.* New York: Vintage.

———. 1990. "Kongo Influences on African-American Artistic Culture." In *Africanisms in American Culture,* ed. Joseph E. Holloway, 148–84. Bloominn: Indiana University Press.

Thornton, John K. 1991. "African Dimensions of the Stono Rebellion." *American Historical Review* 96: 1101–13.

———. 1993. "Central African Names and African-American Naming Patterns." *William and Mary Quarterly,* 3d ser., 50, no. 4: 727–42.

———. 1993. "'I Am the Subject of the King of Congo': African Political Ideology and the Haitian Revolution." *Journal of World History* 4, no. 2: 181–214.

———. 1998a. *Africa and Africans in the Making of the Atlantic World, 1400–1800.* 2d ed. Cambridge: Cambridge University Press.

———. 1998b. "The African Experience of the '20. and Odd Negroes' Arriving in Virginia in 1619." *William and Mary Quarterly,* 3d ser., 55, no. 3: 421–34.

Three Negro Classics. 1965. New York: Avon.

Tucker, George. 1816. *Letters from Virginia.* Baltimore, Md.: Fielding Lewis.

Turner, Lorenzo Dow. 1949. *Africanisms in the Gullah Dialect.* Chicago: University of Chicago Press.

Twining, Mary A., and Keith E. Baird, eds. 1991. *Sea Island Roots: African Presence in the Carolinas and Georgia.* Trenton, N.J.: Africa World.

Tyler, Lyon G., ed. 1900. "Chart Pedigree of Madison Family." *William and Mary Quarterly,* 1st ser., 9, no. 1: 37–40.

Ukwu, Ukwu I. 1967. "The Development of Trade and Marketing in Iboland." *Journal of the Historical Society of Nigeria* 3, no. 4: 647–62.

Umeh, John A. 1997. *After God Is Dibia: Igbo Cosmology, Divination, and Sacred Science in Nigeria.* London: Karnak.

Upton, Dell. 1982. "Vernacular Domestic Architecture in Eighteenth-Century Virginia." *Winterthur Portfolio* 17, nos. 2–3: 95–119.

———. 1985. "White and Black Landscapes in Eighteenth-Century Virginia." *Places* 2, no. 2: 59–72.

U.S. Census Bureau. *Heads of Families of the First Census of the United States Taken in the Year 1790: Records of the State Enumerations, 1782 to 1785.* Washington, D.C.: U.S. Government Printing Office, 1908. Reprint, Bountiful, Utah: Accelerated Indexing Systems, 1978.

Uzozie, L. C. 1978. "Agricultural Land Use in the Nsukka Area." In *The Nsukka Environment,* ed. G. E. K. Ofomata, 153–72. Enugu, Nigeria: Fourth Dimension.

Vansina, Jan. 1990. *Paths in the Rainforests: Toward a History of Political Tradition in Equatorial Africa.* Madison: University of Wisconsin Press.

Vass, Winifred K. 1979. *The Bantu Speaking Heritage of the United States.* Los Angeles: Center for Afro-American Studies.

Vlach, John Michael. 1991. *By the Work of Their Hands: Studies in Afro-American Folklife.* Charlottesville: University Press of Virginia.

———. 1993. *Back of the Big House: The Architecture of Plantation Society.* Chapel Hill: University of North Carolina Press.

Wagner, Mark. 1981. "The Introduction and Early Use of African Plants in the New World." *Tennessee Anthropologist* 6, no. 2: 112–23.

Walser, Richard. 1971. "His Worship the John Kuner." *North Carolina Folklore* 19, no. 4: 160–72.

Walsh, Lorena S. 1989. "Plantation Management in the Chesapeake, 1620–1820." *Journal of Economic History* 49, no. 2: 393–406.

———. 1997. *From Calabar to Carter's Grove: The History of a Virginia Slave Community.* Charlottesville: University Press of Virginia.

———. 1999. "Summing the Parts: Implications for Estimating Chesapeake Output and Income Regionally." *William and Mary Quarterly,* 3d ser., 56, no. 1: 53–94.

———. 2001. "The Chesapeake Slave Trade: Regional Patterns, African Origins, and Some Implications." *William and Mary Quarterly,* 3d ser., 58, no. 1: 139–70.

Warren, Edward. 1885. *A Doctor's Experiences in Three Continents.* Baltimore, Md.: Cushings and Bailey.

Washington, Booker. 1901. *Up from Slavery.* Intro. Louis R. Harlan. Repr., New York: Penguin, 1986.

Wheaton, Thomas R. 2002. "Colonial African American Plantation Villages." In *Another's Country: Archaeological and Historical Perspectives on Cultural Interactions in the Southern Colonies*, ed. J. W. Joseph and Martha Zierden, 30–44. Tuscaloosa: University of Alabama Press.

Wieschoff, H. A. 1941. "The Social Significance of Names among the Ibo of Nigeria." *American Anthropologist* 43, no. 2: 212–22.

Wilkie, Laurie A. 1995. "Magic and Empowerment on the Plantation: An Archaeological Consideration of African-American World View." *Southeastern Archaeology* 14, no. 2: 136–48.

———. 1997. "Secret and Sacred: Contextualizing the Artifacts of African-American Magic and Religion." *Historical Archaeology* 31, no. 4: 81–106.

"Will of Ambrose Madison." 1899 [1732]. *Virginia Magazine of History and Biography* 6: 434–35.

Williams, D. Alan. 1983. "The Small Farmer in Eighteenth-Century Virginia Politics." In *Colonial America: Essays in Politics and Social Development*, 3d ed., ed. Stanley N. Katz and John H. Murrin, 410–21. New York: Knopf.

Willis, John C. 1991. "From the Dictates of Pride to the Paths of Righteousness: Slave Honor and Christianity in Antebellum Virginia." In *The Edge of the South: Life in Nineteenth-Century Virginia*, ed. Edward L. Ayers and John C. Willis, 37–55. Charlottesville: University Press of Virginia.

Windley, Lathan A., ed. 1983. *Runaway Slave Advertisements: A Documentary History from the 1730s to 1790*. 4 vols. Westport, Conn.: Greenwood.

Woolman, John. 1774. *The Journal of John Woolman*. Philadelphia: Crukshank; Repr., Gloucester, Mass.: Peter Smith, 1971.

Young, Amy L. 1996. "Archaeological Evidence of African-Style Ritual and Healing Practices in the Upland South." *Tennessee Anthropologist* 21, no. 2: 139–55.

UNPUBLISHED SECONDARY SOURCES

Baron, Robert. 1994. "Africa in the Americas: Melville J. Herskovits' Folkloristic and Anthropological Scholarship, 1923–1941." Ph.D. diss., University of Pennsylvania.

Bear, James A., Jr. N.d. *Thomas Jefferson's Account Books [1767–1826]*. 5 vols. Special Collections, Alderman Library, University of Virginia, Charlottesville.

Bettelheim, Judith. 1979. "The Afro-Jamaica Jonkonnu Festival: Playing the Forces and Operating the Cloth." Ph.D. diss., Yale University.

Chambers, Douglas B. 1991. "The Making of Montpelier: Col. James Madison and the Development of a Piedmont Plantation, 1741 To 1774." Master's thesis, University of Virginia.

———. 1996. "'He Gwine Sing He Country': Africans, Afro-Virginians, and the Development of Slave Culture in Virginia, 1690–1810." Ph.D. diss., University of Virginia.

———, ed. 2001. "Madison Slaves Biographical Database." In possession of author.

Chew, Enos, and Emma Mae Chew. 1987. "Antient Burial Ground of Chew, Beverley, Stanard Families Overlooking the Po River on Larkin Chew, Sr.'s Plantation." In possession of author.

Dandridge, Anne Spotswood. 1901–2. "Family Notes, Taylor, etc., Written for Betty Taylor Dandridge—with Love—by Anne Spotswood Dandridge, 1901–1902. Copied for Mrs. Betty Taylor Stauffer in Pleasant Remembrance of Auld Lang Syne—by 'The Dou' [Philip Pendleton Dandridge] 1915–1916 (with Addenda)." In possession of author.

———. 1915–16. "Addenda: Taylor—Births, Marriages and Deaths from Mrs. Betty Taylor Dandridge's Notes, Copied, in 1915, by Philip Pendleton Dandridge from the original Ms. of Mrs. Betty Taylor Dandridge." Original in possession of Helen Marie Taylor, Meadowfarm, Orange County, Va.

"Each a Mighty Voice: The African-American Presence in Albemarle County." 1996. Museum exhibition for Black History Month, Albemarle County Historical Society, Charlottesville, Va.

"Jefferson Slaves Database." [1998]. International Center for Jefferson Studies, Thomas Jefferson Foundation, Monticello, Va.

King and Queen County Committee. 1957. "A True Relation of the History of King and Queen County in Virginia, 1607–1790." Jamestown 350th Anniversary Festival, King and Queen Courthouse, Va..

Klein, Michael. 1988. *The Montpelier Periphery: An Archaeological Survey.* Archaeological Survey Monograph 4. Charlottesville: Department of Anthropology, University of Virginia.

Lewis, Lynne G., and Scott K. Parker. 1987. *From Aborigenes to Aristocrats: Archaeological Survey in Orange County, Virginia, 1987.* Richmond: Virginia Division of Historic Landmarks.

Mebuge-Obaa II, Prince P. N. 2002. "An Oral History Research Project: History of Scarification (Tattoo) in Nri as Narrated by Ichie Anago Okoye a.k.a. Onwanetilora of Nri." In possession of author.

Miller, Ann L. 1984. "Counterpoints to Montpelier: The Homes of President Madison's Brothers." AIV 25. Charlottesville: School of Architecture, Fiske Kimball Library, University of Virginia.

Montpelier Fact Sheet 2: The Montpelier Gardens. 1991. Montpelier Station, Va.: National Trust for Historic Preservation.

Montpelier Fact Sheet 3: Archaeology at Montpelier. 1991. Montpelier Station, Va.: National Trust for Historic Preservation.

Montpelier Fact Sheet 5: Origin of the Montpelier Name. Montpelier Station, Va.: National Trust for Historic Preservation.

Nwokeji, G. Ugo. 1999. "The Biafran Frontier: Trade, Slaves, and Aro Society, c. 1750–1905." Ph.D. diss., University of Toronto.

Parker, Kathleen A., and Jacqueline L. Hernigle. 1990. *Portici: Portrait of a Middling Plantation in Piedmont Virginia.* Occasional Report 3. Washington, D.C.: Regional Archaeology Program, National Capital Region, National Park Service.

Parker, Scott K., Lynne G. Lewis, Larry D. Dermody, and Ann L. Miller. 1992. "Crafty Businessmen: A New Perspective on Eighteenth-Century Plantation Economics." Paper presented at the Council of Virginia Archaeologists Symposium VI: The Historical Archaeology of Eighteenth-Century Virginia, Charlottesville, May.

Pearce, Laurie E. 1992. "The Cowrie Shell in Virginia: A Critical Evaluation of Potential Archaeological Significance." Master's thesis, College of William and Mary.

Samford, Patricia Merle. 2000. "Power Runs in Many Channels: Subfloor Pits and West African–Based Spiritual Traditions in Colonial Virginia." Ph.D. diss., University of North Carolina at Chapel Hill.

Schlotterbeck, John T. 1980. "Plantation and Farm: Social and Economic Change in Orange and Green Counties, Virginia, 1716 to 1860." Ph.D. diss., Johns Hopkins University.

White, Esther C. 1992. " 'To Indulge Themselves in All the Luxuries as Well as Necessaries of Life': Comparison of Slave Quarter and Kitchen Midden Assemblages from George Washington's Mt. Vernon." Paper presented at the Society for Historical Archaeology Annual Meeting, Kingston, Jamaica, January.

Works Progress Administration of Virginia. 1936. "Virginia Historical Inventory, Orange County." Microfilm, Alderman Library, University of Virginia, Charlottesville.

INDEX

Africans
Akan, 11–12, 101
Central Africans (Western Bantu,
  Angola, Congo), 11, 12, 13, 40,
  100, 159, 161–62, 180
Ekoi, 45
FulBe, 11, 13, 162
Malagasy (Madagascars), 11
Mande, 11–12, 13, 162, 184
Moko, 102
Muslims, 162
Yoruba, 11
Agriculture. *See also individual plants*
in Igboland, 39–40, 45, 103;
  women, 103
in Virginia, 103, 166
American Colonization Society, 133,
  137–38, 156
Archaeology
blue glass beads, 70, 173, 183–84
buttons, 183–84
cowries, 184–85
in Igboland, 30–31
at Monticello, 183–84

at Montpelier, 70–71, 86–89
root-cellars, 88–89, 183–85
Architecture
in Igboland, 40–41
at Montpelier, 116–17, 123, 129,
  153, 155–56
in Virginia, 86–87
Aro
colonies of, 25, 27–28
general, 15, 17, 23–24, 26, 46
markets of, 26–27
merchant warlords in, 27–28, 29,
  35, 47
mmuba concept, 27, 28, 57
slave trade by, 25, 26, 33, 35, 44
as a state, 27–28
Arochukwu, 25, 27
Asparagus, 168–69
Astronomy, 185
Atlantic Africans, 13, 14, 15–16, 19,
  71, 98, 112, 143, 188, 192

Banjo, 42, 179–80
Barbot, James, 128

CPSIA information can be obtained
at www.ICGtesting.com
Printed in the USA
LVHW010906100222
710101LV00001B/1

9 781604 732467